FALL OF THE HULKS

RED HULK

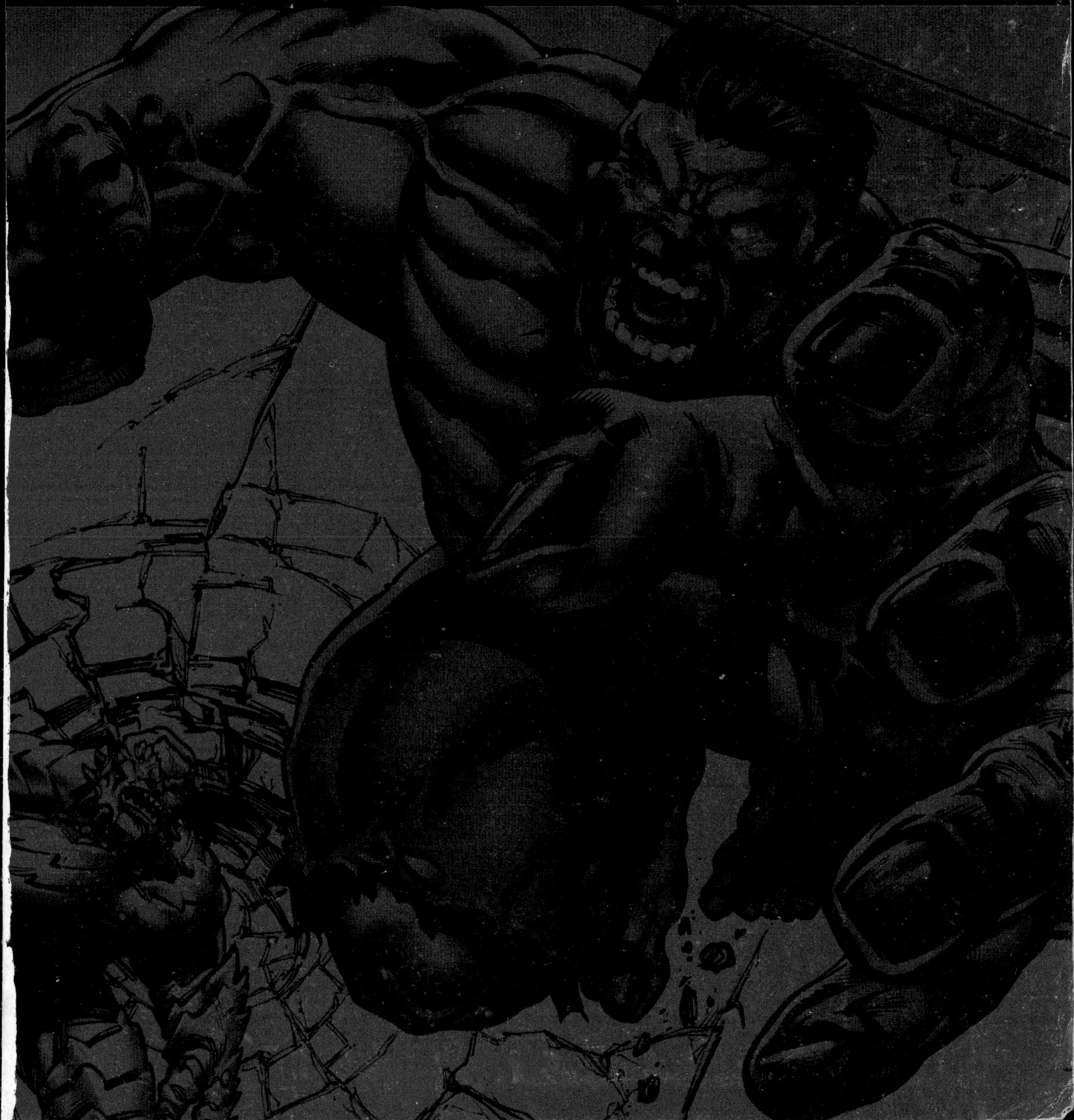

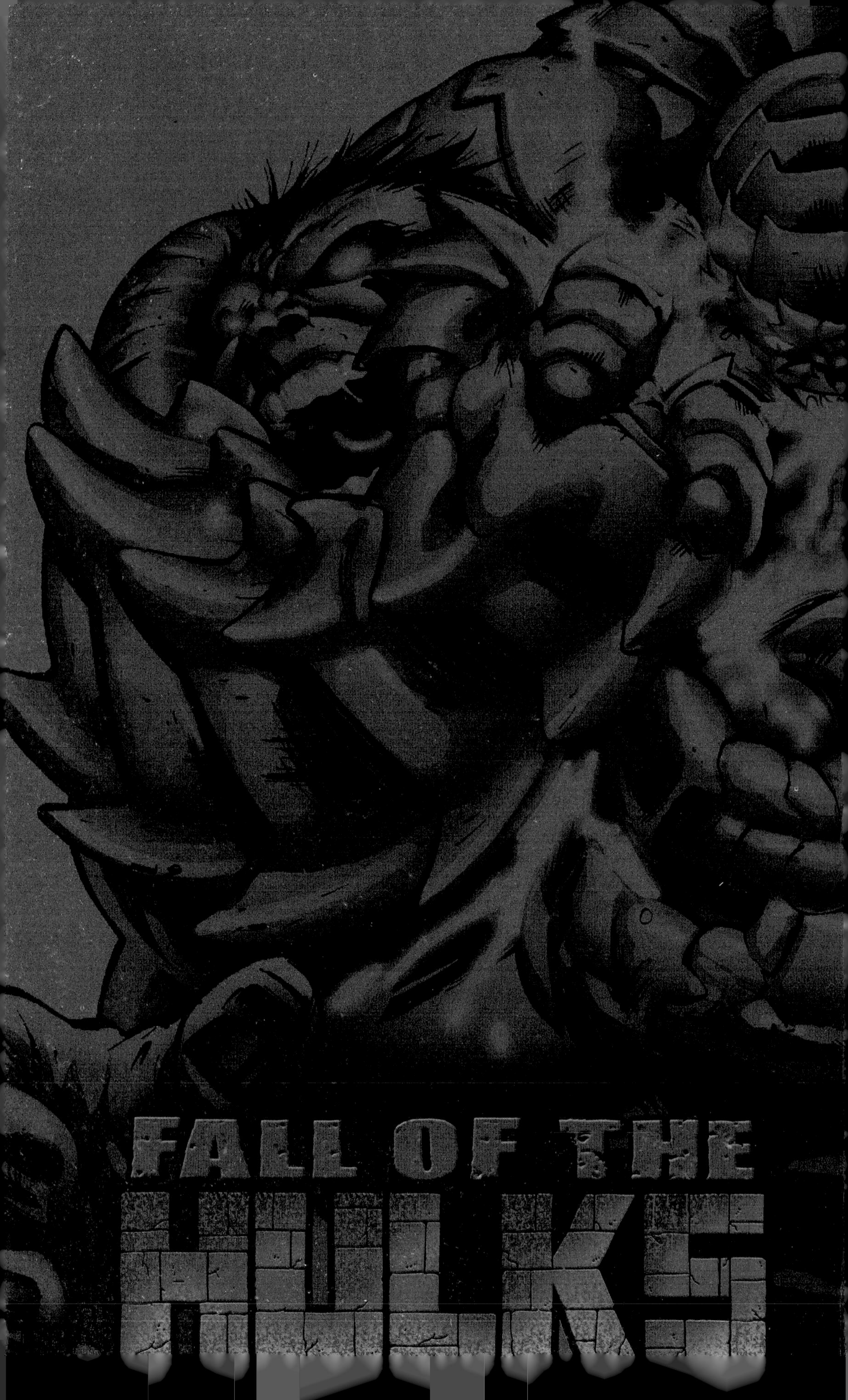

FALL OF THE
HULKS

RED HULK

Writer: **Jeff Parker**

Pencils: **Carlos Rodriguez**
& **Fernando Blanco**

Inks: **Vicente Cifuentes,**
Jason Paz & **Fernando Blanco**

Colors: **Guru eFX**

Letters: **Simon Bowland**

Cover Artists: **Ed McGuinness** & **Chris Sotomayor;**
John Romita Jr., Klaus Janson & **Dean White;**
and **Paul Pelletier** & **Frank D'Armata**

Assistant Editor: **Jordan D. White**

Associate Editor: **Nathan Cosby**

Editor: **Mark Paniccia**

RED SHE-HULK BACKUPS
from Incredible Hulk #606-608

Writer: **Harrison Wilcox**

Pencils: **Ryan Stegman**

Inks: **Tom Palmer**

Colors: **Guru eFX**

Letters: **Simon Bowland**

Cover Artists: **John Romita Jr., Klaus Janson**
& **Dean White**

Assistant Editor: **Jordan D. White**

Editor: **Mark Paniccia**

Collection Editor & Design: **Cory Levine**
Editorial Assistants: **James Emmett** & **Joe Hochstein**
Assistant Editor: **Alex Starbuck**
Associate Editor: **John Denning**
Editors, Special Projects: **Jennifer Grünwald** & **Mark D. Beazley**
Senior Editor, Special Projects: **Jeff Youngquist**
Senior Vice President of Sales: **David Gabriel**

Editor in Chief: **Joe Quesada**
Publisher: **Dan Buckley**
Executive Producer: **Alan Fine**

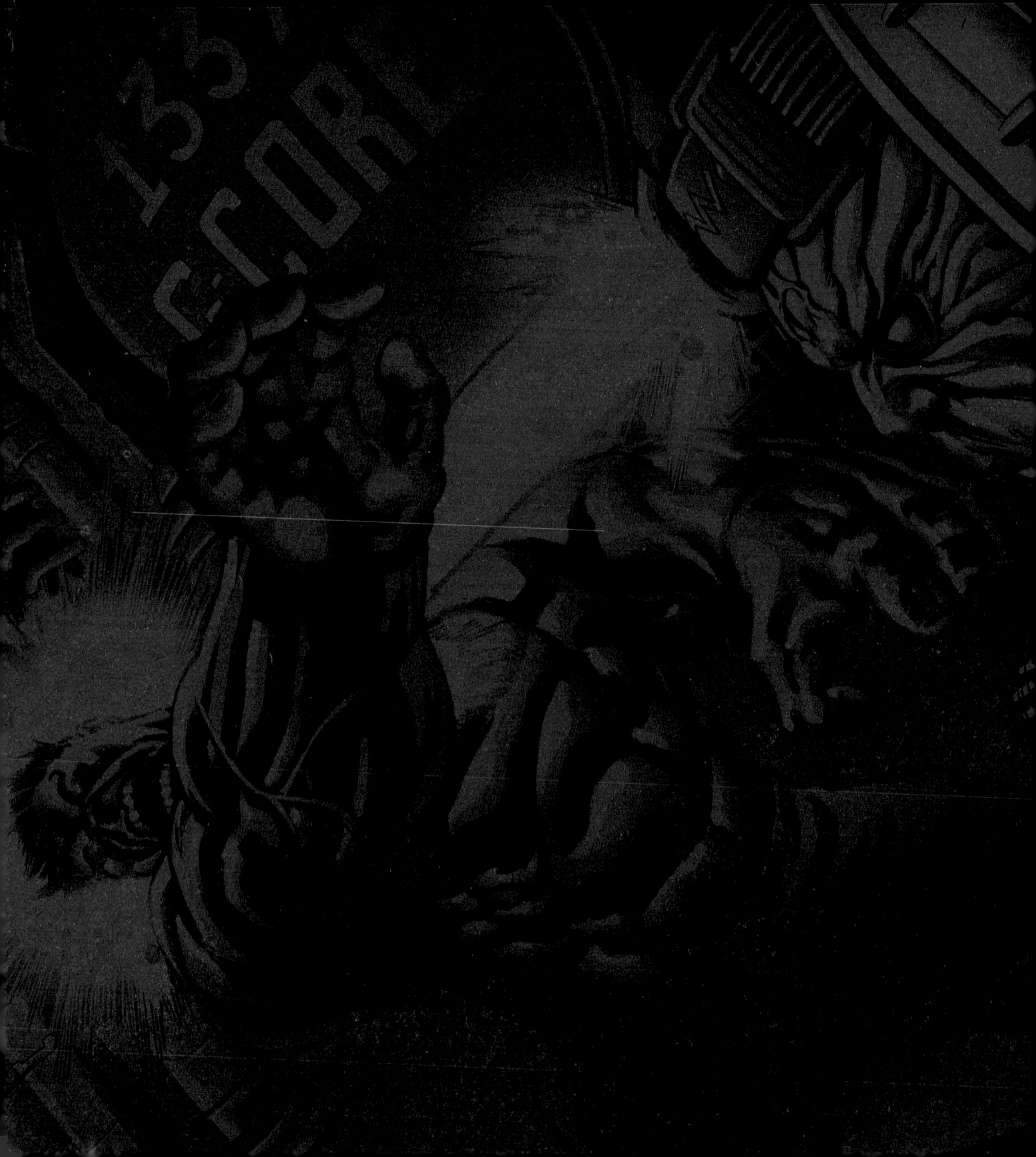

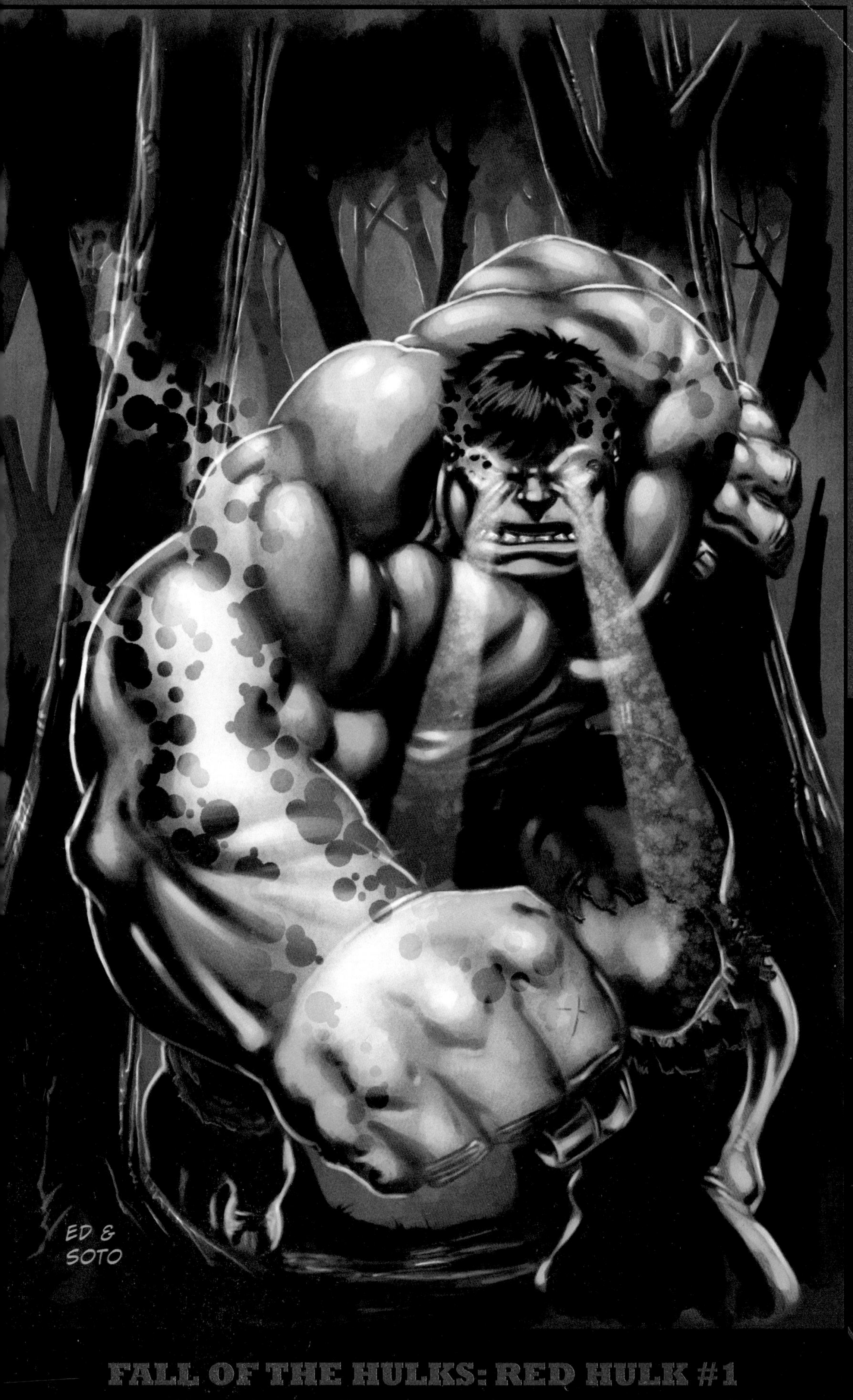
ED &
SOTO

FALL OF THE HULKS: RED HULK #1

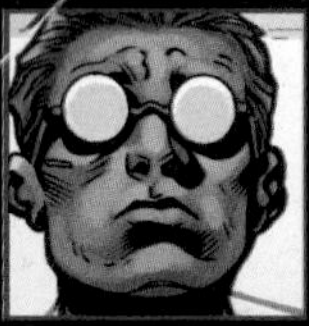

BRUCE BANNER

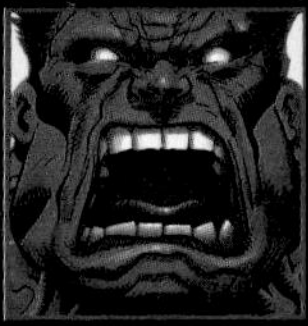

RED HULK

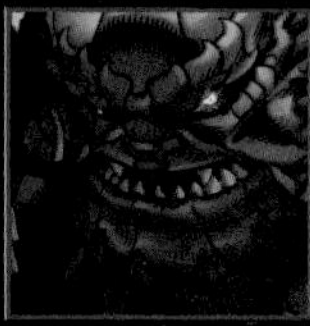

A-BOMB
(RICK JONES)

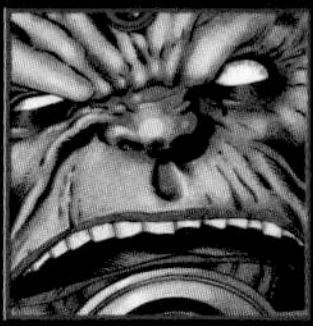

M.O.D.O.K.

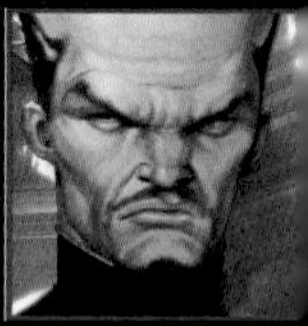

THE LEADE

PREVIOUSLY ON HULK

M.O.D.O.K. and the Leader have formed a team to kidnap the Eight Smartest Men.

Bruce Banner and Red Hulk have allied to stop them.

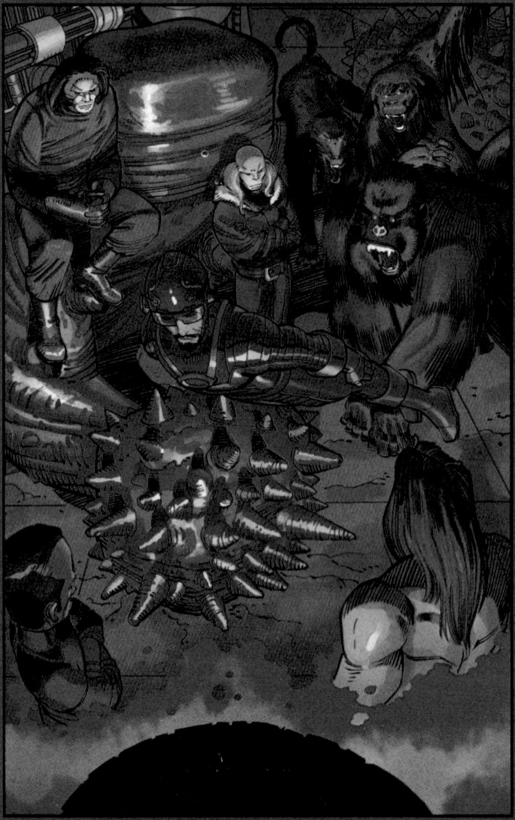

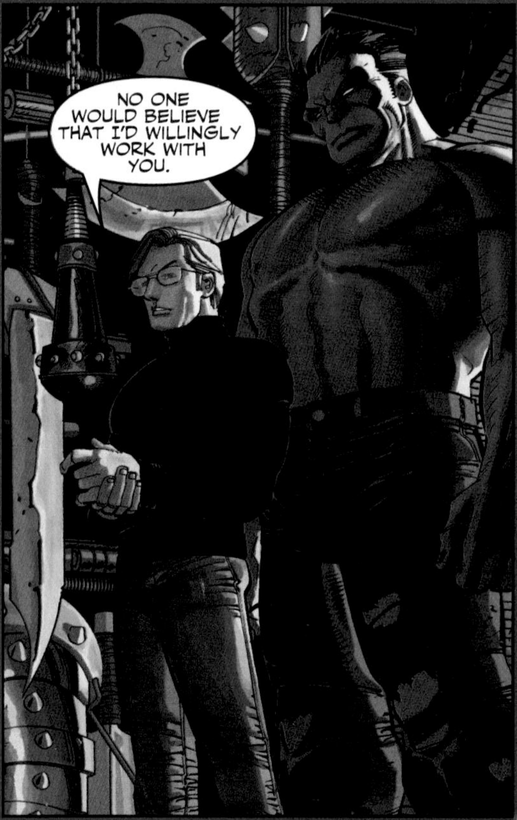
NO ONE WOULD BELIEVE THAT I'D WILLINGLY WORK WITH YOU.

The events of this story occur before Incredible Hulk #606

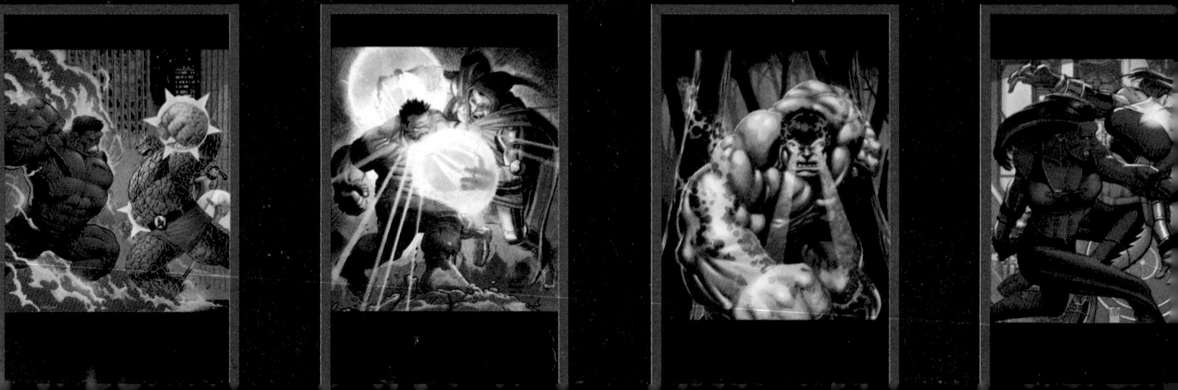

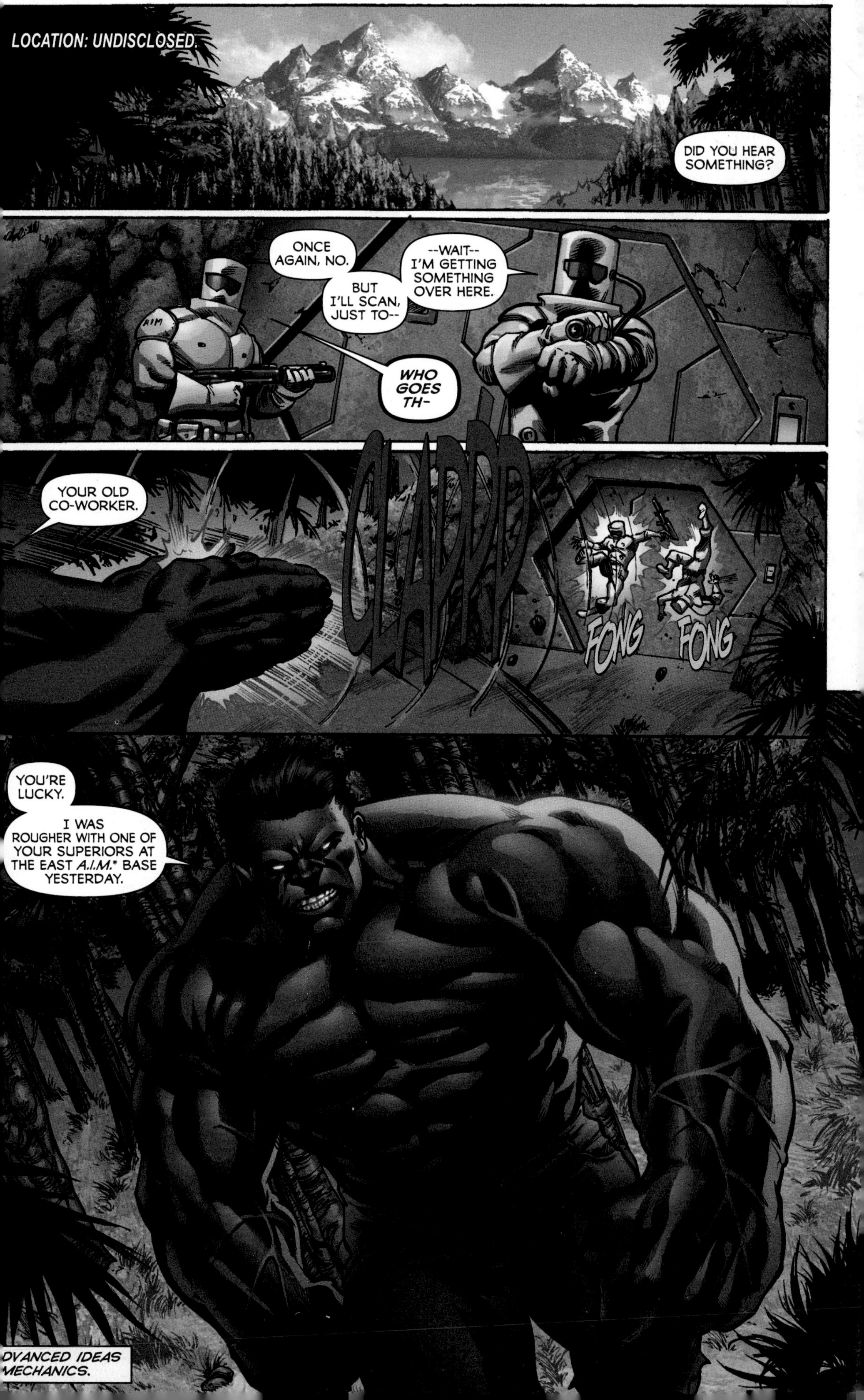
LOCATION: UNDISCLOSED.
DID YOU HEAR SOMETHING?
ONCE AGAIN, NO.
BUT I'LL SCAN, JUST TO--
--WAIT-- I'M GETTING SOMETHING OVER HERE.
WHO GOES TH-
YOUR OLD CO-WORKER.
CLAPPP
FONG
FONG
YOU'RE LUCKY.
I WAS ROUGHER WITH ONE OF YOUR SUPERIORS AT THE EAST A.I.M.* BASE YESTERDAY.
DVANCED IDEAS MECHANICS.

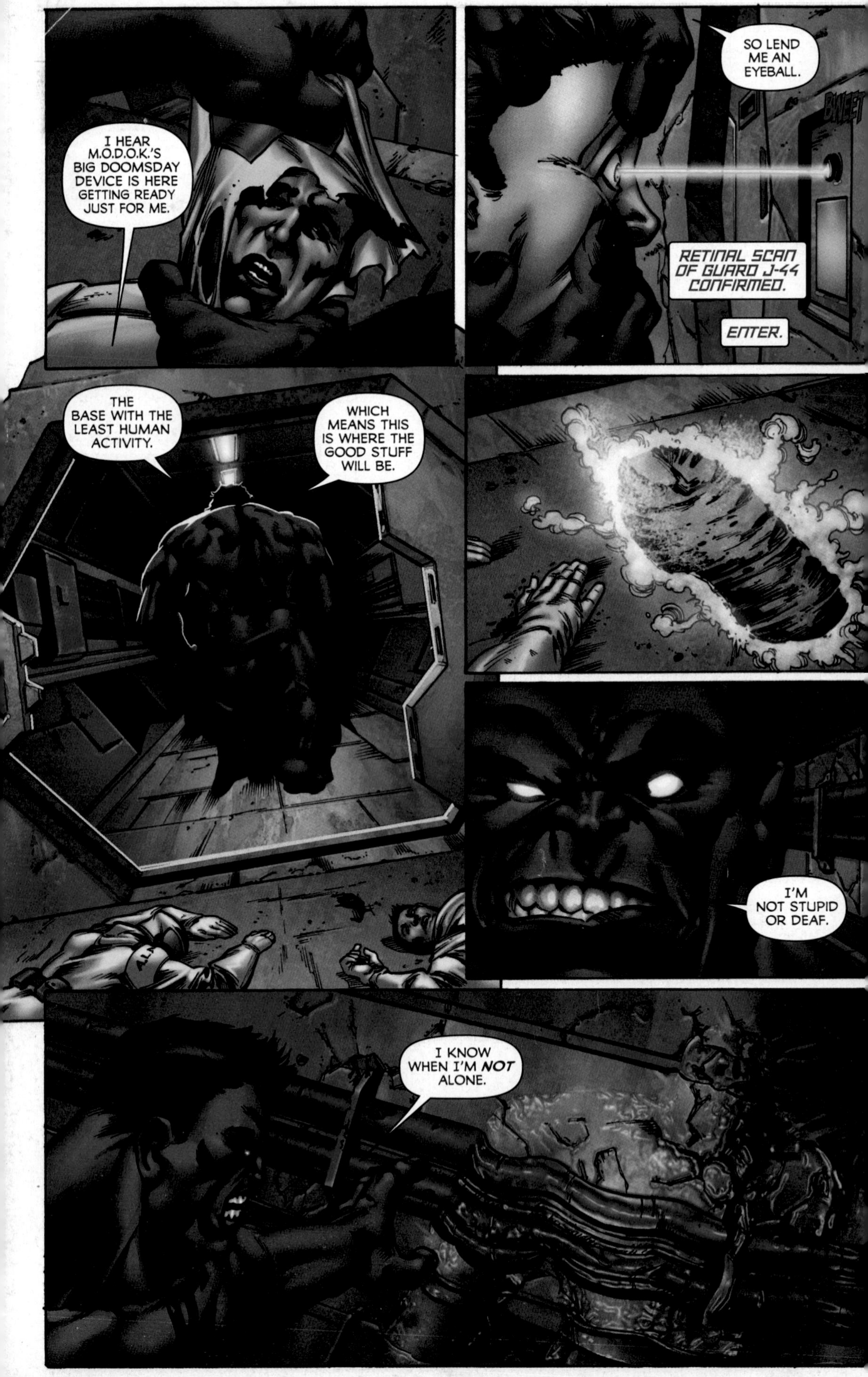
I HEAR M.O.D.O.K.'S BIG DOOMSDAY DEVICE IS HERE GETTING READY JUST FOR ME.
SO LEND ME AN EYEBALL.
BWEET
RETINAL SCAN OF GUARD J-44 CONFIRMED.
ENTER.
THE BASE WITH THE LEAST HUMAN ACTIVITY.
WHICH MEANS THIS IS WHERE THE GOOD STUFF WILL BE.
I'M NOT STUPID OR DEAF.
I KNOW WHEN I'M ***NOT*** ALONE.

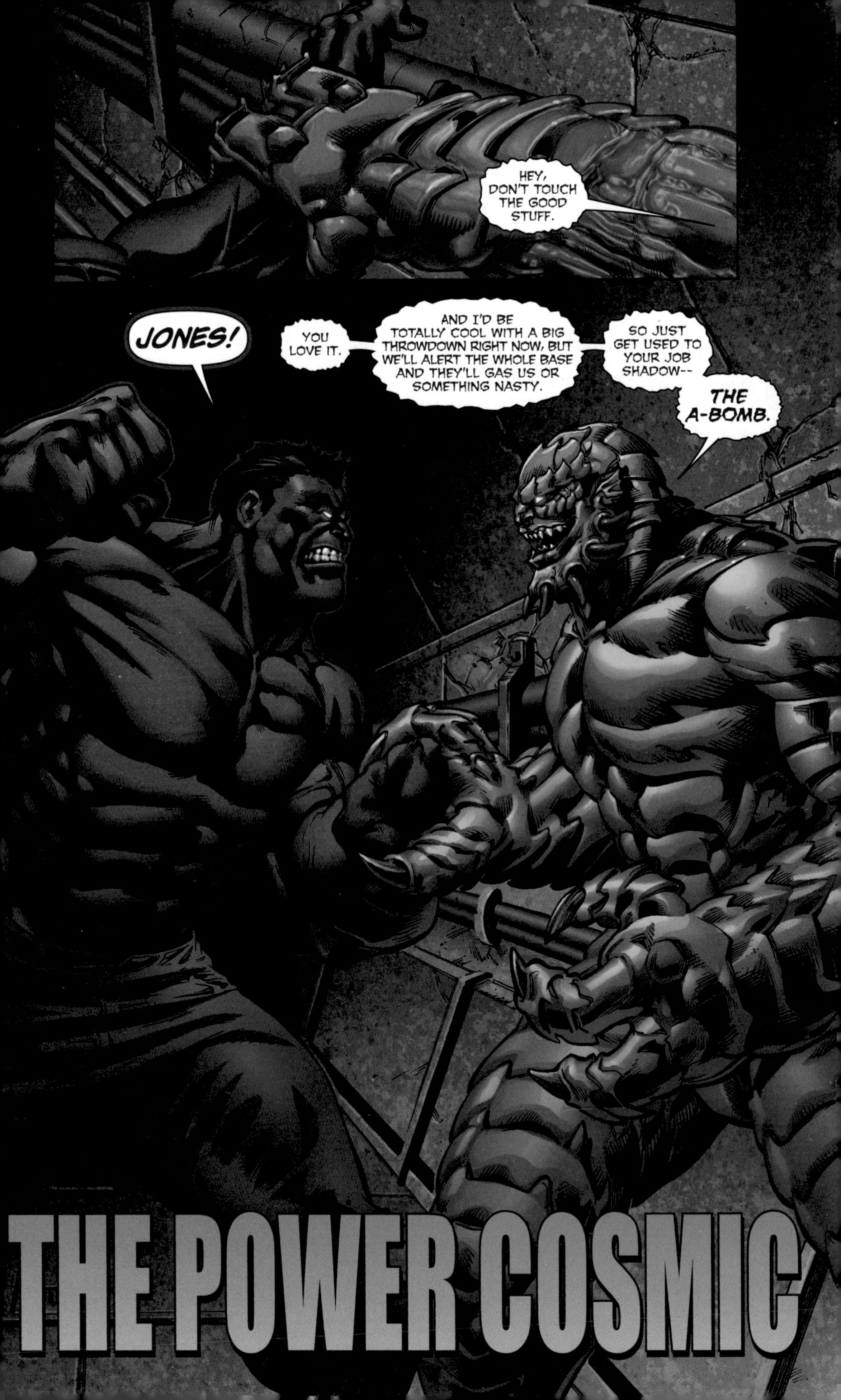
HEY, DON'T TOUCH THE GOOD STUFF.
JONES!
YOU LOVE IT.
AND I'D BE TOTALLY COOL WITH A BIG THROWDOWN RIGHT NOW, BUT WE'LL ALERT THE WHOLE BASE AND THEY'LL GAS US OR SOMETHING NASTY.
SO JUST GET USED TO YOUR JOB SHADOW--
THE A-BOMB.
THE POWER COSMIC

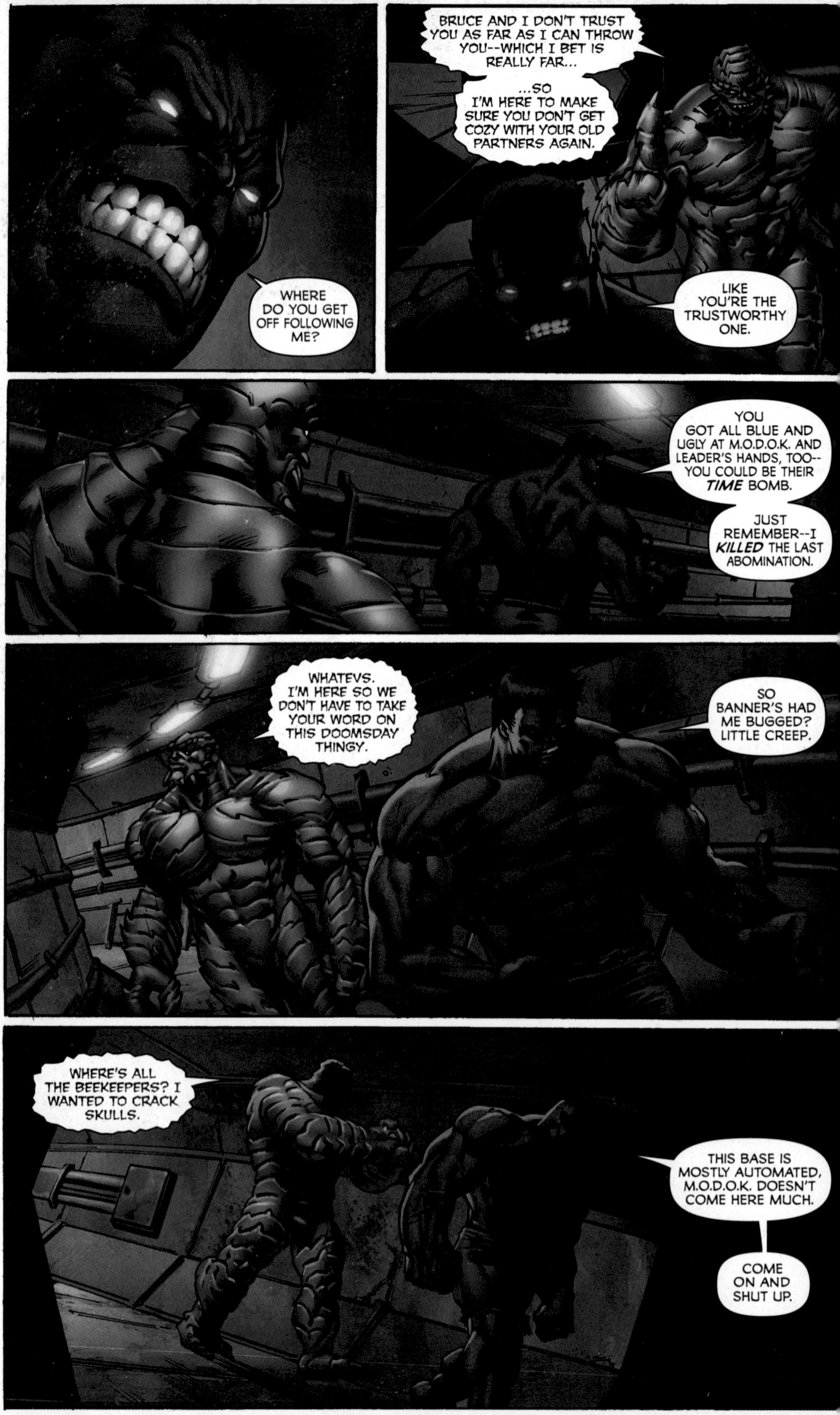
WHERE DO YOU GET OFF FOLLOWING ME?
BRUCE AND I DON'T TRUST YOU AS FAR AS I CAN THROW YOU--WHICH I BET IS REALLY FAR...
...SO I'M HERE TO MAKE SURE YOU DON'T GET COZY WITH YOUR OLD PARTNERS AGAIN.
LIKE YOU'RE THE TRUSTWORTHY ONE.
YOU GOT ALL BLUE AND UGLY AT M.O.D.O.K. AND LEADER'S HANDS, TOO--YOU COULD BE THEIR TIME BOMB.
JUST REMEMBER--I KILLED THE LAST ABOMINATION.
WHATEVS. I'M HERE SO WE DON'T HAVE TO TAKE YOUR WORD ON THIS DOOMSDAY THINGY.
SO BANNER'S HAD ME BUGGED? LITTLE CREEP.
WHERE'S ALL THE BEEKEEPERS? I WANTED TO CRACK SKULLS.
THIS BASE IS MOSTLY AUTOMATED, M.O.D.O.K. DOESN'T COME HERE MUCH.
COME ON AND SHUT UP.

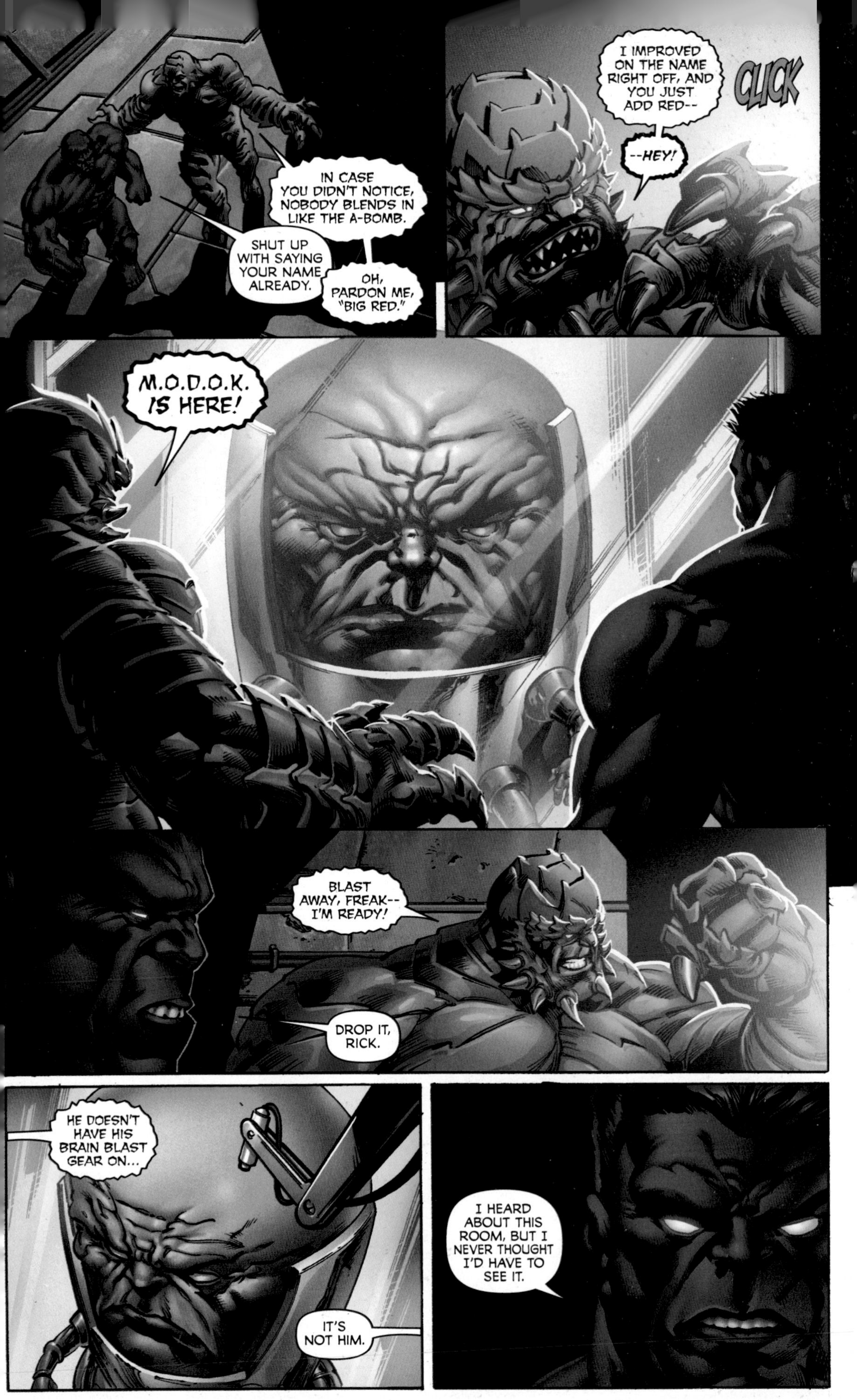

IN CASE YOU DIDN'T NOTICE, NOBODY BLENDS IN LIKE THE A-BOMB.
SHUT UP WITH SAYING YOUR NAME ALREADY.
OH, PARDON ME, "BIG RED."
I IMPROVED ON THE NAME RIGHT OFF, AND YOU JUST ADD RED--
CLICK
--HEY!
M.O.D.O.K. IS HERE!
BLAST AWAY, FREAK-- I'M READY!
DROP IT, RICK.
HE DOESN'T HAVE HIS BRAIN BLAST GEAR ON...
IT'S NOT HIM.
I HEARD ABOUT THIS ROOM, BUT I NEVER THOUGHT I'D HAVE TO SEE IT.

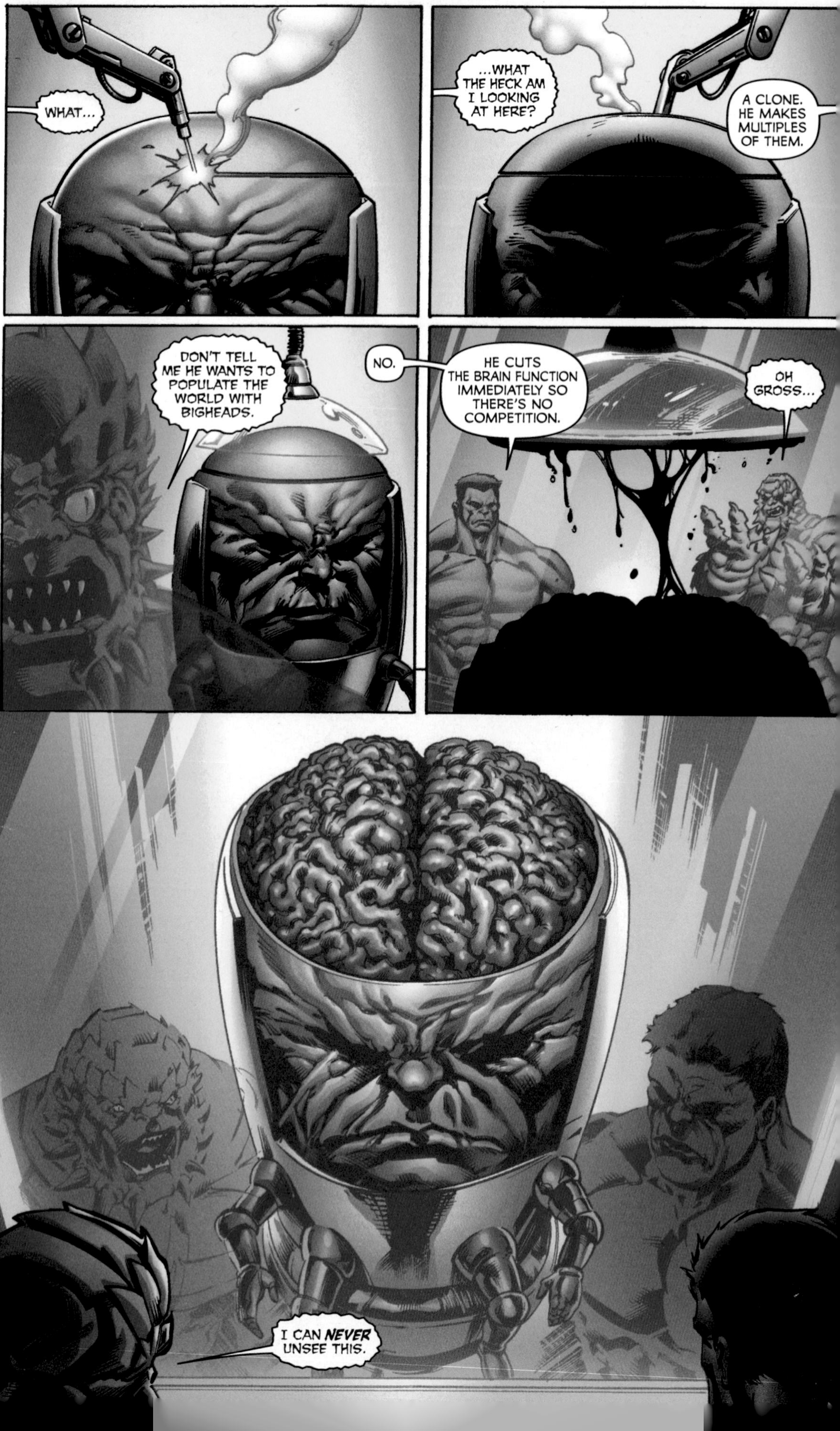
WHAT...
...WHAT THE HECK AM I LOOKING AT HERE?
A CLONE. HE MAKES MULTIPLES OF THEM.
DON'T TELL ME HE WANTS TO POPULATE THE WORLD WITH BIGHEADS.
NO.
HE CUTS THE BRAIN FUNCTION IMMEDIATELY SO THERE'S NO COMPETITION.
OH GROSS...
I CAN *NEVER* UNSEE THIS.

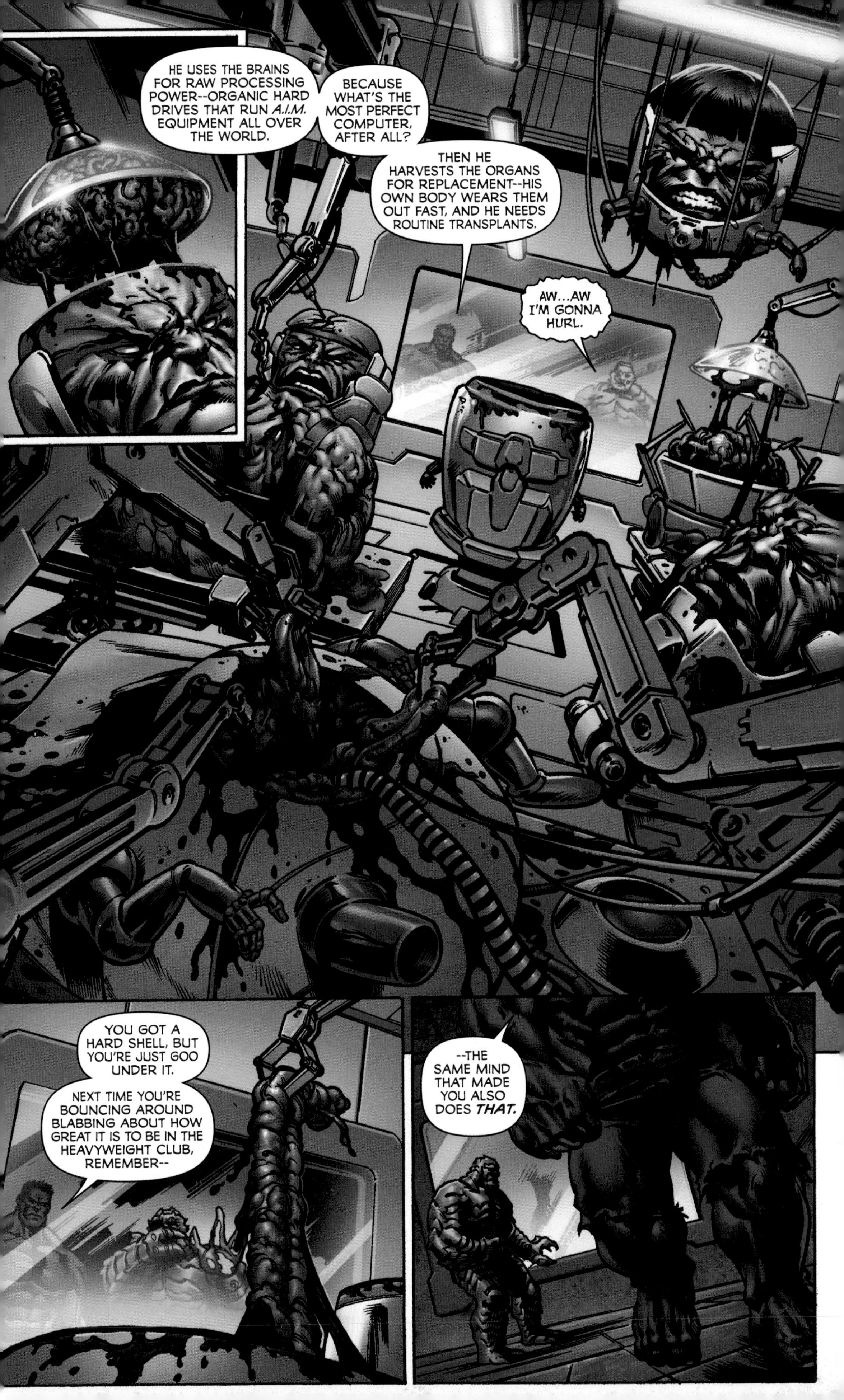
HE USES THE BRAINS FOR RAW PROCESSING POWER--ORGANIC HARD DRIVES THAT RUN *A.I.M.* EQUIPMENT ALL OVER THE WORLD.
BECAUSE WHAT'S THE MOST PERFECT COMPUTER, AFTER ALL?
THEN HE HARVESTS THE ORGANS FOR REPLACEMENT--HIS OWN BODY WEARS THEM OUT FAST, AND HE NEEDS ROUTINE TRANSPLANTS.
AW...AW I'M GONNA HURL.
YOU GOT A HARD SHELL, BUT YOU'RE JUST GOO UNDER IT.
NEXT TIME YOU'RE BOUNCING AROUND BLABBING ABOUT HOW GREAT IT IS TO BE IN THE HEAVYWEIGHT CLUB, REMEMBER--
--THE SAME MIND THAT MADE YOU ALSO DOES *THAT.*

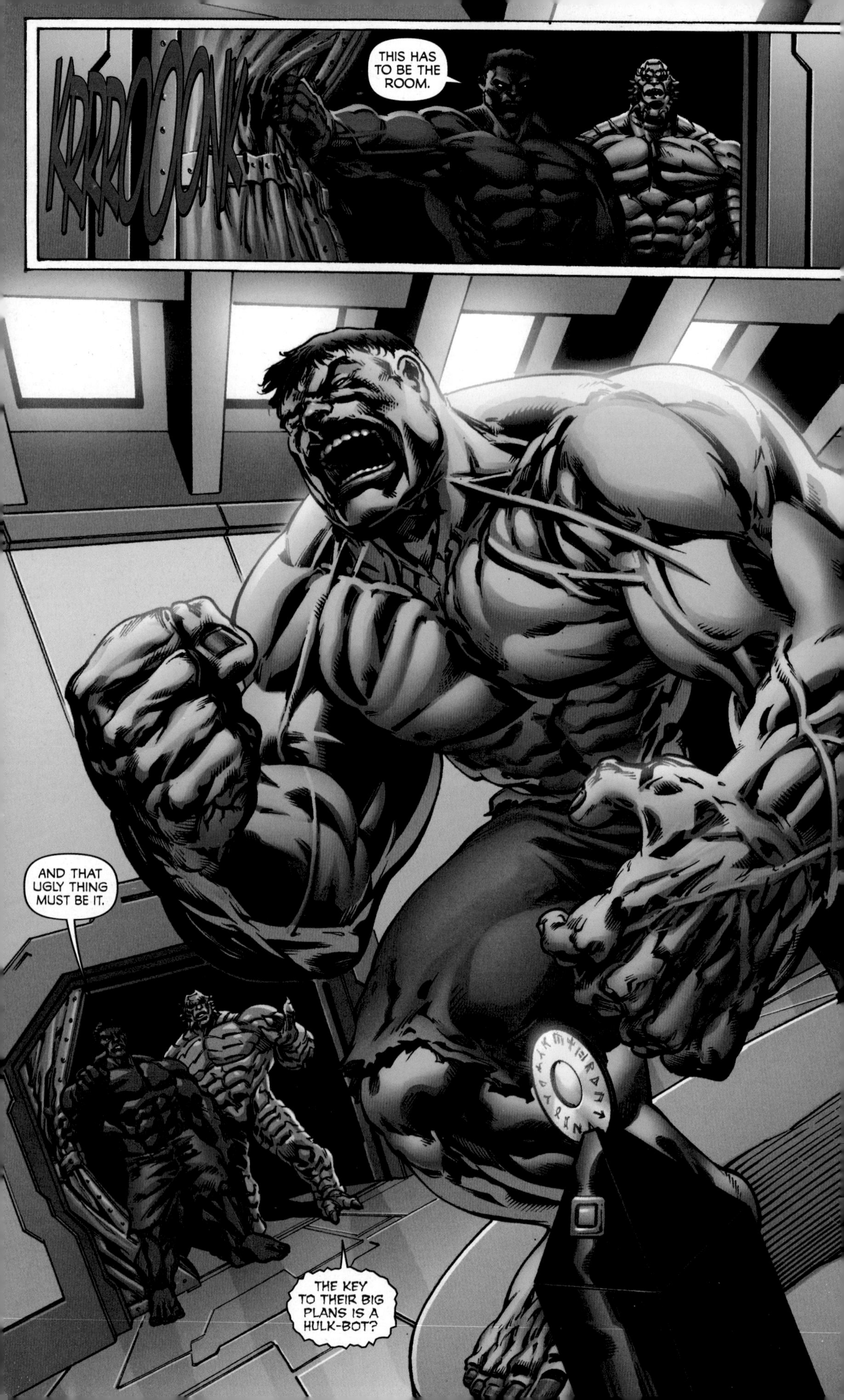
KRRROOONK!
THIS HAS TO BE THE ROOM.
AND THAT UGLY THING MUST BE IT.
THE KEY TO THEIR BIG PLANS IS A HULK-BOT?

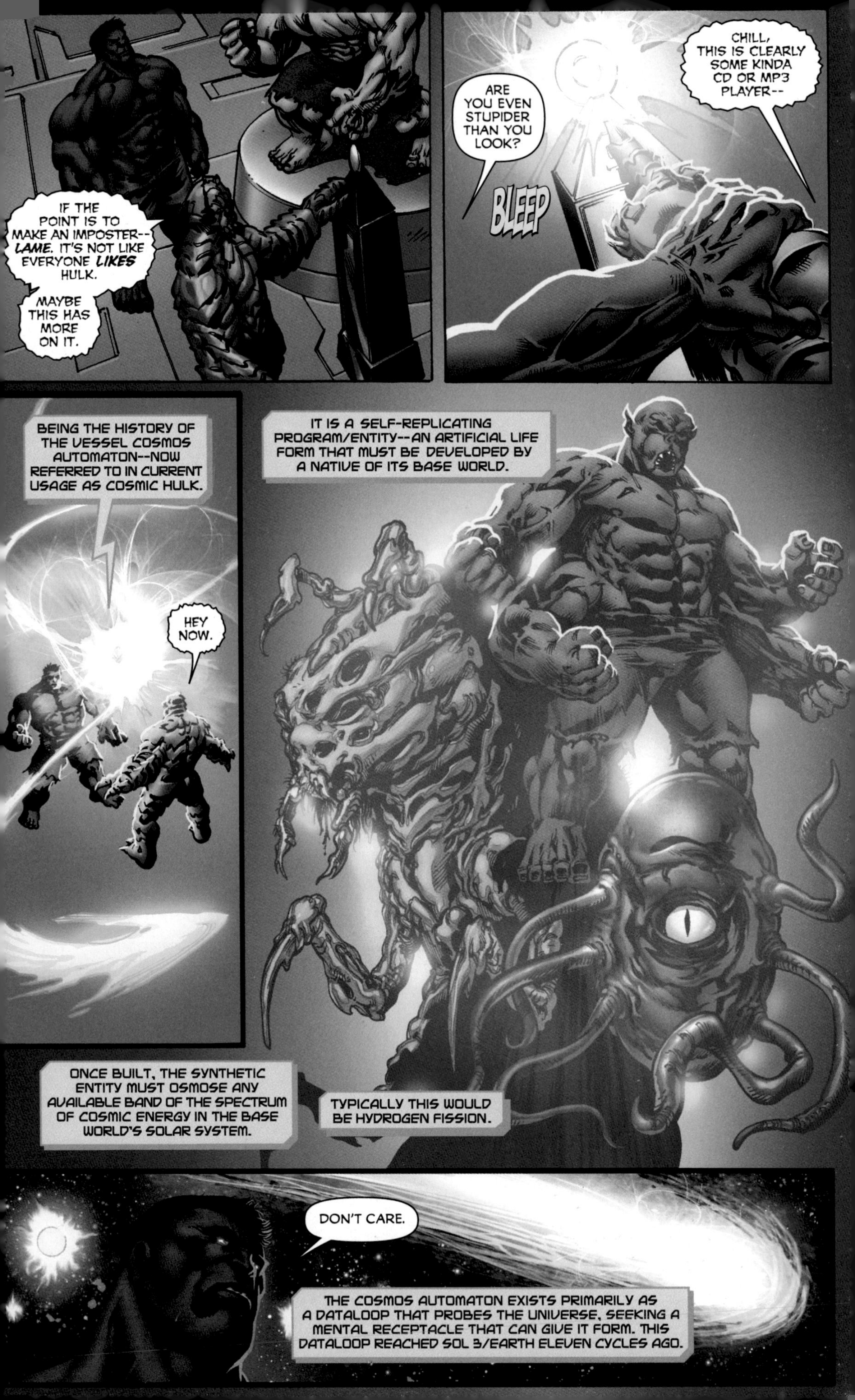
IF THE POINT IS TO MAKE AN IMPOSTER-- LAME. IT'S NOT LIKE EVERYONE LIKES HULK.
MAYBE THIS HAS MORE ON IT.
ARE YOU EVEN STUPIDER THAN YOU LOOK?
CHILL, THIS IS CLEARLY SOME KINDA CD OR MP3 PLAYER--
BLEEP
BEING THE HISTORY OF THE VESSEL COSMOS AUTOMATON--NOW REFERRED TO IN CURRENT USAGE AS COSMIC HULK.
HEY NOW.
IT IS A SELF-REPLICATING PROGRAM/ENTITY--AN ARTIFICIAL LIFE FORM THAT MUST BE DEVELOPED BY A NATIVE OF ITS BASE WORLD.
ONCE BUILT, THE SYNTHETIC ENTITY MUST OSMOSE ANY AVAILABLE BAND OF THE SPECTRUM OF COSMIC ENERGY IN THE BASE WORLD'S SOLAR SYSTEM.
TYPICALLY THIS WOULD BE HYDROGEN FISSION.
DON'T CARE.
THE COSMOS AUTOMATON EXISTS PRIMARILY AS A DATALOOP THAT PROBES THE UNIVERSE, SEEKING A MENTAL RECEPTACLE THAT CAN GIVE IT FORM. THIS DATALOOP REACHED SOL 3/EARTH ELEVEN CYCLES AGO.

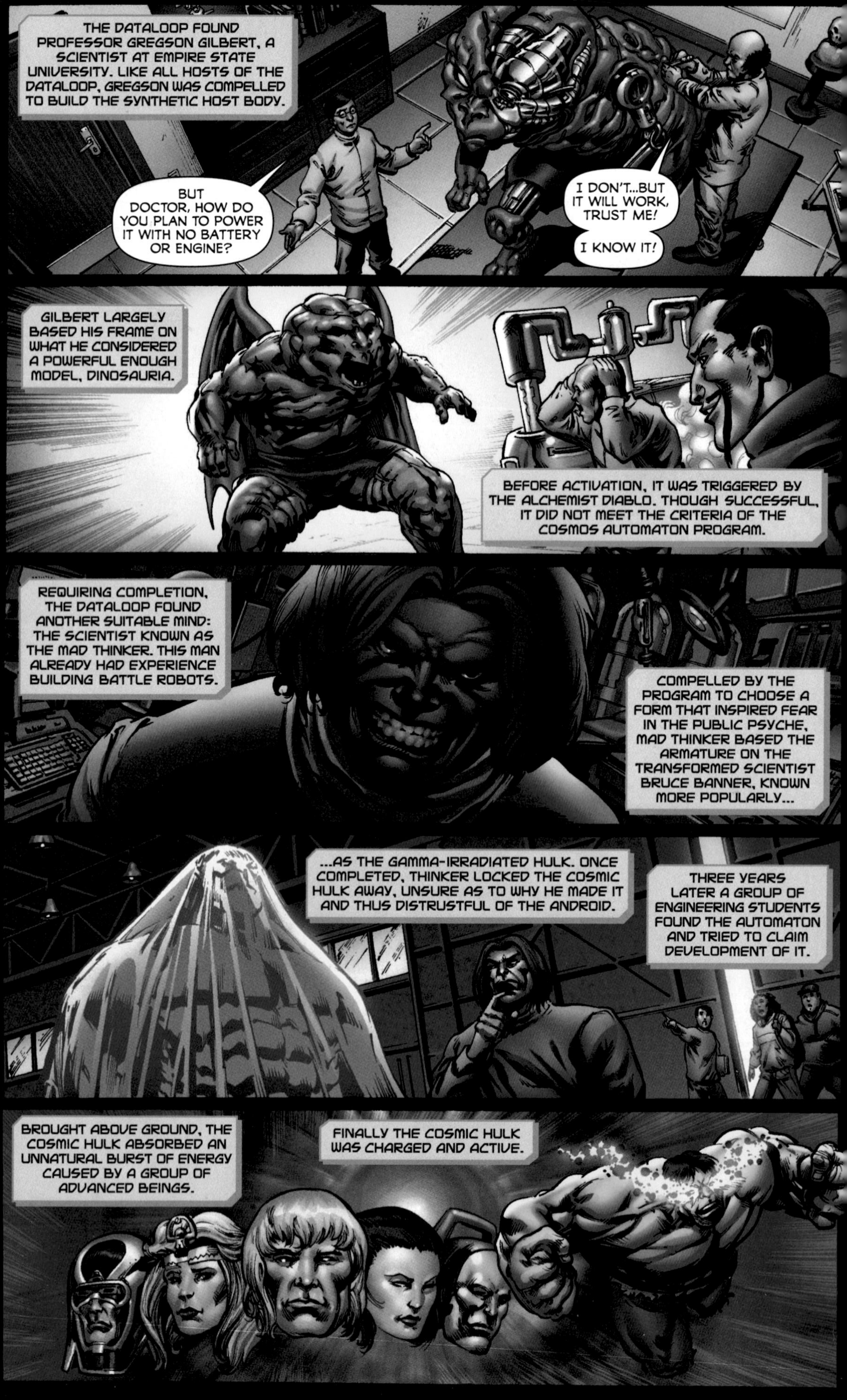
THE DATALOOP FOUND PROFESSOR GREGSON GILBERT, A SCIENTIST AT EMPIRE STATE UNIVERSITY. LIKE ALL HOSTS OF THE DATALOOP, GREGSON WAS COMPELLED TO BUILD THE SYNTHETIC HOST BODY.
BUT DOCTOR, HOW DO YOU PLAN TO POWER IT WITH NO BATTERY OR ENGINE?
I DON'T...BUT IT WILL WORK, TRUST ME!
I KNOW IT!
GILBERT LARGELY BASED HIS FRAME ON WHAT HE CONSIDERED A POWERFUL ENOUGH MODEL, DINOSAURIA.
BEFORE ACTIVATION, IT WAS TRIGGERED BY THE ALCHEMIST DIABLO. THOUGH SUCCESSFUL, IT DID NOT MEET THE CRITERIA OF THE COSMOS AUTOMATON PROGRAM.
REQUIRING COMPLETION, THE DATALOOP FOUND ANOTHER SUITABLE MIND: THE SCIENTIST KNOWN AS THE MAD THINKER. THIS MAN ALREADY HAD EXPERIENCE BUILDING BATTLE ROBOTS.
COMPELLED BY THE PROGRAM TO CHOOSE A FORM THAT INSPIRED FEAR IN THE PUBLIC PSYCHE, MAD THINKER BASED THE ARMATURE ON THE TRANSFORMED SCIENTIST BRUCE BANNER, KNOWN MORE POPULARLY...
...AS THE GAMMA-IRRADIATED HULK. ONCE COMPLETED, THINKER LOCKED THE COSMIC HULK AWAY, UNSURE AS TO WHY HE MADE IT AND THUS DISTRUSTFUL OF THE ANDROID.
THREE YEARS LATER A GROUP OF ENGINEERING STUDENTS FOUND THE AUTOMATON AND TRIED TO CLAIM DEVELOPMENT OF IT.
BROUGHT ABOVE GROUND, THE COSMIC HULK ABSORBED AN UNNATURAL BURST OF ENERGY CAUSED BY A GROUP OF ADVANCED BEINGS.
FINALLY THE COSMIC HULK WAS CHARGED AND ACTIVE.

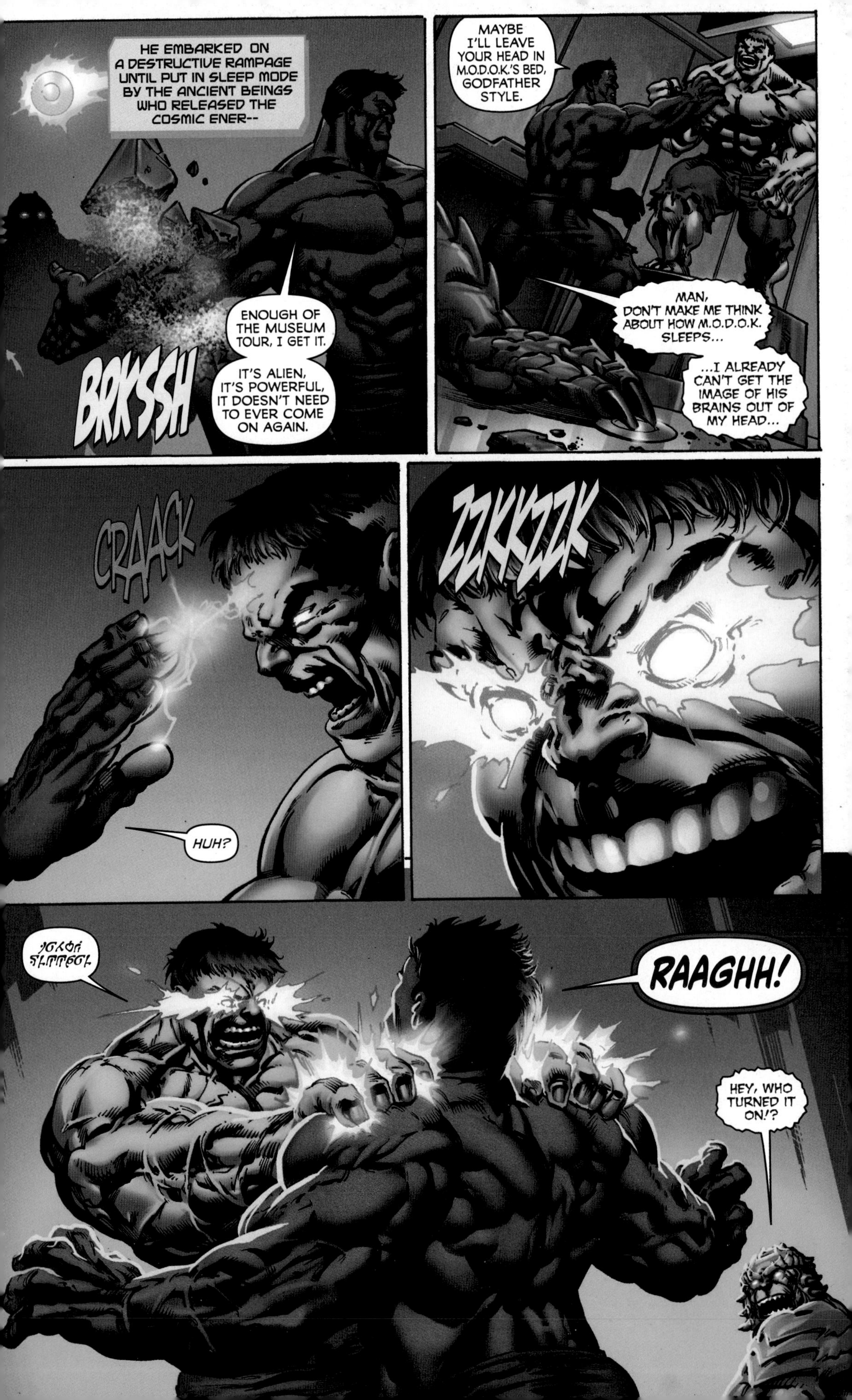
HE EMBARKED ON A DESTRUCTIVE RAMPAGE UNTIL PUT IN SLEEP MODE BY THE ANCIENT BEINGS WHO RELEASED THE COSMIC ENER--
BRKSSH
ENOUGH OF THE MUSEUM TOUR, I GET IT.
IT'S ALIEN, IT'S POWERFUL, IT DOESN'T NEED TO EVER COME ON AGAIN.
MAYBE I'LL LEAVE YOUR HEAD IN M.O.D.O.K.'S BED, GODFATHER STYLE.
MAN, DON'T MAKE ME THINK ABOUT HOW M.O.D.O.K. SLEEPS...
...I ALREADY CAN'T GET THE IMAGE OF HIS BRAINS OUT OF MY HEAD...
CRAACK
HUH?
ZZKKZZK
RAAGHH!
HEY, WHO TURNED IT ON!?

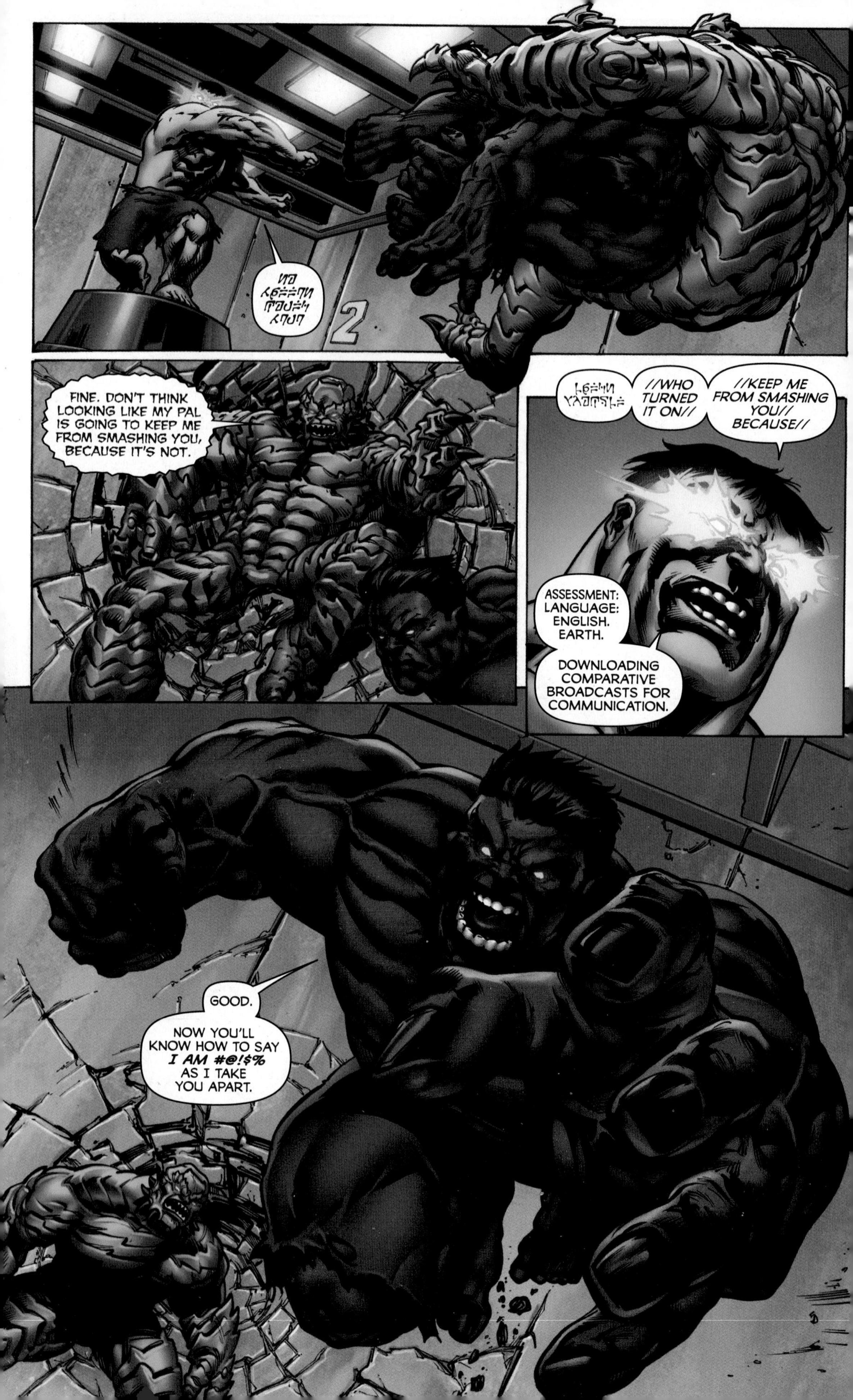

2
FINE. DON'T THINK LOOKING LIKE MY PAL IS GOING TO KEEP ME FROM SMASHING YOU, BECAUSE IT'S NOT.
//WHO TURNED IT ON//
//KEEP ME FROM SMASHING YOU// BECAUSE//
ASSESSMENT: LANGUAGE: ENGLISH. EARTH.
DOWNLOADING COMPARATIVE BROADCASTS FOR COMMUNICATION.
GOOD.
NOW YOU'LL KNOW HOW TO SAY *I AM #@!$%* AS I TAKE YOU APART.

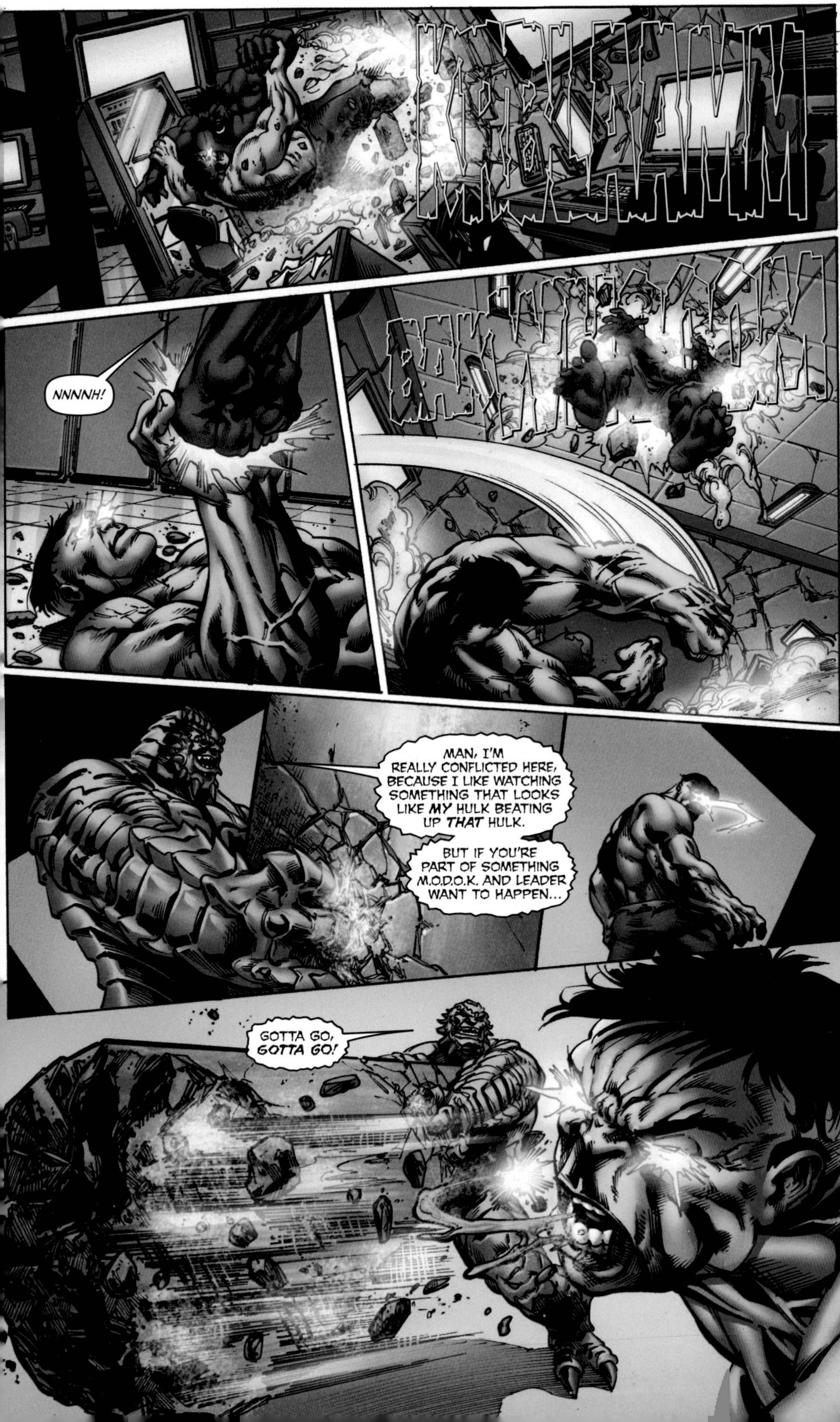
NNNNH!
MAN, I'M REALLY CONFLICTED HERE, BECAUSE I LIKE WATCHING SOMETHING THAT LOOKS LIKE *MY* HULK BEATING UP *THAT* HULK.
BUT IF YOU'RE PART OF SOMETHING M.O.D.O.K. AND LEADER WANT TO HAPPEN...
GOTTA GO, *GOTTA GO!*

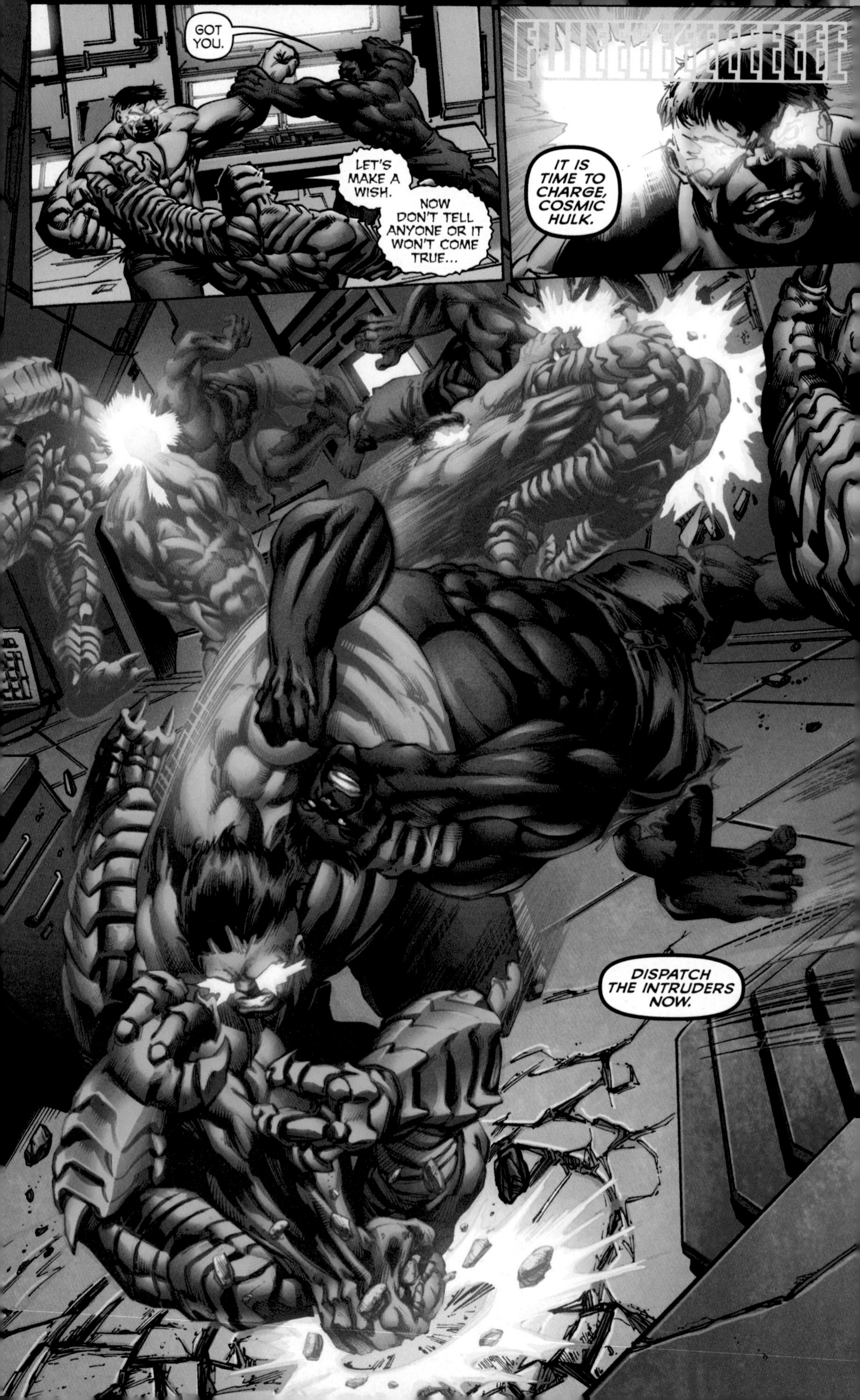
GOT YOU.
LET'S MAKE A WISH.
NOW DON'T TELL ANYONE OR IT WON'T COME TRUE...
FWEEEEEEEEE
IT IS TIME TO CHARGE, COSMIC HULK.
DISPATCH THE INTRUDERS NOW.

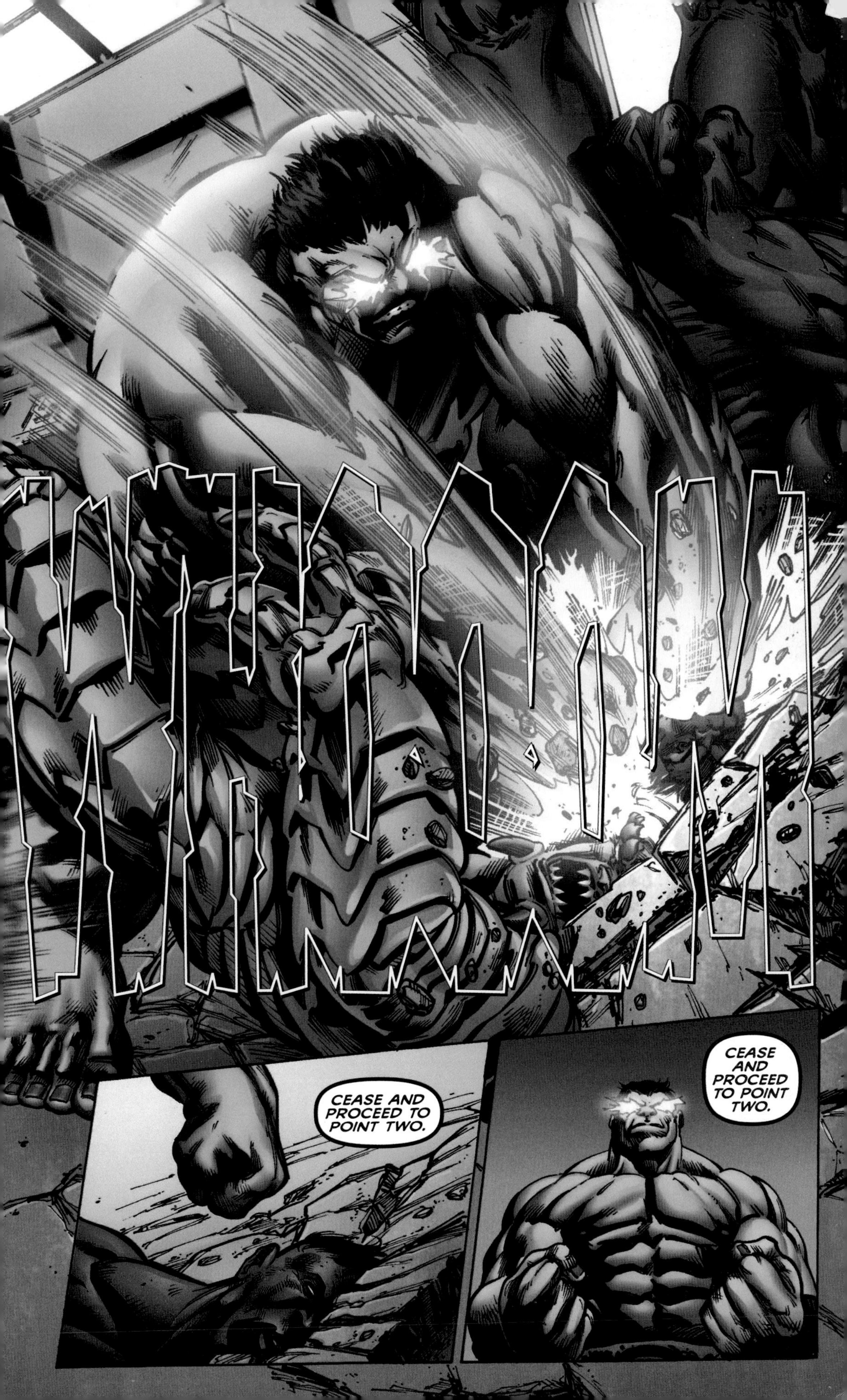
WHOOOM
CEASE AND PROCEED TO POINT TWO.
CEASE AND PROCEED TO POINT TWO.

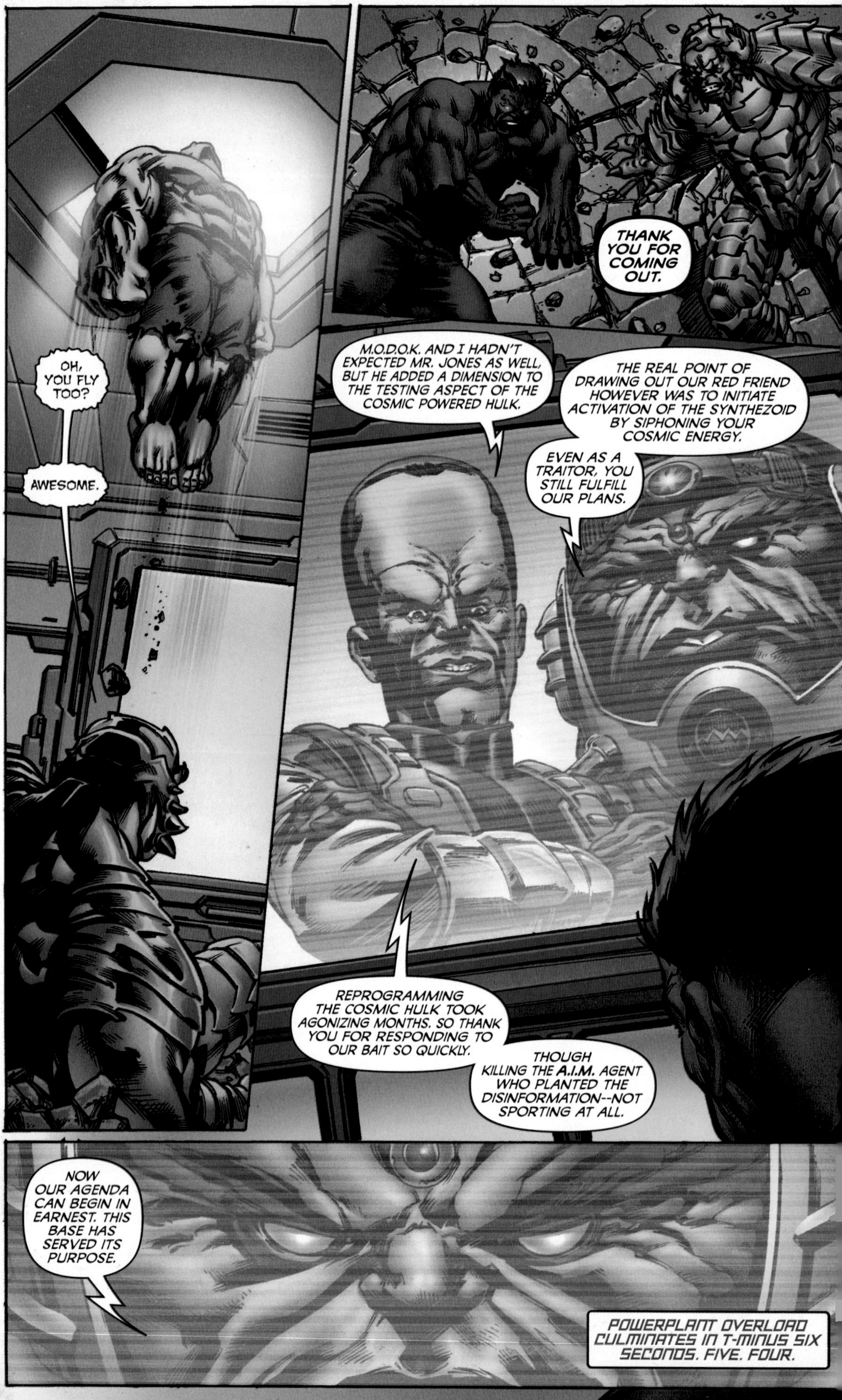
THANK YOU FOR COMING OUT.
OH, YOU FLY TOO?
AWESOME.
M.O.D.O.K. AND I HADN'T EXPECTED MR. JONES AS WELL, BUT HE ADDED A DIMENSION TO THE TESTING ASPECT OF THE COSMIC POWERED HULK.
THE REAL POINT OF DRAWING OUT OUR RED FRIEND HOWEVER WAS TO INITIATE ACTIVATION OF THE SYNTHEZOID BY SIPHONING YOUR COSMIC ENERGY.
EVEN AS A TRAITOR, YOU STILL FULFILL OUR PLANS.
REPROGRAMMING THE COSMIC HULK TOOK AGONIZING MONTHS. SO THANK YOU FOR RESPONDING TO OUR BAIT SO QUICKLY.
THOUGH KILLING THE A.I.M. AGENT WHO PLANTED THE DISINFORMATION--NOT SPORTING AT ALL.
NOW OUR AGENDA CAN BEGIN IN EARNEST. THIS BASE HAS SERVED ITS PURPOSE.
POWERPLANT OVERLOAD CULMINATES IN T-MINUS SIX SECONDS. FIVE. FOUR.

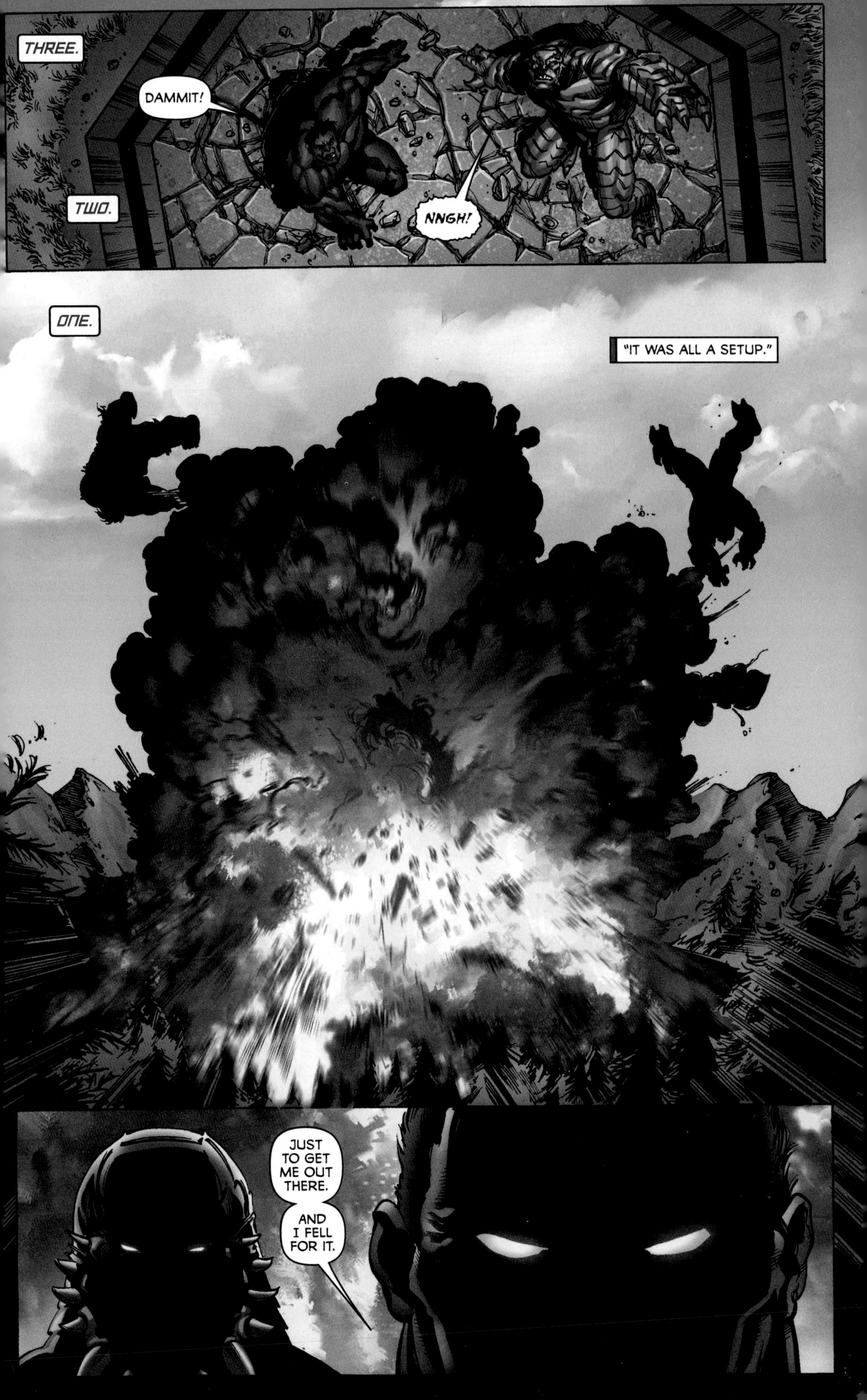
THREE.
DAMMIT!
TWO.
NNGH!
ONE.
"IT WAS ALL A SETUP."
JUST TO GET ME OUT THERE.
AND I FELL FOR IT.

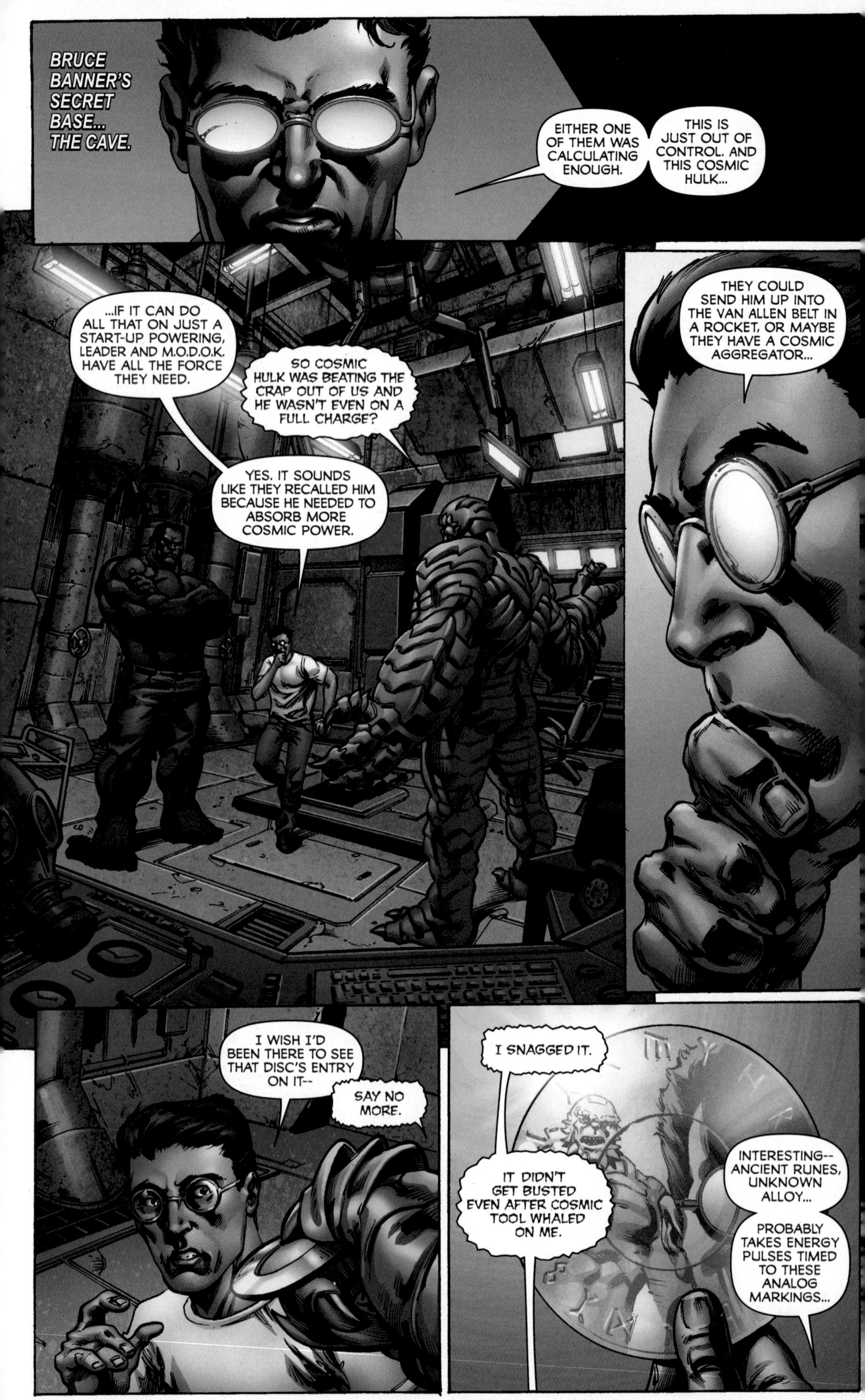
BRUCE BANNER'S SECRET BASE... THE CAVE.
EITHER ONE OF THEM WAS CALCULATING ENOUGH.
THIS IS JUST OUT OF CONTROL. AND THIS COSMIC HULK...
...IF IT CAN DO ALL THAT ON JUST A START-UP POWERING, LEADER AND M.O.D.O.K. HAVE ALL THE FORCE THEY NEED.
SO COSMIC HULK WAS BEATING THE CRAP OUT OF US AND HE WASN'T EVEN ON A FULL CHARGE?
YES. IT SOUNDS LIKE THEY RECALLED HIM BECAUSE HE NEEDED TO ABSORB MORE COSMIC POWER.
THEY COULD SEND HIM UP INTO THE VAN ALLEN BELT IN A ROCKET, OR MAYBE THEY HAVE A COSMIC AGGREGATOR...
I WISH I'D BEEN THERE TO SEE THAT DISC'S ENTRY ON IT--
SAY NO MORE.
I SNAGGED IT.
IT DIDN'T GET BUSTED EVEN AFTER COSMIC TOOL WHALED ON ME.
INTERESTING-- ANCIENT RUNES, UNKNOWN ALLOY...
PROBABLY TAKES ENERGY PULSES TIMED TO THESE ANALOG MARKINGS...

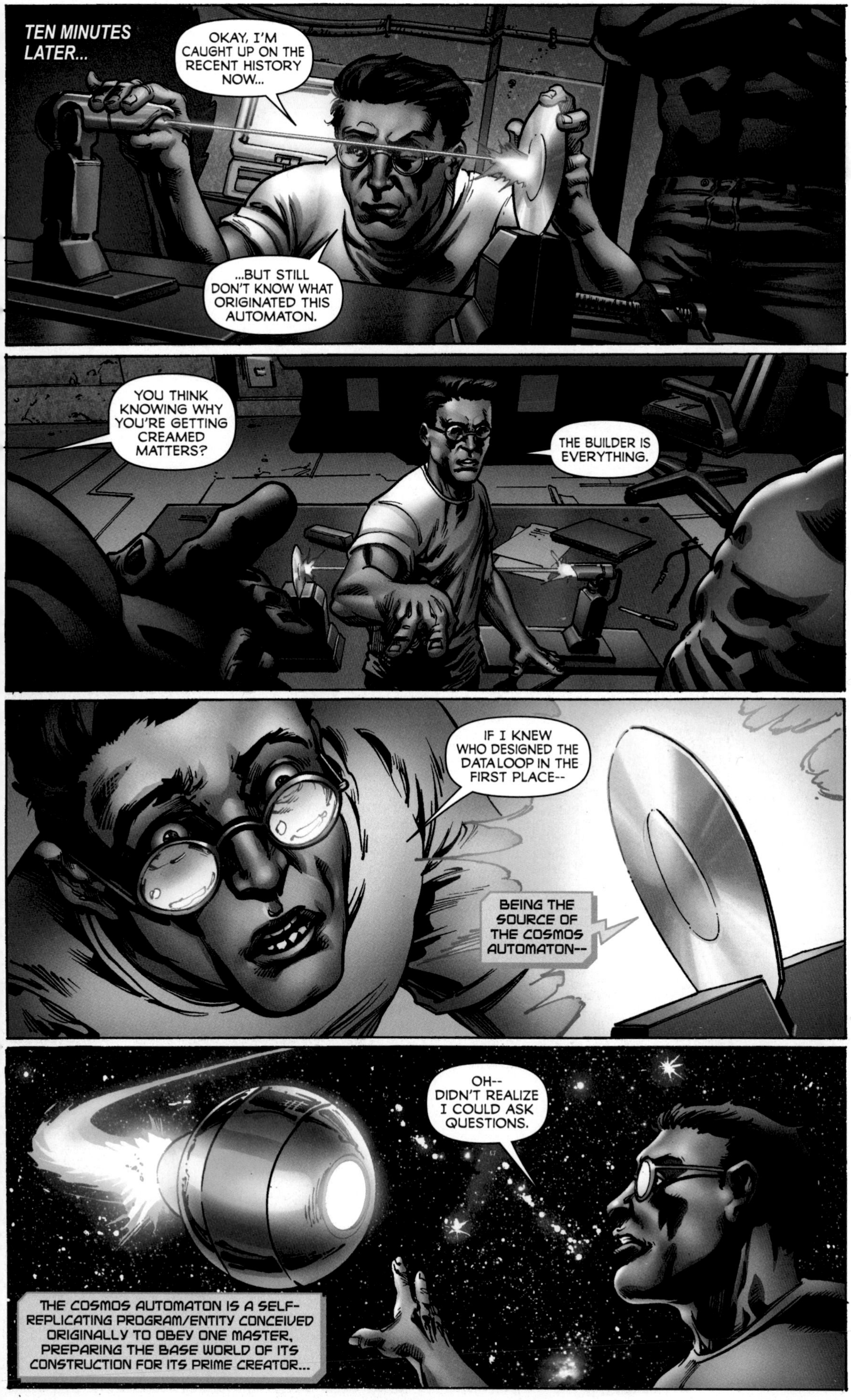
TEN MINUTES LATER...
OKAY, I'M CAUGHT UP ON THE RECENT HISTORY NOW...
...BUT STILL DON'T KNOW WHAT ORIGINATED THIS AUTOMATON.
YOU THINK KNOWING WHY YOU'RE GETTING CREAMED MATTERS?
THE BUILDER IS EVERYTHING.
IF I KNEW WHO DESIGNED THE DATALOOP IN THE FIRST PLACE--
BEING THE SOURCE OF THE COSMOS AUTOMATON--
OH-- DIDN'T REALIZE I COULD ASK QUESTIONS.
THE COSMOS AUTOMATON IS A SELF-REPLICATING PROGRAM/ENTITY CONCEIVED ORIGINALLY TO OBEY ONE MASTER, PREPARING THE BASE WORLD OF ITS CONSTRUCTION FOR ITS PRIME CREATOR...

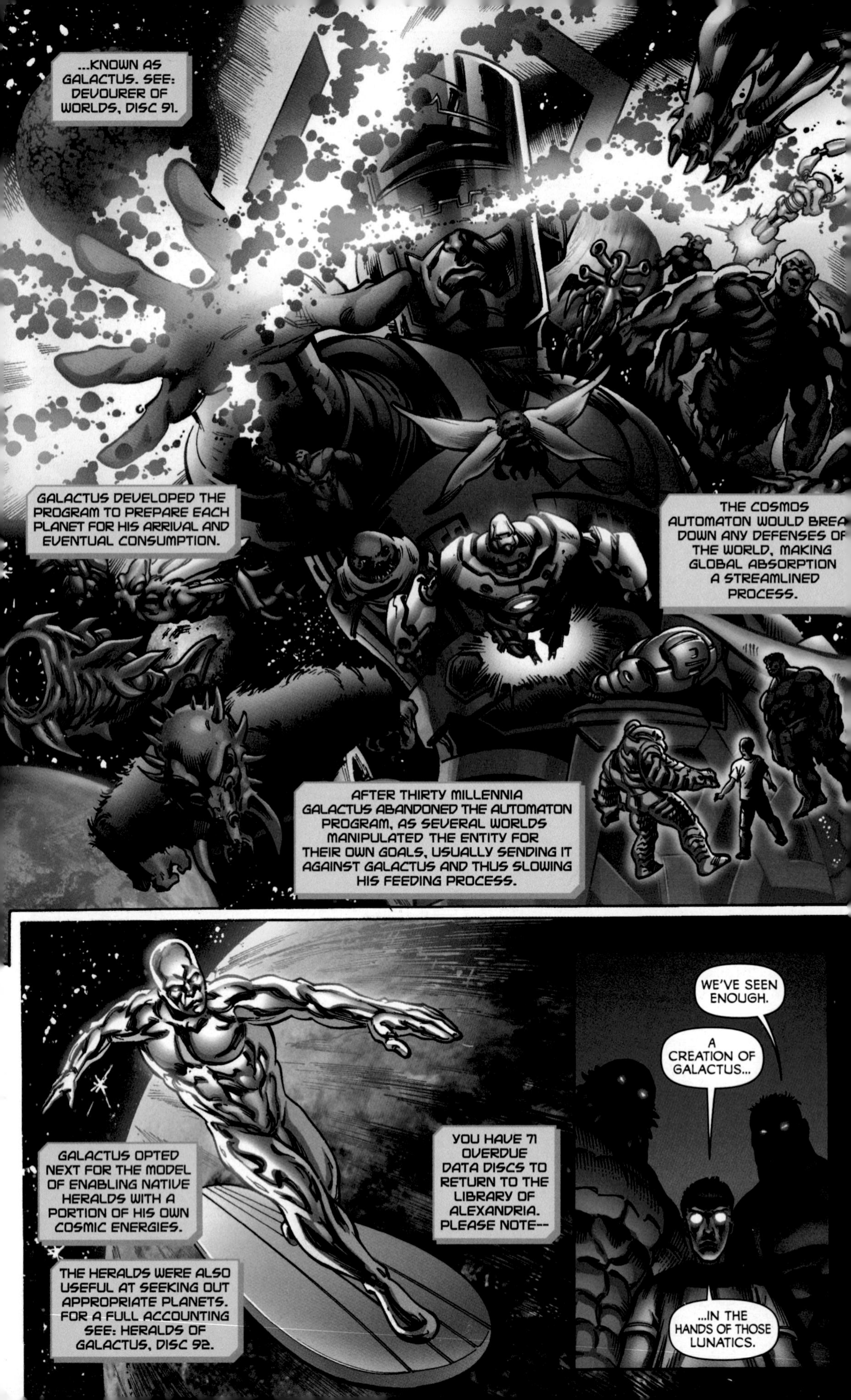
...KNOWN AS GALACTUS. SEE: DEVOURER OF WORLDS, DISC 91.
GALACTUS DEVELOPED THE PROGRAM TO PREPARE EACH PLANET FOR HIS ARRIVAL AND EVENTUAL CONSUMPTION.
THE COSMOS AUTOMATON WOULD BREA DOWN ANY DEFENSES OF THE WORLD, MAKING GLOBAL ABSORPTION A STREAMLINED PROCESS.
AFTER THIRTY MILLENNIA GALACTUS ABANDONED THE AUTOMATON PROGRAM, AS SEVERAL WORLDS MANIPULATED THE ENTITY FOR THEIR OWN GOALS, USUALLY SENDING IT AGAINST GALACTUS AND THUS SLOWING HIS FEEDING PROCESS.
GALACTUS OPTED NEXT FOR THE MODEL OF ENABLING NATIVE HERALDS WITH A PORTION OF HIS OWN COSMIC ENERGIES.
THE HERALDS WERE ALSO USEFUL AT SEEKING OUT APPROPRIATE PLANETS. FOR A FULL ACCOUNTING SEE: HERALDS OF GALACTUS, DISC 92.
YOU HAVE 71 OVERDUE DATA DISCS TO RETURN TO THE LIBRARY OF ALEXANDRIA. PLEASE NOTE--
WE'VE SEEN ENOUGH.
A CREATION OF GALACTUS...
...IN THE HANDS OF THOSE LUNATICS.

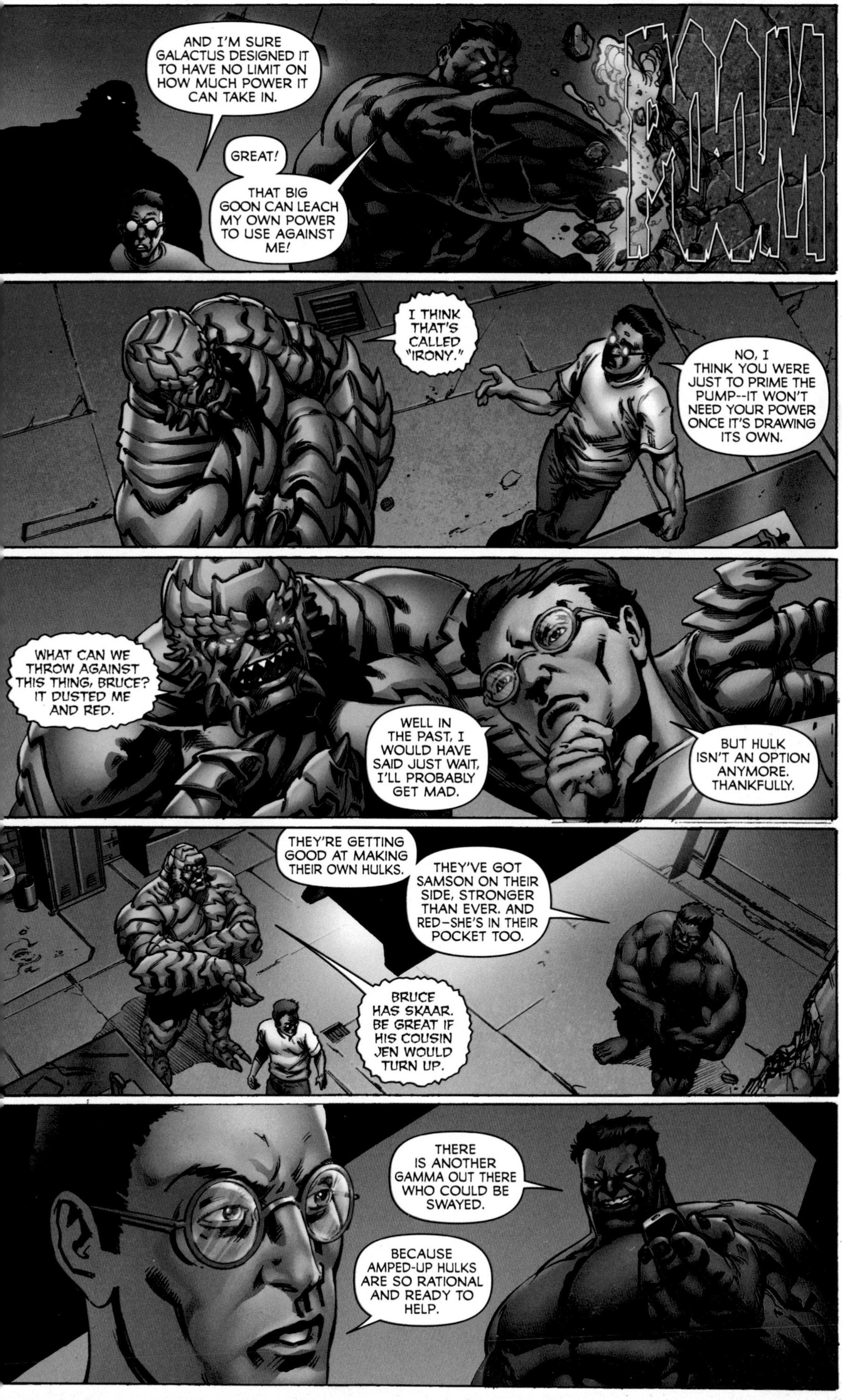
AND I'M SURE GALACTUS DESIGNED IT TO HAVE NO LIMIT ON HOW MUCH POWER IT CAN TAKE IN.
GREAT!
THAT BIG GOON CAN LEACH MY OWN POWER TO USE AGAINST ME!
I THINK THAT'S CALLED "IRONY."
NO, I THINK YOU WERE JUST TO PRIME THE PUMP--IT WON'T NEED YOUR POWER ONCE IT'S DRAWING ITS OWN.
WHAT CAN WE THROW AGAINST THIS THING, BRUCE? IT DUSTED ME AND RED.
WELL IN THE PAST, I WOULD HAVE SAID JUST WAIT, I'LL PROBABLY GET MAD.
BUT HULK ISN'T AN OPTION ANYMORE. THANKFULLY.
THEY'RE GETTING GOOD AT MAKING THEIR OWN HULKS.
THEY'VE GOT SAMSON ON THEIR SIDE, STRONGER THAN EVER. AND RED–SHE'S IN THEIR POCKET TOO.
BRUCE HAS SKAAR. BE GREAT IF HIS COUSIN JEN WOULD TURN UP.
THERE IS ANOTHER GAMMA OUT THERE WHO COULD BE SWAYED.
BECAUSE AMPED-UP HULKS ARE SO RATIONAL AND READY TO HELP.

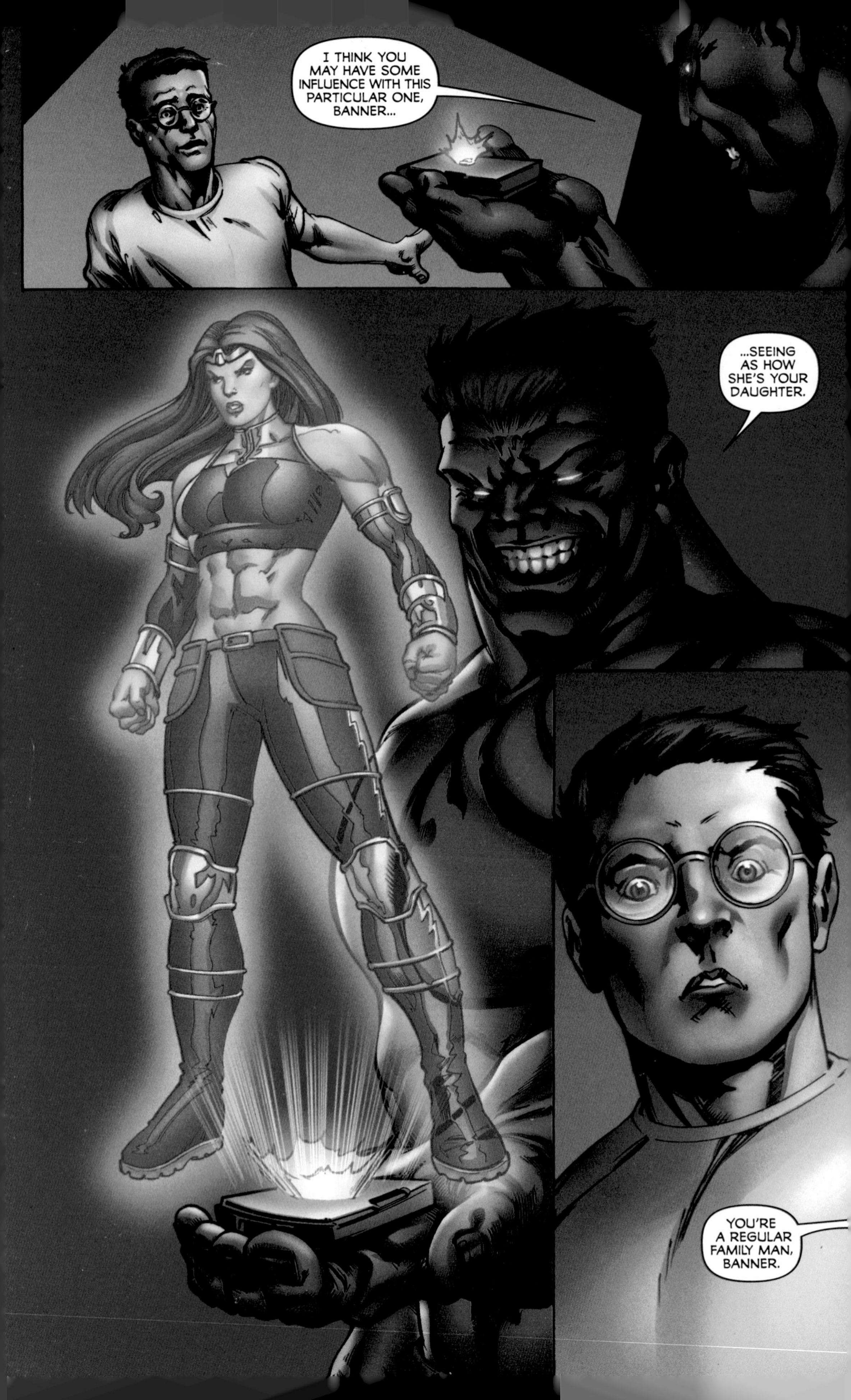
I THINK YOU MAY HAVE SOME INFLUENCE WITH THIS PARTICULAR ONE, BANNER...
...SEEING AS HOW SHE'S YOUR DAUGHTER.
YOU'RE A REGULAR FAMILY MAN, BANNER.

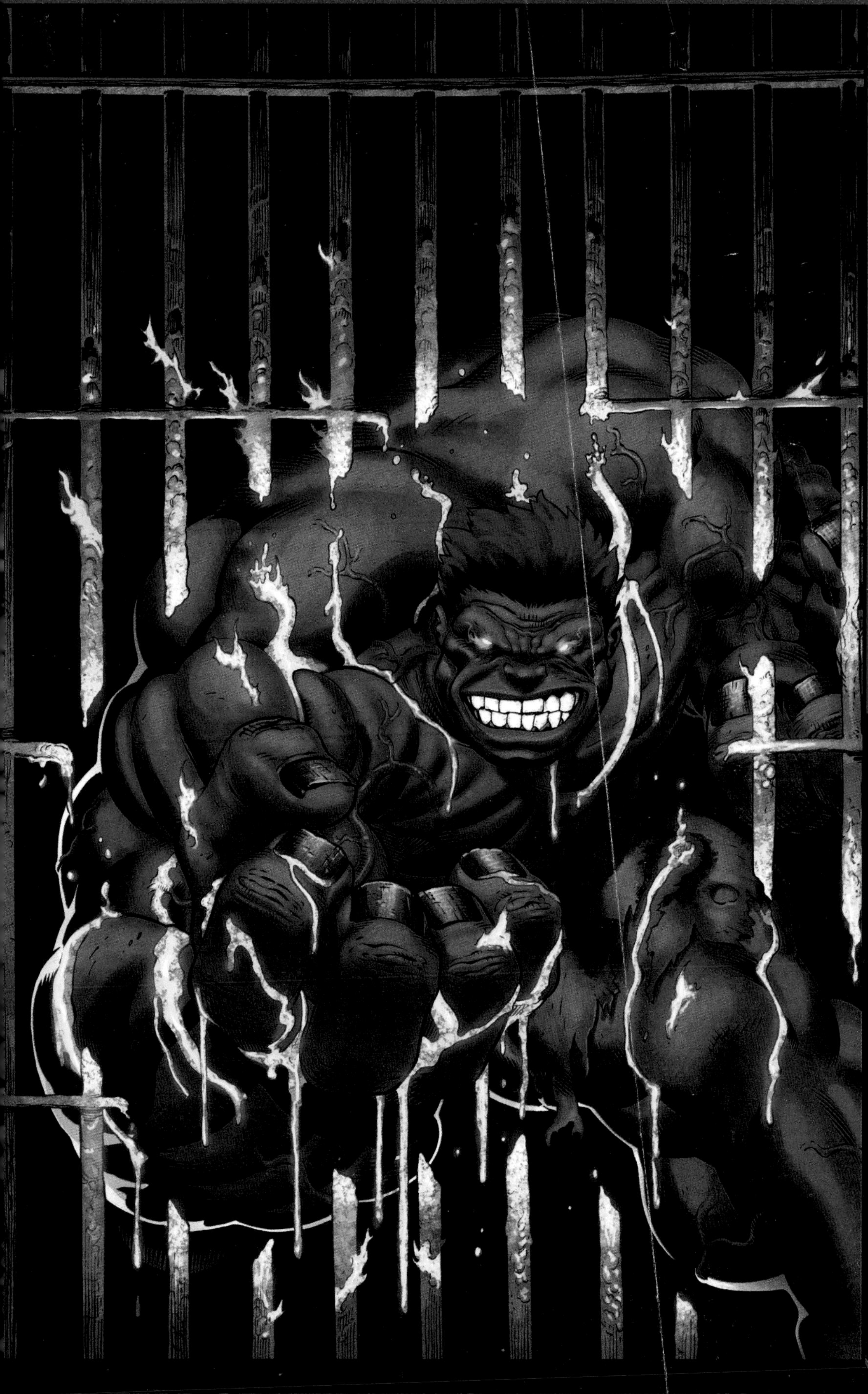

FALL OF THE HULKS: RED HULK #2

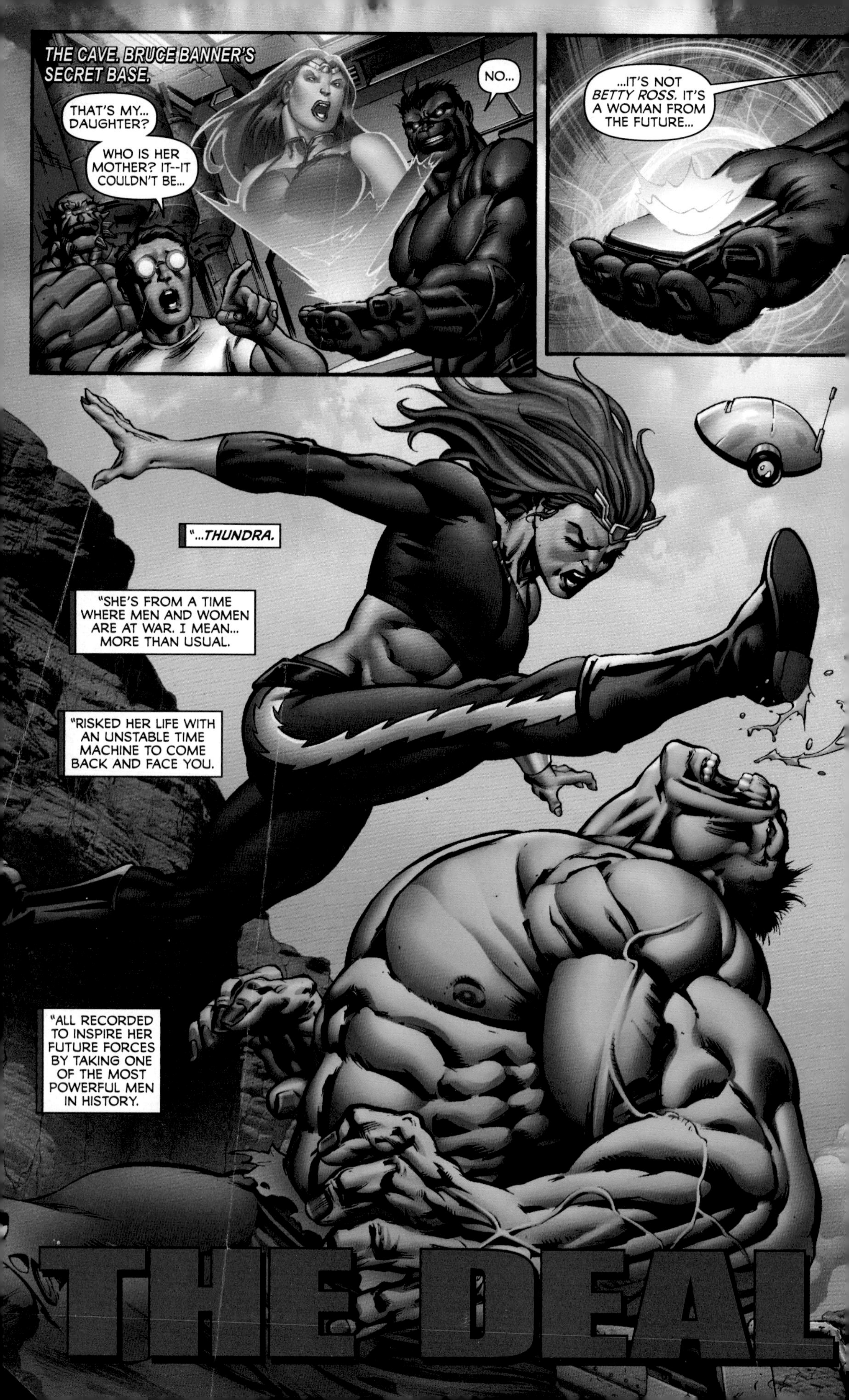
THE CAVE. BRUCE BANNER'S SECRET BASE.
THAT'S MY... DAUGHTER?
WHO IS HER MOTHER? IT--IT COULDN'T BE...
NO...
...IT'S NOT BETTY ROSS. IT'S A WOMAN FROM THE FUTURE...
"...THUNDRA.
"SHE'S FROM A TIME WHERE MEN AND WOMEN ARE AT WAR. I MEAN... MORE THAN USUAL.
"RISKED HER LIFE WITH AN UNSTABLE TIME MACHINE TO COME BACK AND FACE YOU.
"ALL RECORDED TO INSPIRE HER FUTURE FORCES BY TAKING ONE OF THE MOST POWERFUL MEN IN HISTORY.
THE DEAL

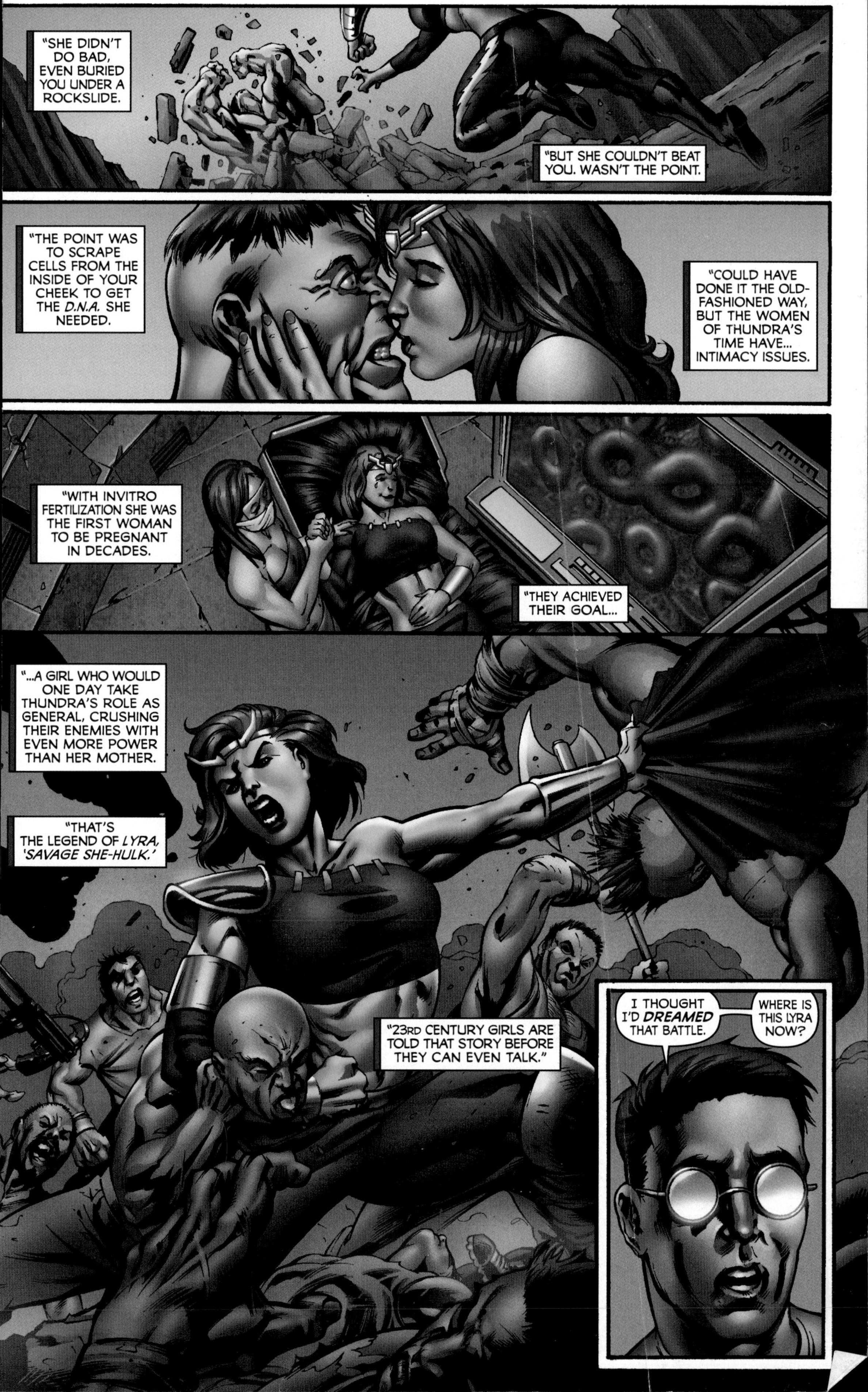
"SHE DIDN'T DO BAD, EVEN BURIED YOU UNDER A ROCKSLIDE.
"BUT SHE COULDN'T BEAT YOU. WASN'T THE POINT.
"THE POINT WAS TO SCRAPE CELLS FROM THE INSIDE OF YOUR CHEEK TO GET THE *D.N.A.* SHE NEEDED.
"COULD HAVE DONE IT THE OLD-FASHIONED WAY, BUT THE WOMEN OF THUNDRA'S TIME HAVE... INTIMACY ISSUES.
"WITH INVITRO FERTILIZATION SHE WAS THE FIRST WOMAN TO BE PREGNANT IN DECADES.
"THEY ACHIEVED THEIR GOAL...
"...A GIRL WHO WOULD ONE DAY TAKE THUNDRA'S ROLE AS GENERAL, CRUSHING THEIR ENEMIES WITH EVEN MORE POWER THAN HER MOTHER.
"THAT'S THE LEGEND OF *LYRA, 'SAVAGE SHE-HULK.'*
"23RD CENTURY GIRLS ARE TOLD THAT STORY BEFORE THEY CAN EVEN TALK."
I THOUGHT I'D ***DREAMED*** THAT BATTLE.
WHERE IS THIS LYRA NOW?

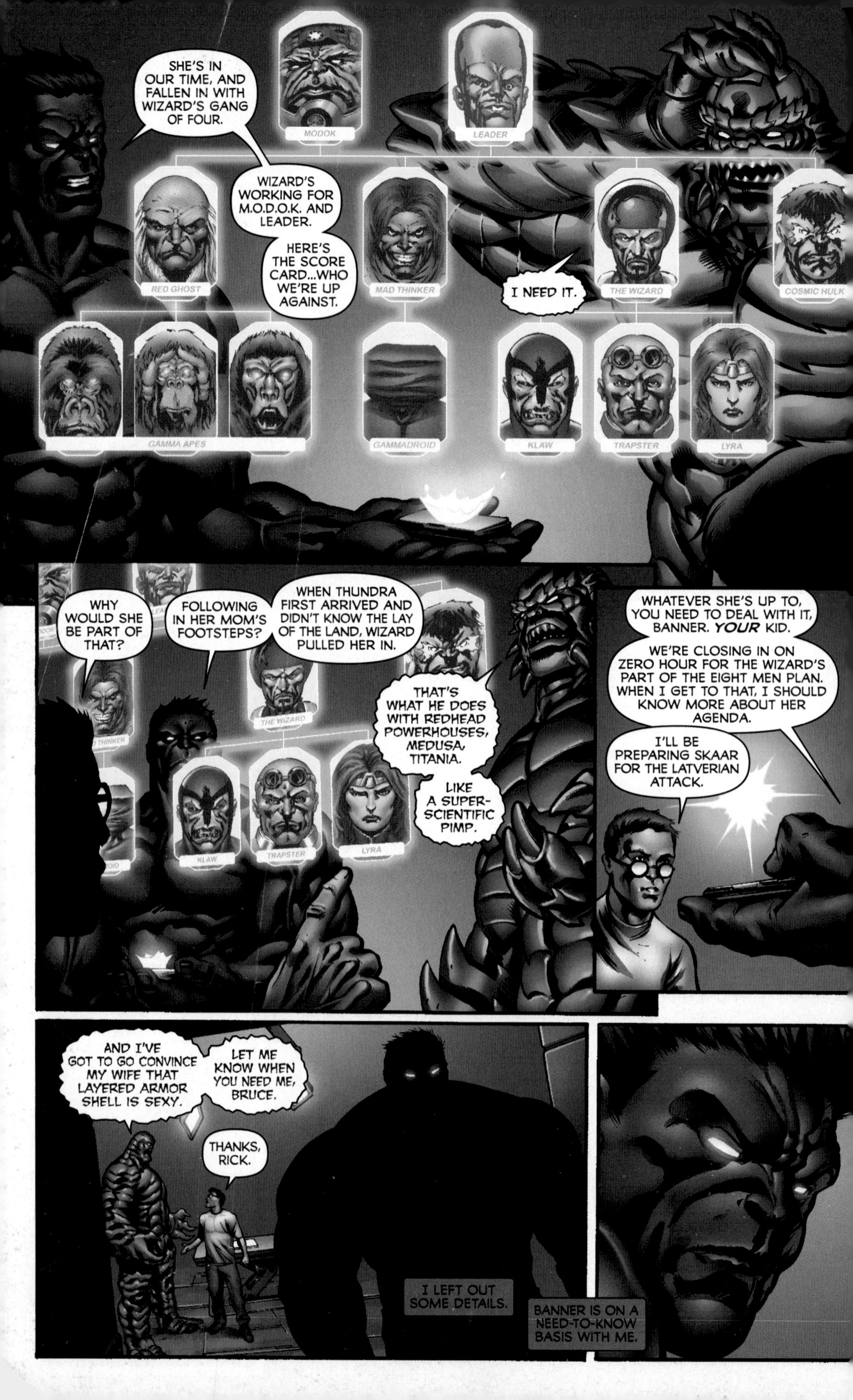
MODOK
LEADER
SHE'S IN OUR TIME, AND FALLEN IN WITH WIZARD'S GANG OF FOUR.
WIZARD'S WORKING FOR M.O.D.O.K. AND LEADER.
HERE'S THE SCORE CARD...WHO WE'RE UP AGAINST.
I NEED IT.
RED GHOST
MAD THINKER
THE WIZARD
COSMIC HULK
GAMMA APES
GAMMADROID
KLAW
TRAPSTER
LYRA
WHY WOULD SHE BE PART OF THAT?
FOLLOWING IN HER MOM'S FOOTSTEPS?
WHEN THUNDRA FIRST ARRIVED AND DIDN'T KNOW THE LAY OF THE LAND, WIZARD PULLED HER IN.
THAT'S WHAT HE DOES WITH REDHEAD POWERHOUSES, MEDUSA, TITANIA.
LIKE A SUPER-SCIENTIFIC PIMP.
WHATEVER SHE'S UP TO, YOU NEED TO DEAL WITH IT, BANNER. *YOUR* KID.
WE'RE CLOSING IN ON ZERO HOUR FOR THE WIZARD'S PART OF THE EIGHT MEN PLAN. WHEN I GET TO THAT, I SHOULD KNOW MORE ABOUT HER AGENDA.
I'LL BE PREPARING SKAAR FOR THE LATVERIAN ATTACK.
AND I'VE GOT TO GO CONVINCE MY WIFE THAT LAYERED ARMOR SHELL IS SEXY.
LET ME KNOW WHEN YOU NEED ME, BRUCE.
THANKS, RICK.
I LEFT OUT SOME DETAILS.
BANNER IS ON A NEED-TO-KNOW BASIS WITH ME.

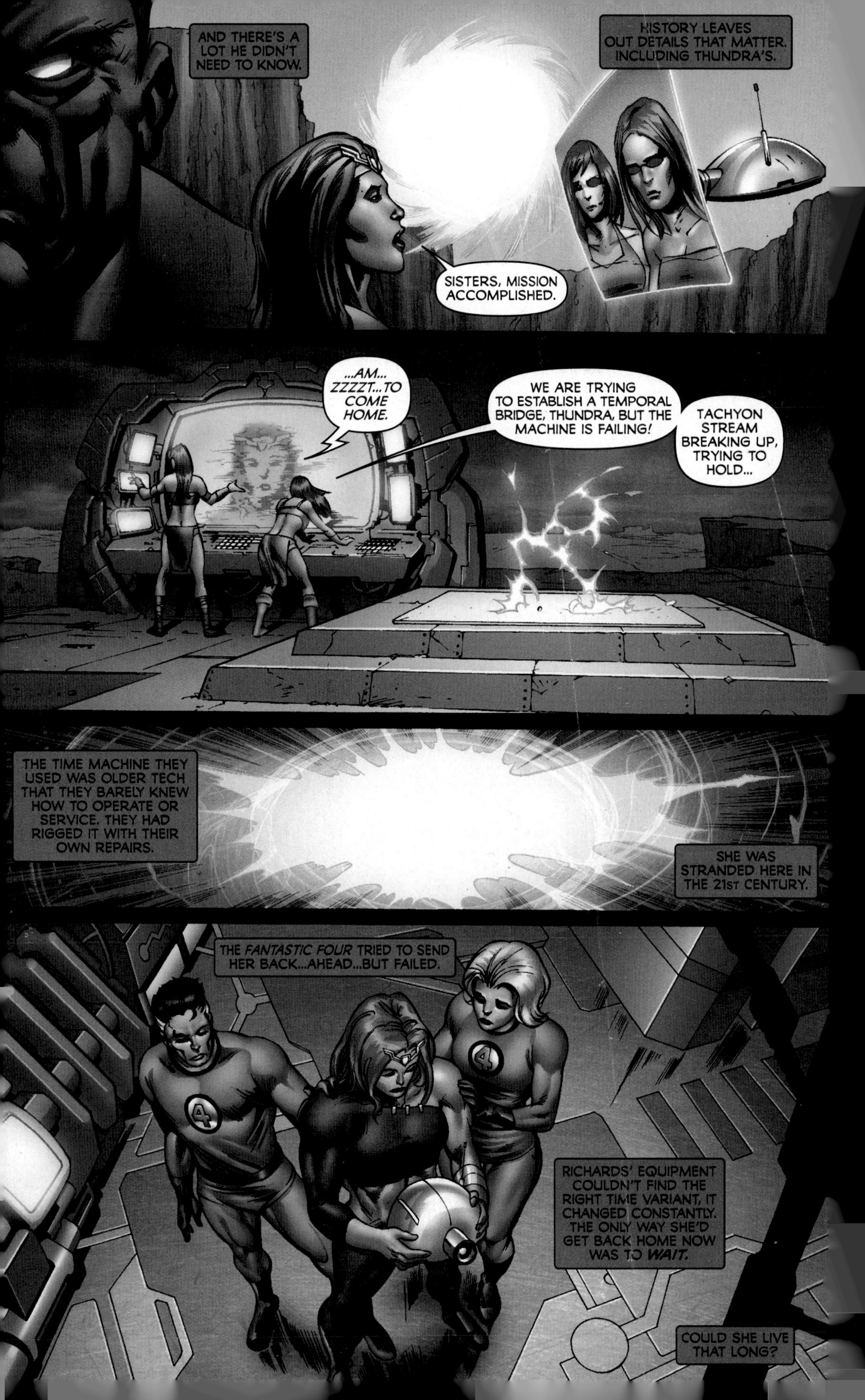
AND THERE'S A LOT HE DIDN'T NEED TO KNOW.
HISTORY LEAVES OUT DETAILS THAT MATTER. INCLUDING THUNDRA'S.
SISTERS, MISSION ACCOMPLISHED.
...AM... ZZZZT...TO COME HOME.
WE ARE TRYING TO ESTABLISH A TEMPORAL BRIDGE, THUNDRA, BUT THE MACHINE IS FAILING!
TACHYON STREAM BREAKING UP, TRYING TO HOLD...
THE TIME MACHINE THEY USED WAS OLDER TECH THAT THEY BARELY KNEW HOW TO OPERATE OR SERVICE. THEY HAD RIGGED IT WITH THEIR OWN REPAIRS.
SHE WAS STRANDED HERE IN THE 21ST CENTURY.
THE *FANTASTIC FOUR* TRIED TO SEND HER BACK...AHEAD...BUT FAILED.
RICHARDS' EQUIPMENT COULDN'T FIND THE RIGHT TIME VARIANT, IT CHANGED CONSTANTLY. THE ONLY WAY SHE'D GET BACK HOME NOW WAS TO ***WAIT.***
COULD SHE LIVE THAT LONG?

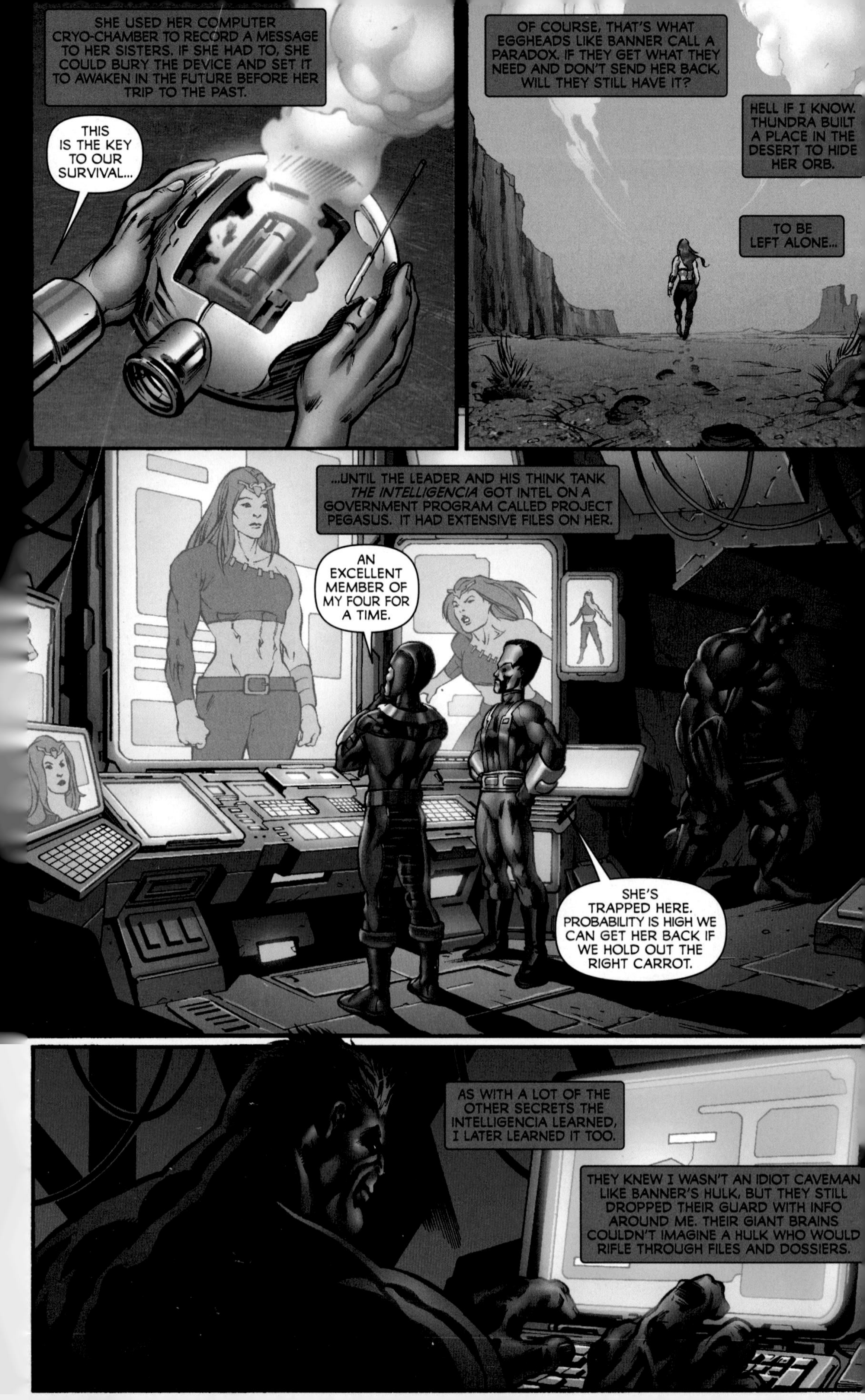
SHE USED HER COMPUTER CRYO-CHAMBER TO RECORD A MESSAGE TO HER SISTERS. IF SHE HAD TO, SHE COULD BURY THE DEVICE AND SET IT TO AWAKEN IN THE FUTURE BEFORE HER TRIP TO THE PAST.
THIS IS THE KEY TO OUR SURVIVAL...
OF COURSE, THAT'S WHAT EGGHEADS LIKE BANNER CALL A PARADOX. IF THEY GET WHAT THEY NEED AND DON'T SEND HER BACK, WILL THEY STILL HAVE IT?
HELL IF I KNOW. THUNDRA BUILT A PLACE IN THE DESERT TO HIDE HER ORB.
TO BE LEFT ALONE...
...UNTIL THE LEADER AND HIS THINK TANK *THE INTELLIGENCIA* GOT INTEL ON A GOVERNMENT PROGRAM CALLED PROJECT PEGASUS. IT HAD EXTENSIVE FILES ON HER.
AN EXCELLENT MEMBER OF MY FOUR FOR A TIME.
SHE'S TRAPPED HERE. PROBABILITY IS HIGH WE CAN GET HER BACK IF WE HOLD OUT THE RIGHT CARROT.
AS WITH A LOT OF THE OTHER SECRETS THE INTELLIGENCIA LEARNED, I LATER LEARNED IT TOO.
THEY KNEW I WASN'T AN IDIOT CAVEMAN LIKE BANNER'S HULK, BUT THEY STILL DROPPED THEIR GUARD WITH INFO AROUND ME. THEIR GIANT BRAINS COULDN'T IMAGINE A HULK WHO WOULD RIFLE THROUGH FILES AND DOSSIERS.

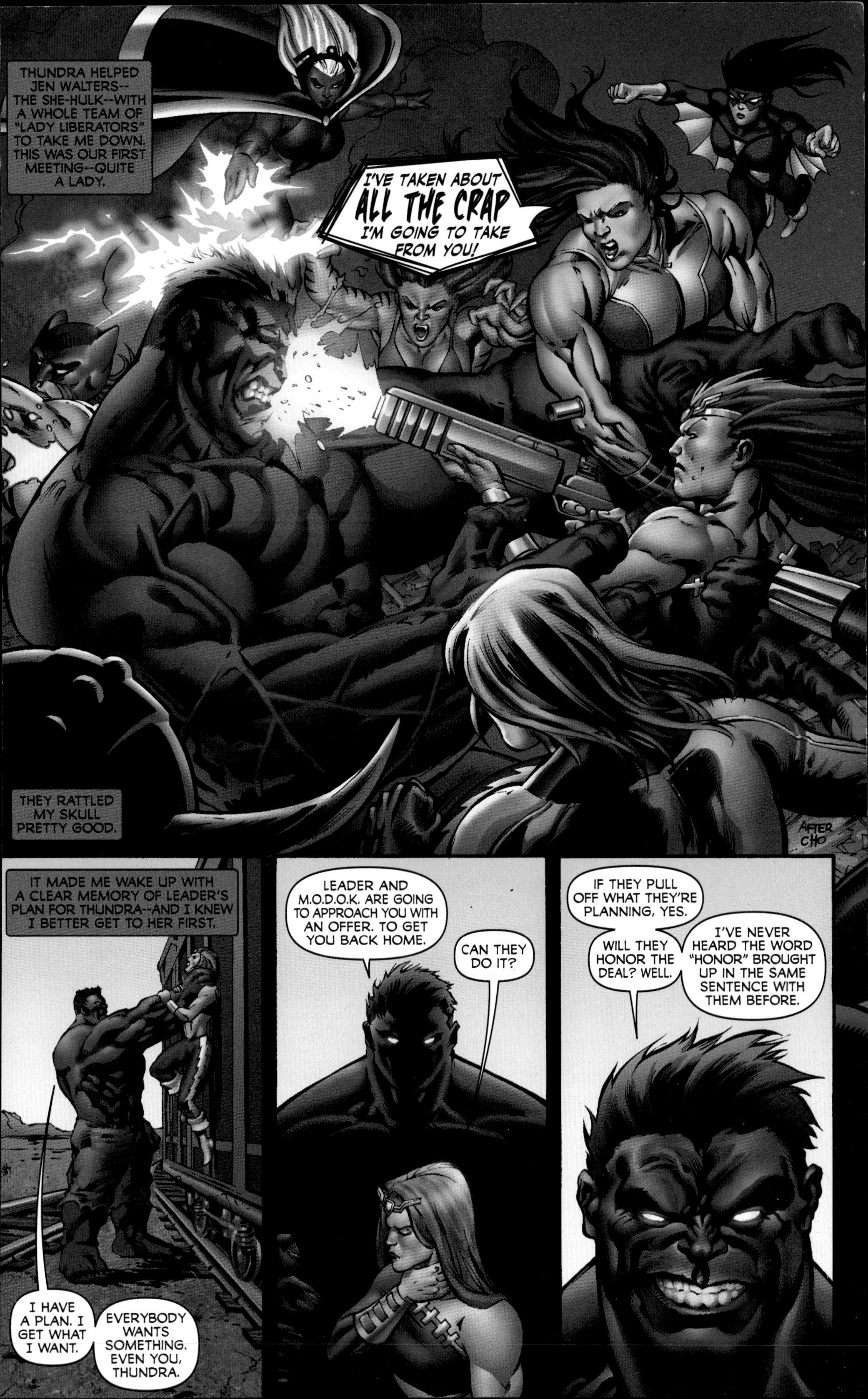
THUNDRA HELPED JEN WALTERS-- THE SHE-HULK--WITH A WHOLE TEAM OF "LADY LIBERATORS" TO TAKE ME DOWN. THIS WAS OUR FIRST MEETING--QUITE A LADY.
I'VE TAKEN ABOUT ALL THE CRAP I'M GOING TO TAKE FROM YOU!
THEY RATTLED MY SKULL PRETTY GOOD.
AFTER CHO
IT MADE ME WAKE UP WITH A CLEAR MEMORY OF LEADER'S PLAN FOR THUNDRA--AND I KNEW I BETTER GET TO HER FIRST.
I HAVE A PLAN. I GET WHAT I WANT.
EVERYBODY WANTS SOMETHING. EVEN YOU, THUNDRA.
LEADER AND M.O.D.O.K. ARE GOING TO APPROACH YOU WITH AN OFFER. TO GET YOU BACK HOME.
CAN THEY DO IT?
IF THEY PULL OFF WHAT THEY'RE PLANNING, YES.
WILL THEY HONOR THE DEAL? WELL.
I'VE NEVER HEARD THE WORD "HONOR" BROUGHT UP IN THE SAME SENTENCE WITH THEM BEFORE.

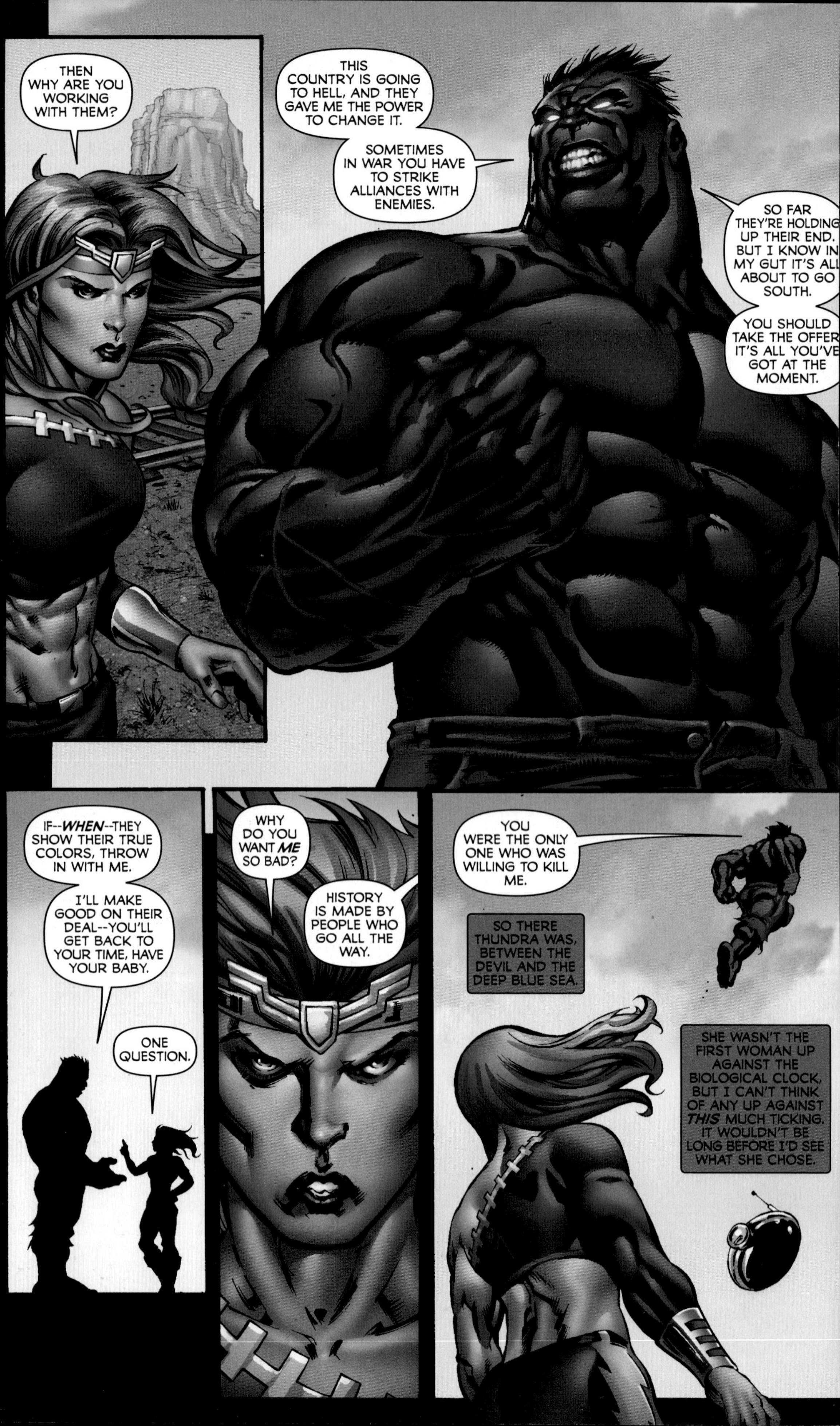
THEN WHY ARE YOU WORKING WITH THEM?
THIS COUNTRY IS GOING TO HELL, AND THEY GAVE ME THE POWER TO CHANGE IT.
SOMETIMES IN WAR YOU HAVE TO STRIKE ALLIANCES WITH ENEMIES.
SO FAR THEY'RE HOLDING UP THEIR END. BUT I KNOW IN MY GUT IT'S ALL ABOUT TO GO SOUTH.
YOU SHOULD TAKE THE OFFER. IT'S ALL YOU'VE GOT AT THE MOMENT.
IF--WHEN--THEY SHOW THEIR TRUE COLORS, THROW IN WITH ME.
I'LL MAKE GOOD ON THEIR DEAL--YOU'LL GET BACK TO YOUR TIME, HAVE YOUR BABY.
ONE QUESTION.
WHY DO YOU WANT ME SO BAD?
HISTORY IS MADE BY PEOPLE WHO GO ALL THE WAY.
YOU WERE THE ONLY ONE WHO WAS WILLING TO KILL ME.
SO THERE THUNDRA WAS, BETWEEN THE DEVIL AND THE DEEP BLUE SEA.
SHE WASN'T THE FIRST WOMAN UP AGAINST THE BIOLOGICAL CLOCK, BUT I CAN'T THINK OF ANY UP AGAINST THIS MUCH TICKING. IT WOULDN'T BE LONG BEFORE I'D SEE WHAT SHE CHOSE.

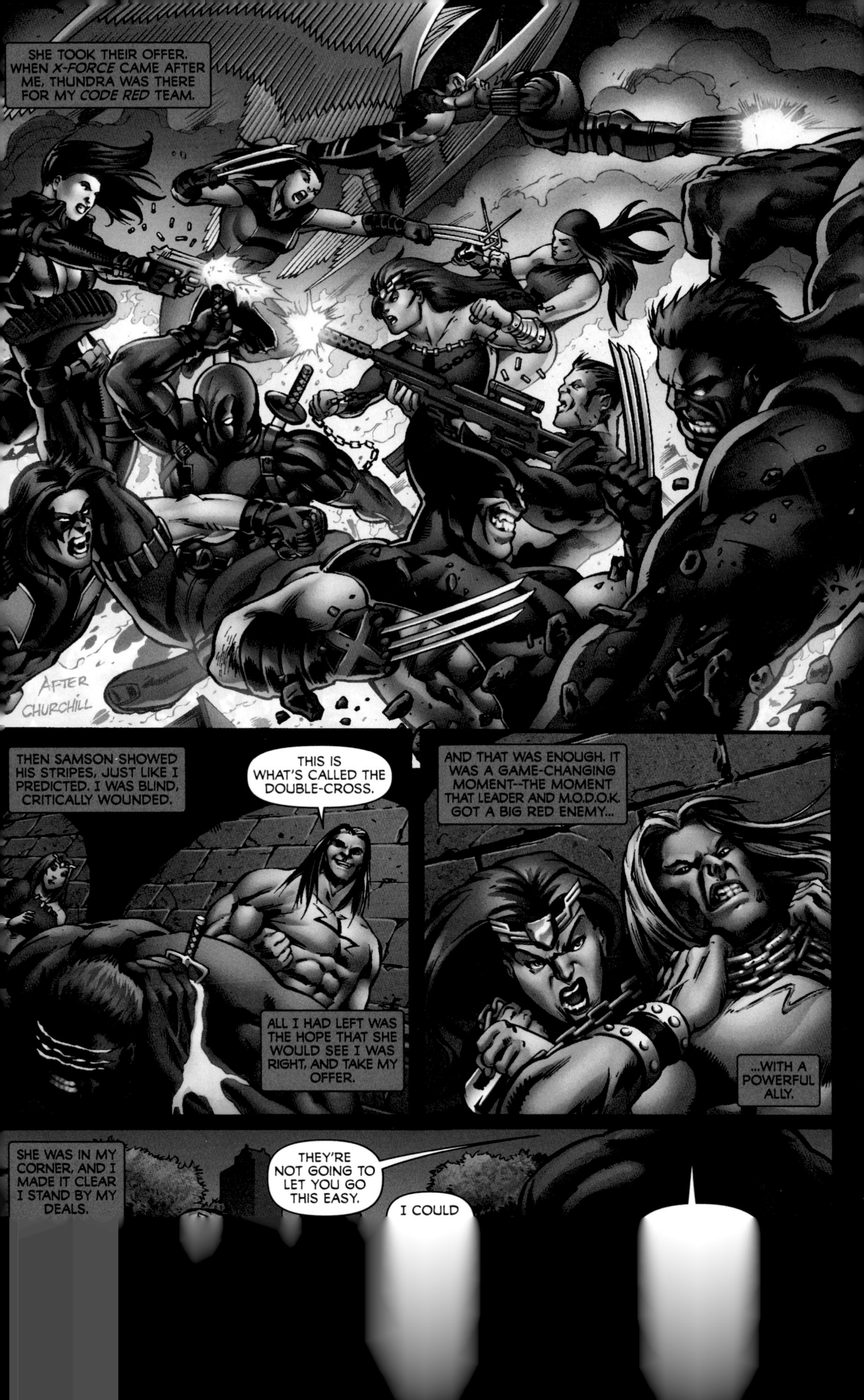
SHE TOOK THEIR OFFER. WHEN X-FORCE CAME AFTER ME, THUNDRA WAS THERE FOR MY CODE RED TEAM.
AFTER CHURCHILL
THEN SAMSON SHOWED HIS STRIPES, JUST LIKE I PREDICTED. I WAS BLIND, CRITICALLY WOUNDED.
THIS IS WHAT'S CALLED THE DOUBLE-CROSS.
ALL I HAD LEFT WAS THE HOPE THAT SHE WOULD SEE I WAS RIGHT, AND TAKE MY OFFER.
AND THAT WAS ENOUGH. IT WAS A GAME-CHANGING MOMENT--THE MOMENT THAT LEADER AND M.O.D.O.K. GOT A BIG RED ENEMY...
...WITH A POWERFUL ALLY.
SHE WAS IN MY CORNER, AND I MADE IT CLEAR I STAND BY MY DEALS.
THEY'RE NOT GOING TO LET YOU GO THIS EASY.
I COULD

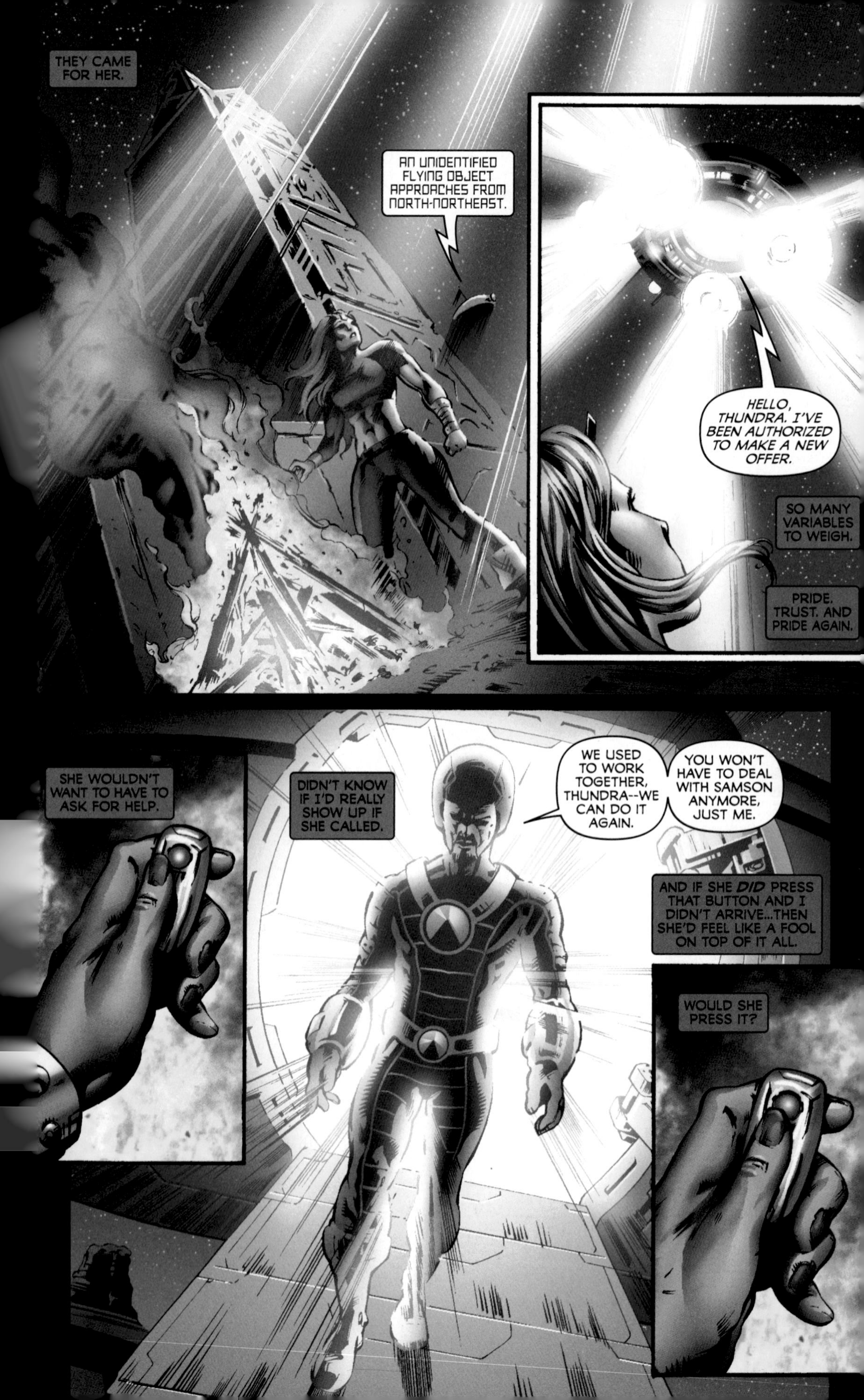
THEY CAME FOR HER.
AN UNIDENTIFIED FLYING OBJECT APPROACHES FROM NORTH-NORTHEAST.
HELLO, THUNDRA. I'VE BEEN AUTHORIZED TO MAKE A NEW OFFER.
SO MANY VARIABLES TO WEIGH.
PRIDE. TRUST. AND PRIDE AGAIN.
SHE WOULDN'T WANT TO HAVE TO ASK FOR HELP.
DIDN'T KNOW IF I'D REALLY SHOW UP IF SHE CALLED.
WE USED TO WORK TOGETHER, THUNDRA--WE CAN DO IT AGAIN.
YOU WON'T HAVE TO DEAL WITH SAMSON ANYMORE, JUST ME.
AND IF SHE DID PRESS THAT BUTTON AND I DIDN'T ARRIVE...THEN SHE'D FEEL LIKE A FOOL ON TOP OF IT ALL.
WOULD SHE PRESS IT?

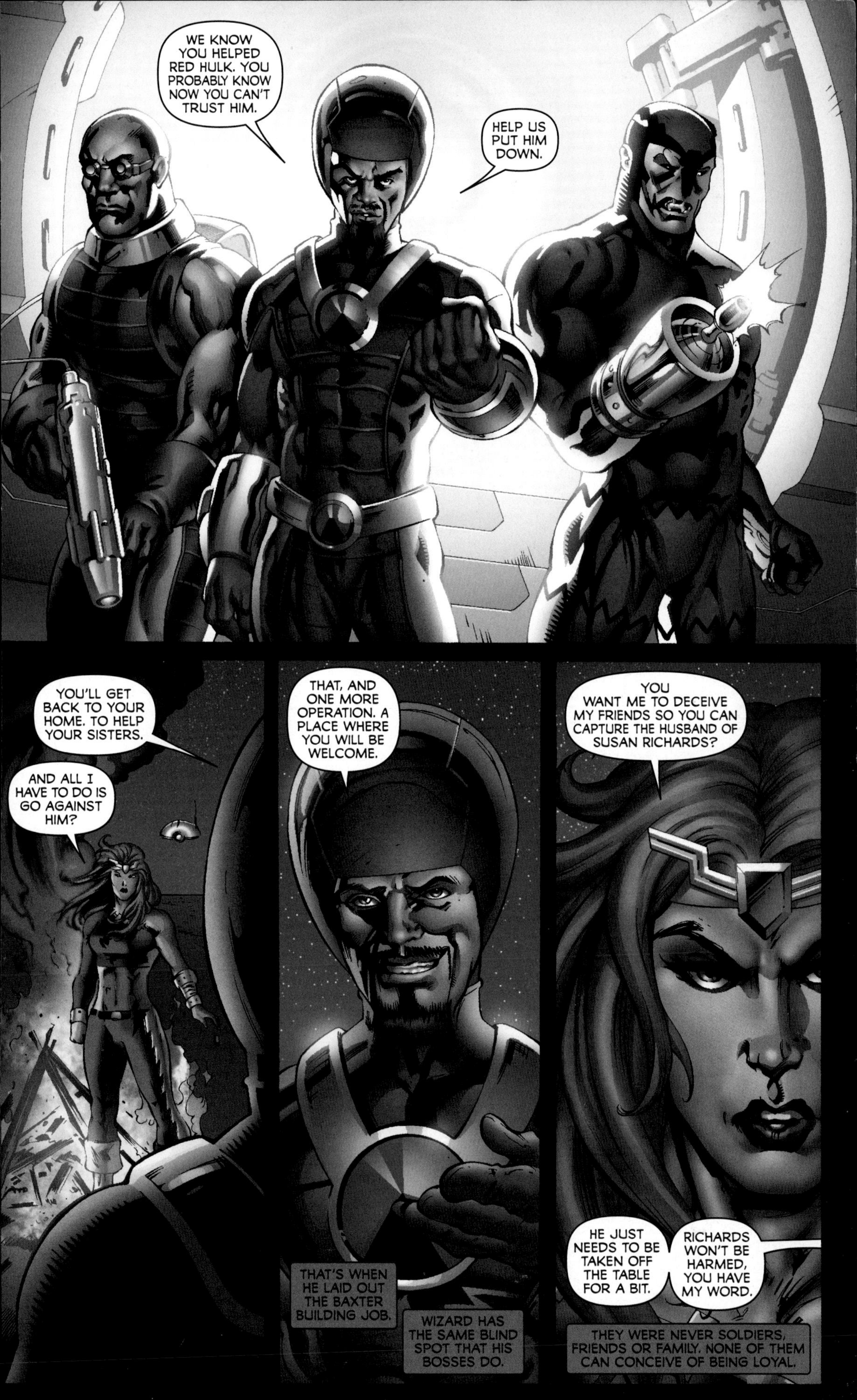
WE KNOW YOU HELPED RED HULK. YOU PROBABLY KNOW NOW YOU CAN'T TRUST HIM.
HELP US PUT HIM DOWN.
YOU'LL GET BACK TO YOUR HOME. TO HELP YOUR SISTERS.
AND ALL I HAVE TO DO IS GO AGAINST HIM?
THAT, AND ONE MORE OPERATION. A PLACE WHERE YOU WILL BE WELCOME.
THAT'S WHEN HE LAID OUT THE BAXTER BUILDING JOB.
WIZARD HAS THE SAME BLIND SPOT THAT HIS BOSSES DO.
YOU WANT ME TO DECEIVE MY FRIENDS SO YOU CAN CAPTURE THE HUSBAND OF SUSAN RICHARDS?
HE JUST NEEDS TO BE TAKEN OFF THE TABLE FOR A BIT.
RICHARDS WON'T BE HARMED, YOU HAVE MY WORD.
THEY WERE NEVER SOLDIERS, FRIENDS OR FAMILY. NONE OF THEM CAN CONCEIVE OF BEING LOYAL.

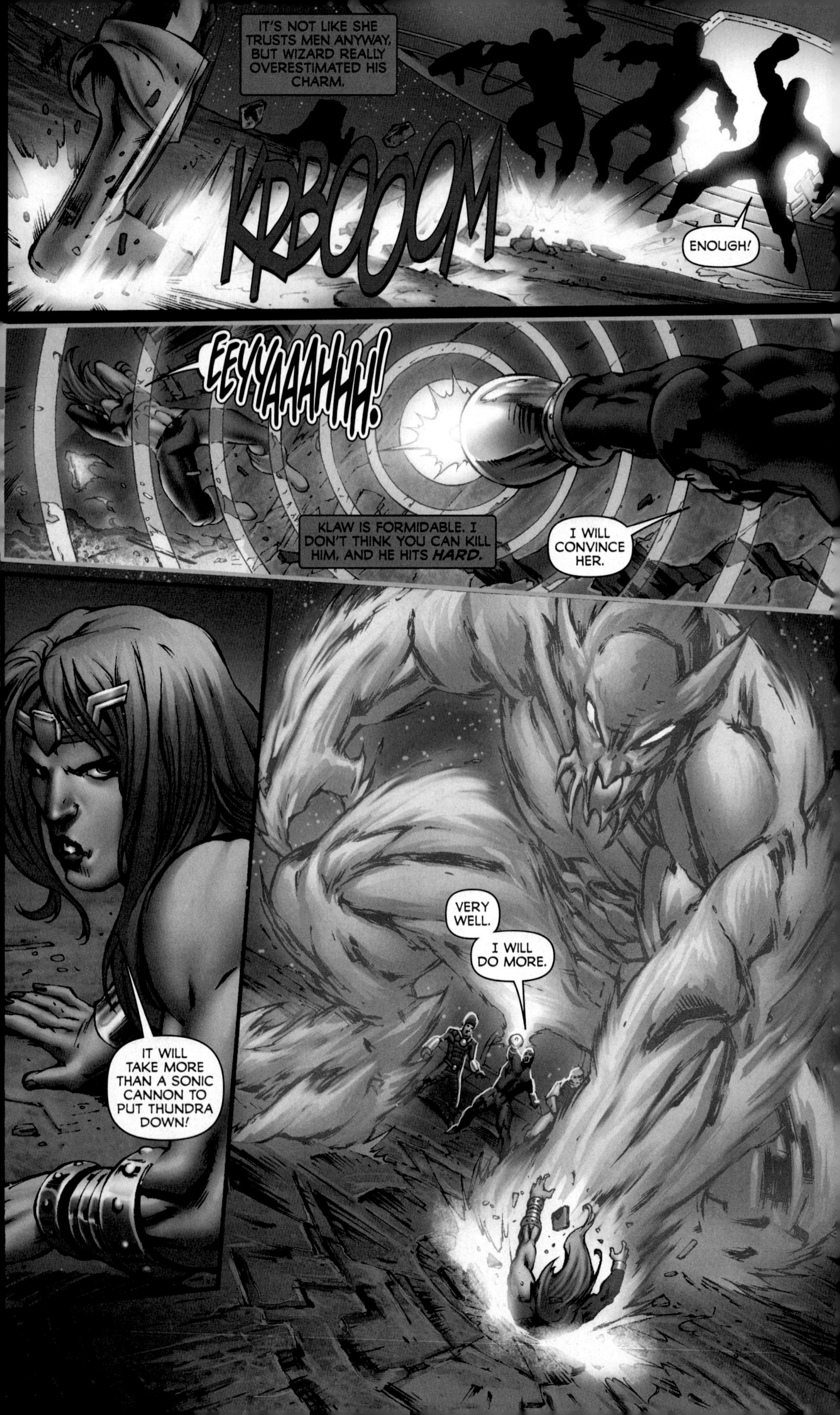

IT'S NOT LIKE SHE TRUSTS MEN ANYWAY, BUT WIZARD REALLY OVERESTIMATED HIS CHARM.
KRBOOOM
ENOUGH!
EEYYAAAHHH!
KLAW IS FORMIDABLE. I DON'T THINK YOU CAN KILL HIM, AND HE HITS HARD.
I WILL CONVINCE HER.
IT WILL TAKE MORE THAN A SONIC CANNON TO PUT THUNDRA DOWN!
VERY WELL.
I WILL DO MORE.

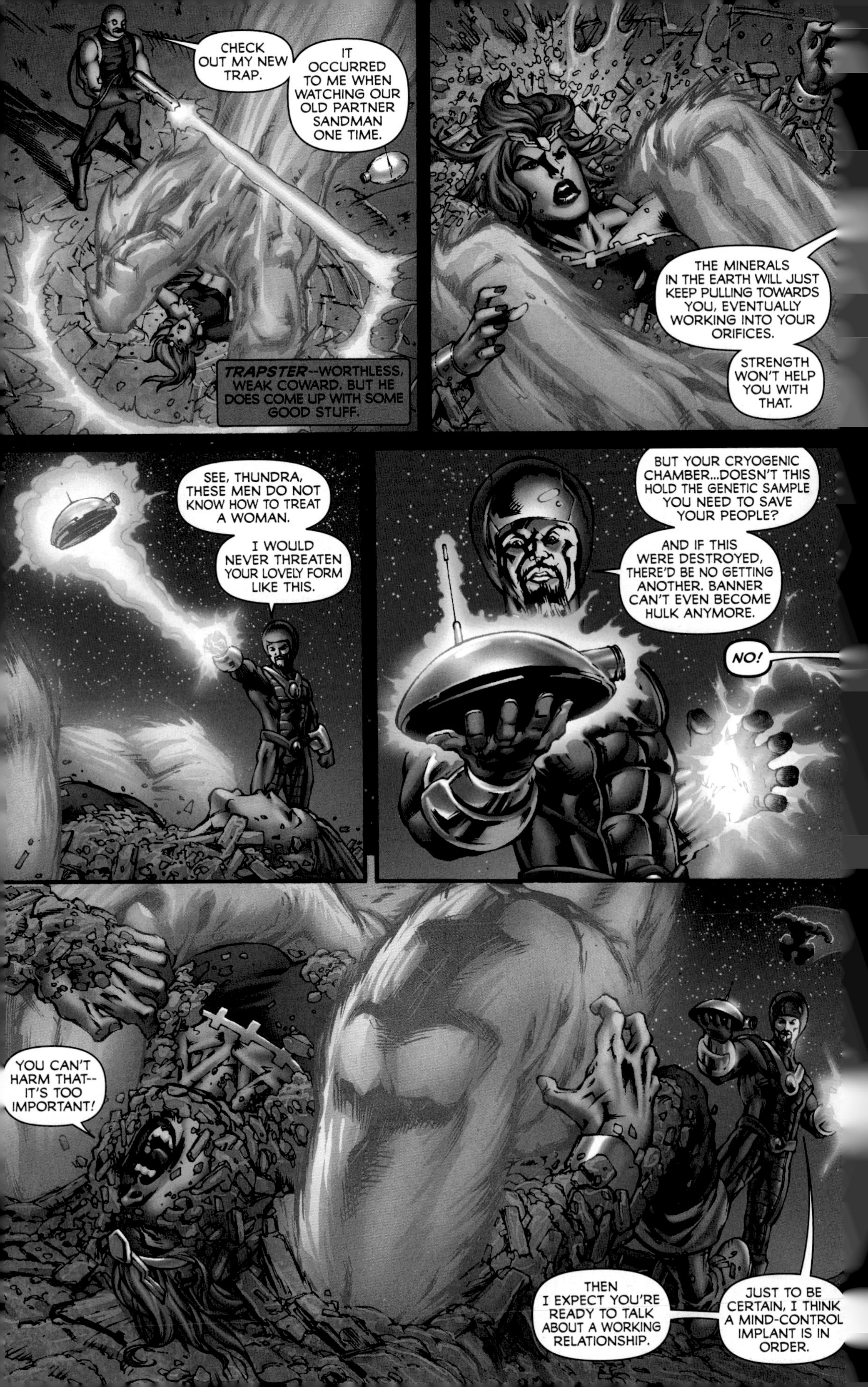

CHECK OUT MY NEW TRAP.
IT OCCURRED TO ME WHEN WATCHING OUR OLD PARTNER SANDMAN ONE TIME.
TRAPSTER--WORTHLESS, WEAK COWARD. BUT HE DOES COME UP WITH SOME GOOD STUFF.
THE MINERALS IN THE EARTH WILL JUST KEEP PULLING TOWARDS YOU, EVENTUALLY WORKING INTO YOUR ORIFICES.
STRENGTH WON'T HELP YOU WITH THAT.
SEE, THUNDRA, THESE MEN DO NOT KNOW HOW TO TREAT A WOMAN.
I WOULD NEVER THREATEN YOUR LOVELY FORM LIKE THIS.
BUT YOUR CRYOGENIC CHAMBER...DOESN'T THIS HOLD THE GENETIC SAMPLE YOU NEED TO SAVE YOUR PEOPLE?
AND IF THIS WERE DESTROYED, THERE'D BE NO GETTING ANOTHER. BANNER CAN'T EVEN BECOME HULK ANYMORE.
NO!
YOU CAN'T HARM THAT-- IT'S TOO IMPORTANT!
THEN I EXPECT YOU'RE READY TO TALK ABOUT A WORKING RELATIONSHIP.
JUST TO BE CERTAIN, I THINK A MIND-CONTROL IMPLANT IS IN ORDER.

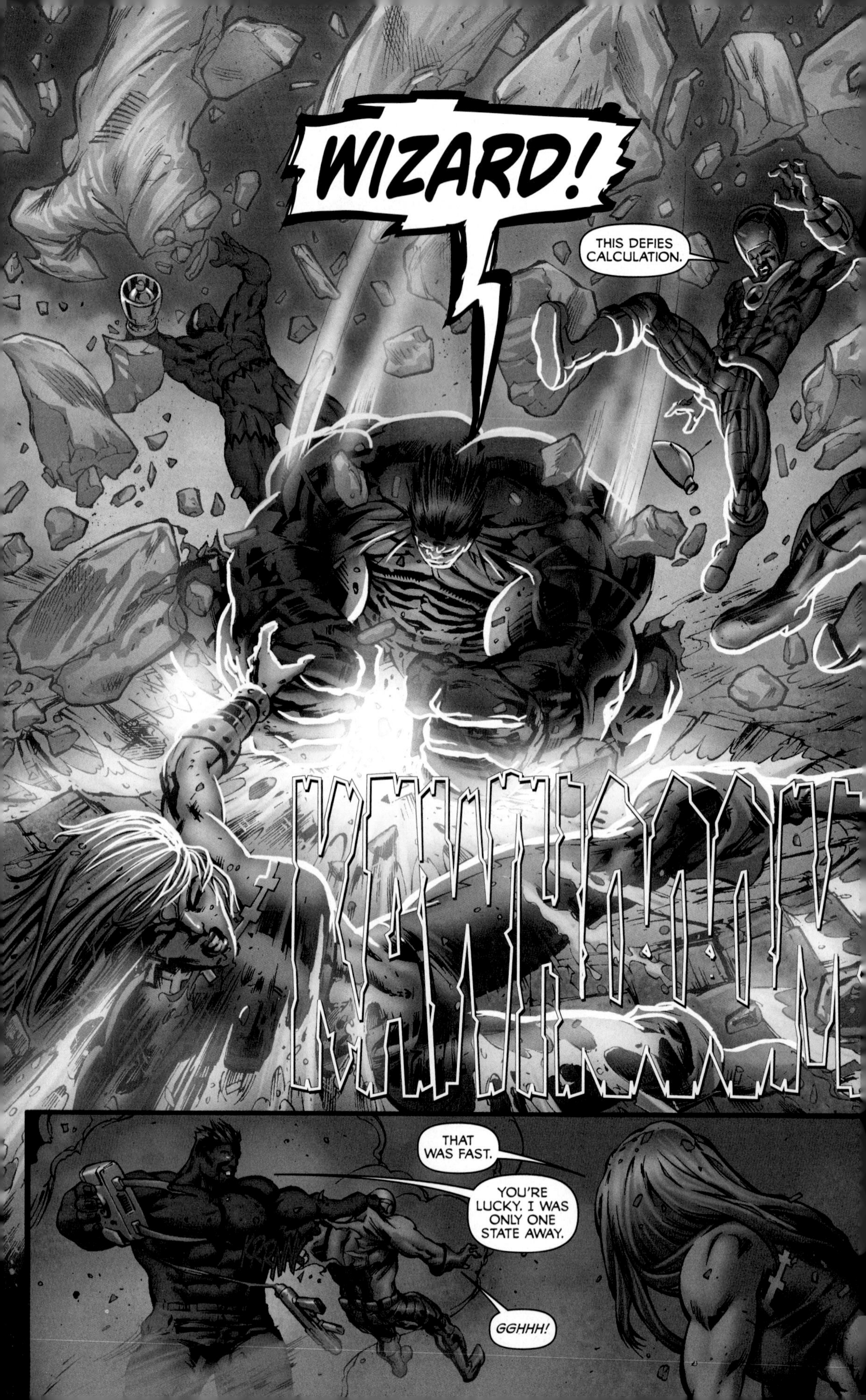
WIZARD!
THIS DEFIES CALCULATION.
THAT WAS FAST.
YOU'RE LUCKY. I WAS ONLY ONE STATE AWAY.
GGHHH!

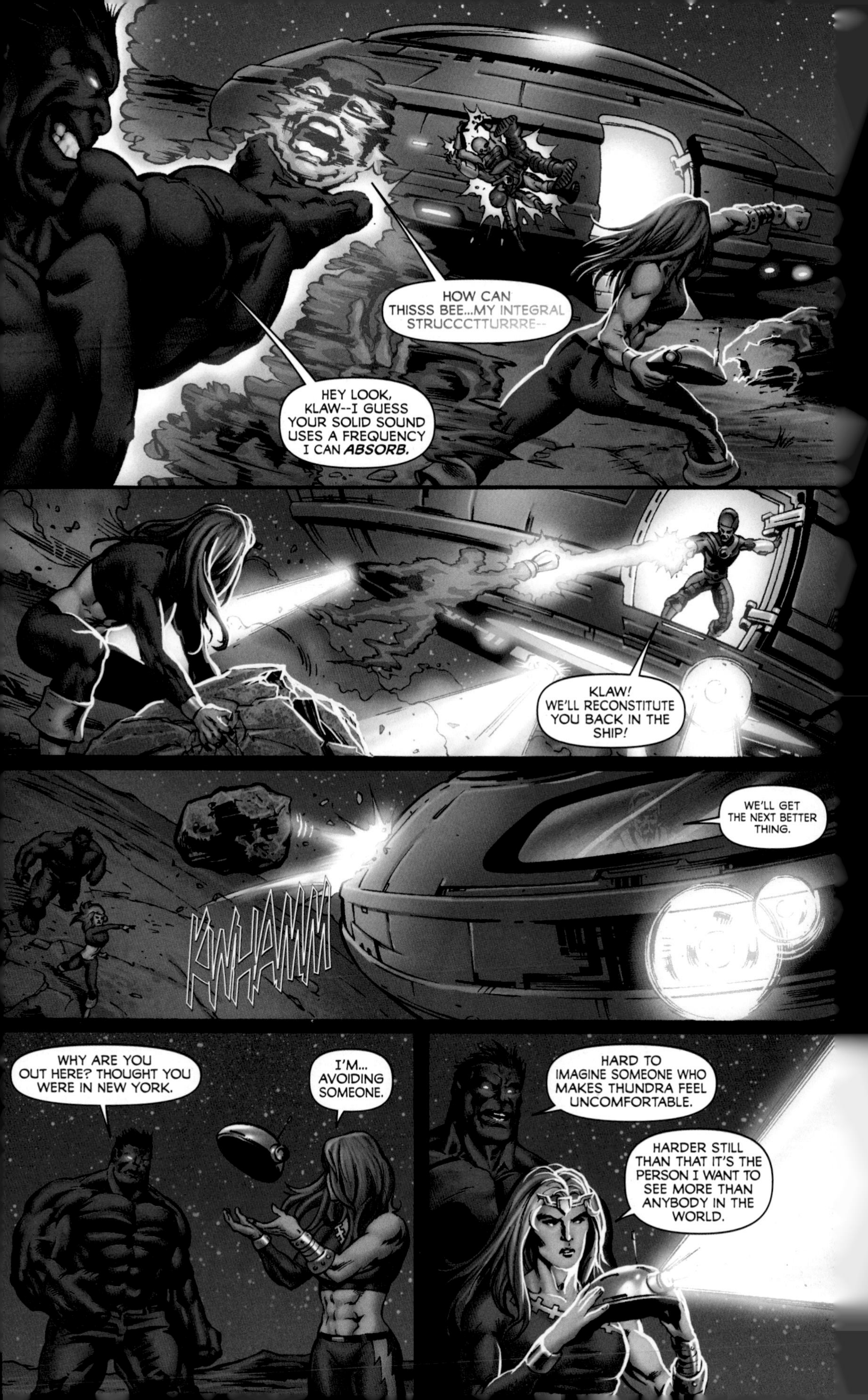
HOW CAN THISSS BEE...MY INTEGRAL STRUCCCTTURRRE--
HEY LOOK, KLAW--I GUESS YOUR SOLID SOUND USES A FREQUENCY I CAN ABSORB.
KLAW! WE'LL RECONSTITUTE YOU BACK IN THE SHIP!
WE'LL GET THE NEXT BETTER THING.
KWHAMM
WHY ARE YOU OUT HERE? THOUGHT YOU WERE IN NEW YORK.
I'M... AVOIDING SOMEONE.
HARD TO IMAGINE SOMEONE WHO MAKES THUNDRA FEEL UNCOMFORTABLE.
HARDER STILL THAN THAT IT'S THE PERSON I WANT TO SEE MORE THAN ANYBODY IN THE WORLD.

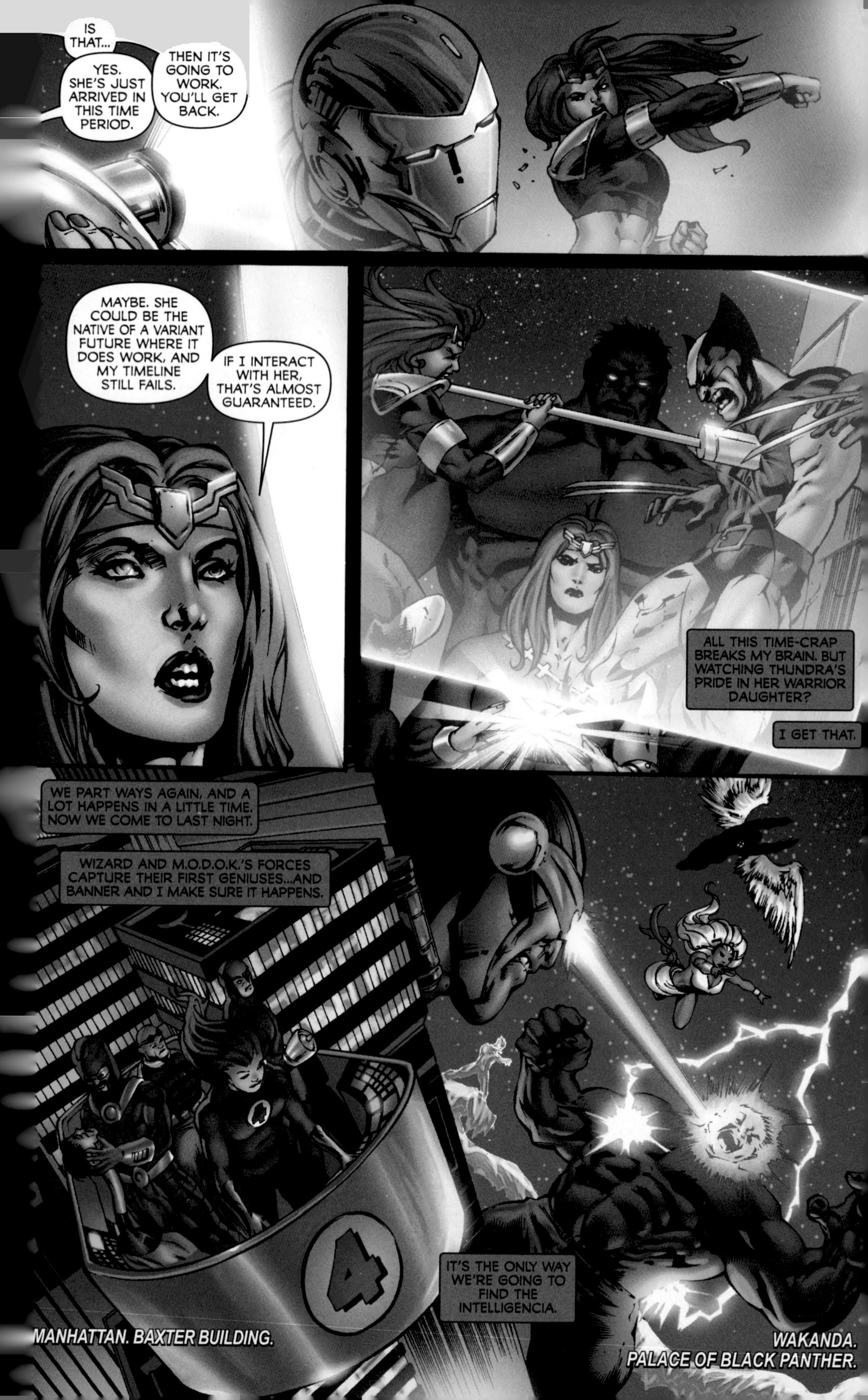
IS THAT...
YES. SHE'S JUST ARRIVED IN THIS TIME PERIOD.
THEN IT'S GOING TO WORK. YOU'LL GET BACK.
MAYBE. SHE COULD BE THE NATIVE OF A VARIANT FUTURE WHERE IT DOES WORK, AND MY TIMELINE STILL FAILS.
IF I INTERACT WITH HER, THAT'S ALMOST GUARANTEED.
ALL THIS TIME-CRAP BREAKS MY BRAIN. BUT WATCHING THUNDRA'S PRIDE IN HER WARRIOR DAUGHTER?
I GET THAT.
WE PART WAYS AGAIN, AND A LOT HAPPENS IN A LITTLE TIME. NOW WE COME TO LAST NIGHT.
WIZARD AND M.O.D.O.K.'S FORCES CAPTURE THEIR FIRST GENIUSES...AND BANNER AND I MAKE SURE IT HAPPENS.
MANHATTAN. BAXTER BUILDING.
IT'S THE ONLY WAY WE'RE GOING TO FIND THE INTELLIGENCIA.
WAKANDA. PALACE OF BLACK PANTHER.

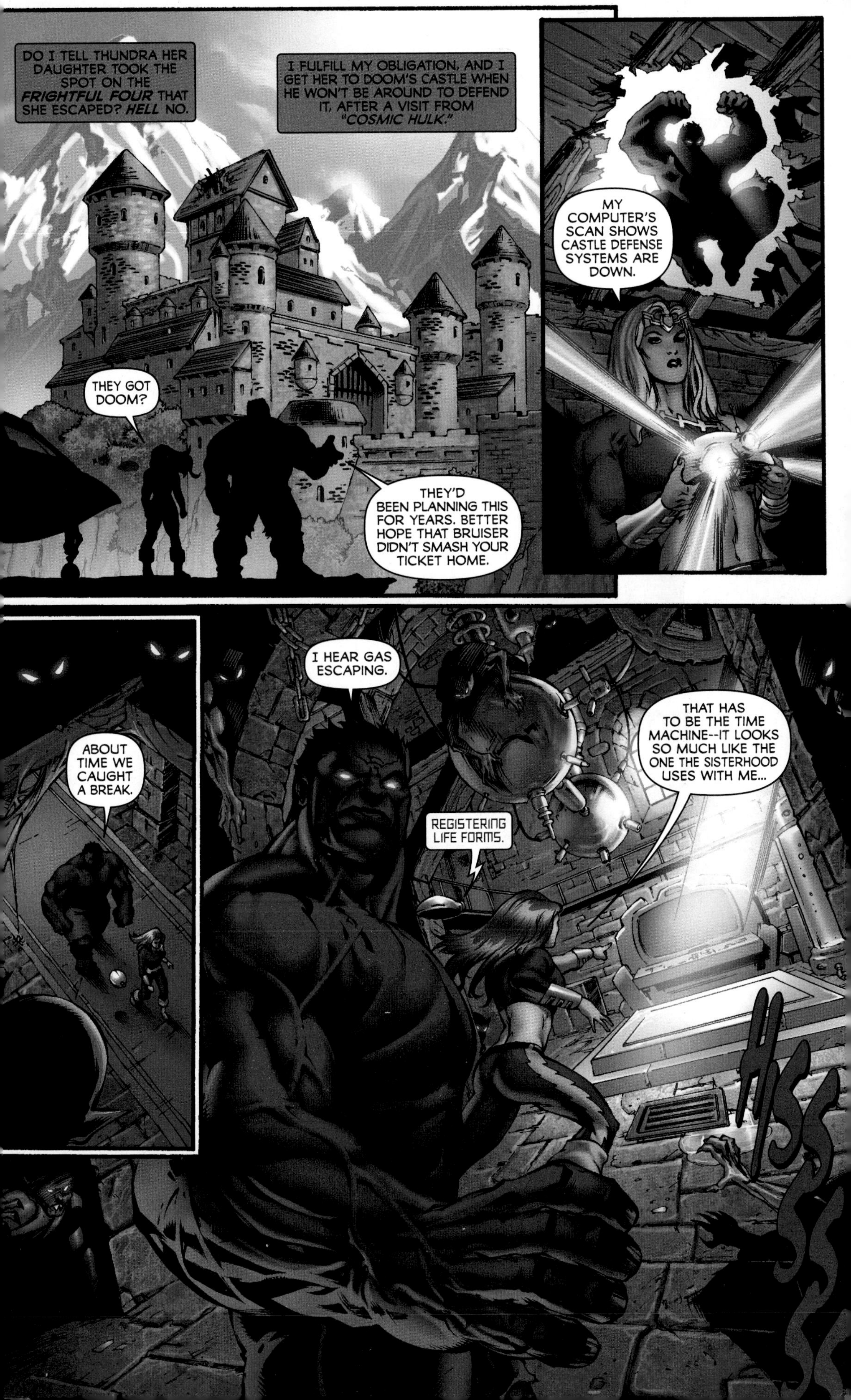
DO I TELL THUNDRA HER DAUGHTER TOOK THE SPOT ON THE FRIGHTFUL FOUR THAT SHE ESCAPED? HELL NO.
I FULFILL MY OBLIGATION, AND I GET HER TO DOOM'S CASTLE WHEN HE WON'T BE AROUND TO DEFEND IT, AFTER A VISIT FROM "COSMIC HULK."
THEY GOT DOOM?
THEY'D BEEN PLANNING THIS FOR YEARS. BETTER HOPE THAT BRUISER DIDN'T SMASH YOUR TICKET HOME.
MY COMPUTER'S SCAN SHOWS CASTLE DEFENSE SYSTEMS ARE DOWN.
ABOUT TIME WE CAUGHT A BREAK.
I HEAR GAS ESCAPING.
REGISTERING LIFE FORMS.
THAT HAS TO BE THE TIME MACHINE--IT LOOKS SO MUCH LIKE THE ONE THE SISTERHOOD USES WITH ME...
HISSS

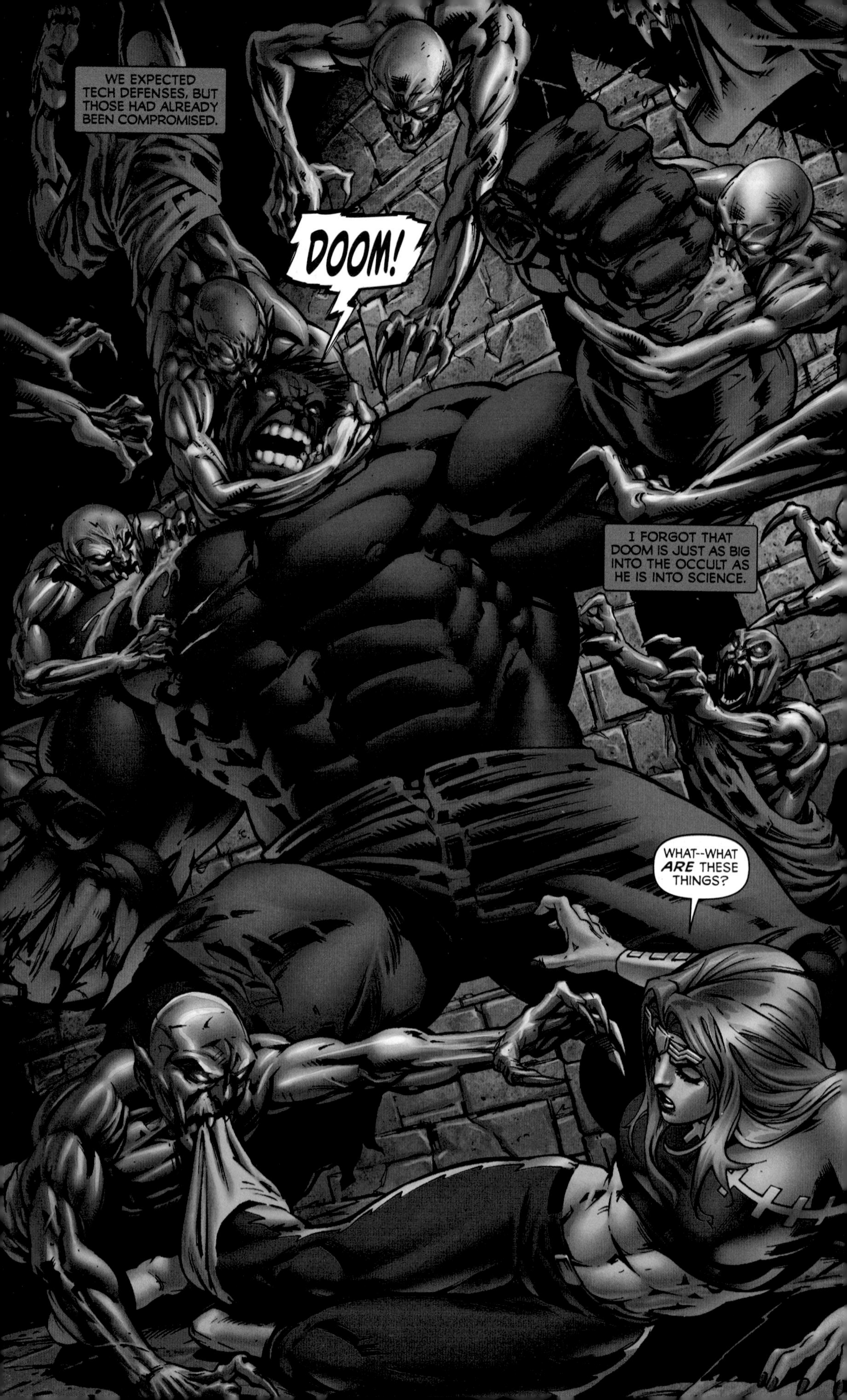

WE EXPECTED TECH DEFENSES, BUT THOSE HAD ALREADY BEEN COMPROMISED.
DOOM!
I FORGOT THAT DOOM IS JUST AS BIG INTO THE OCCULT AS HE IS INTO SCIENCE.
WHAT--WHAT ARE THESE THINGS?

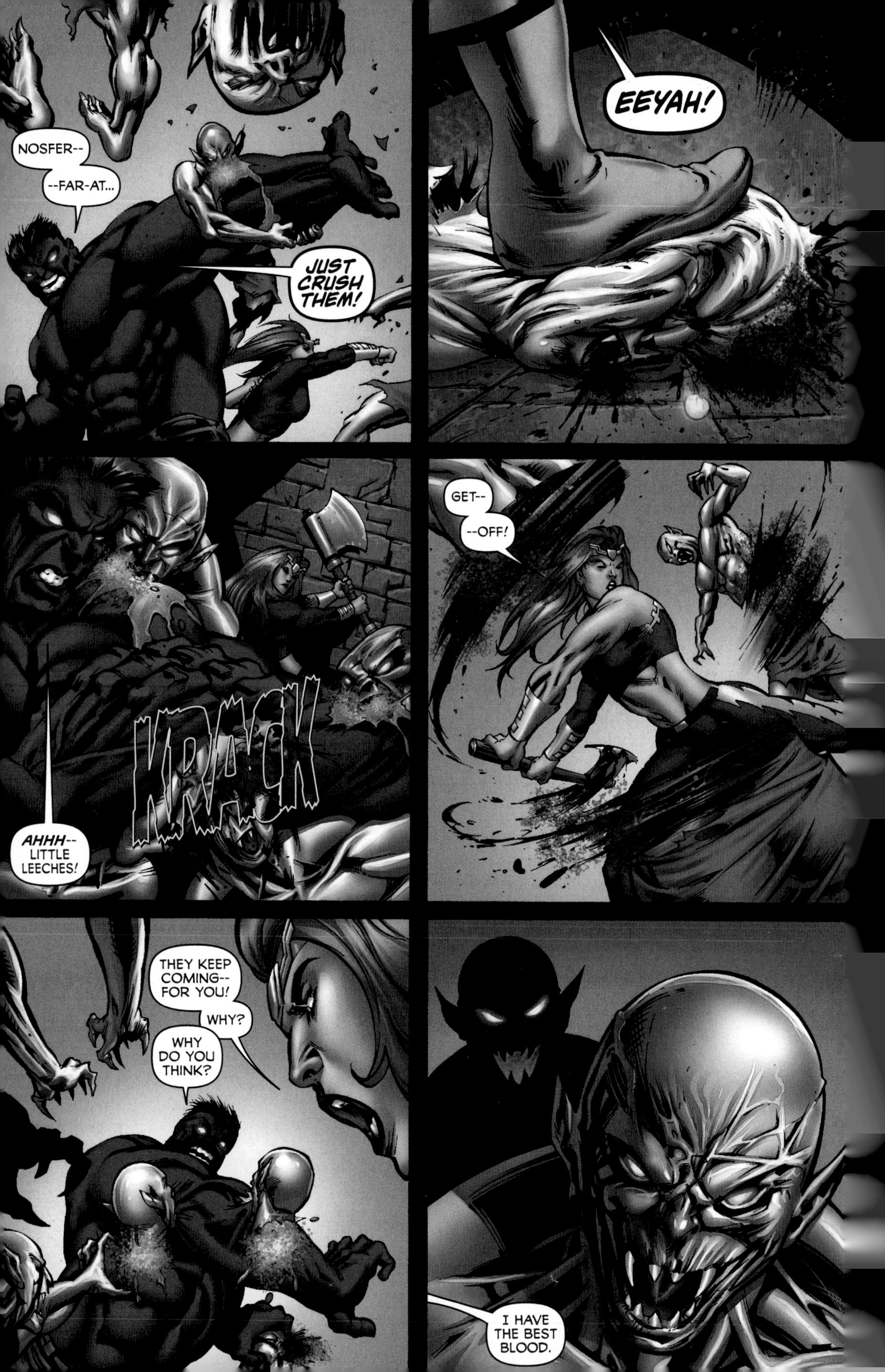
NOSFER--
--FAR-AT...
JUST CRUSH THEM!
EEYAH!
KRACK
AHHH-- LITTLE LEECHES!
GET--
--OFF!
THEY KEEP COMING-- FOR YOU!
WHY?
WHY DO YOU THINK?
I HAVE THE BEST BLOOD.

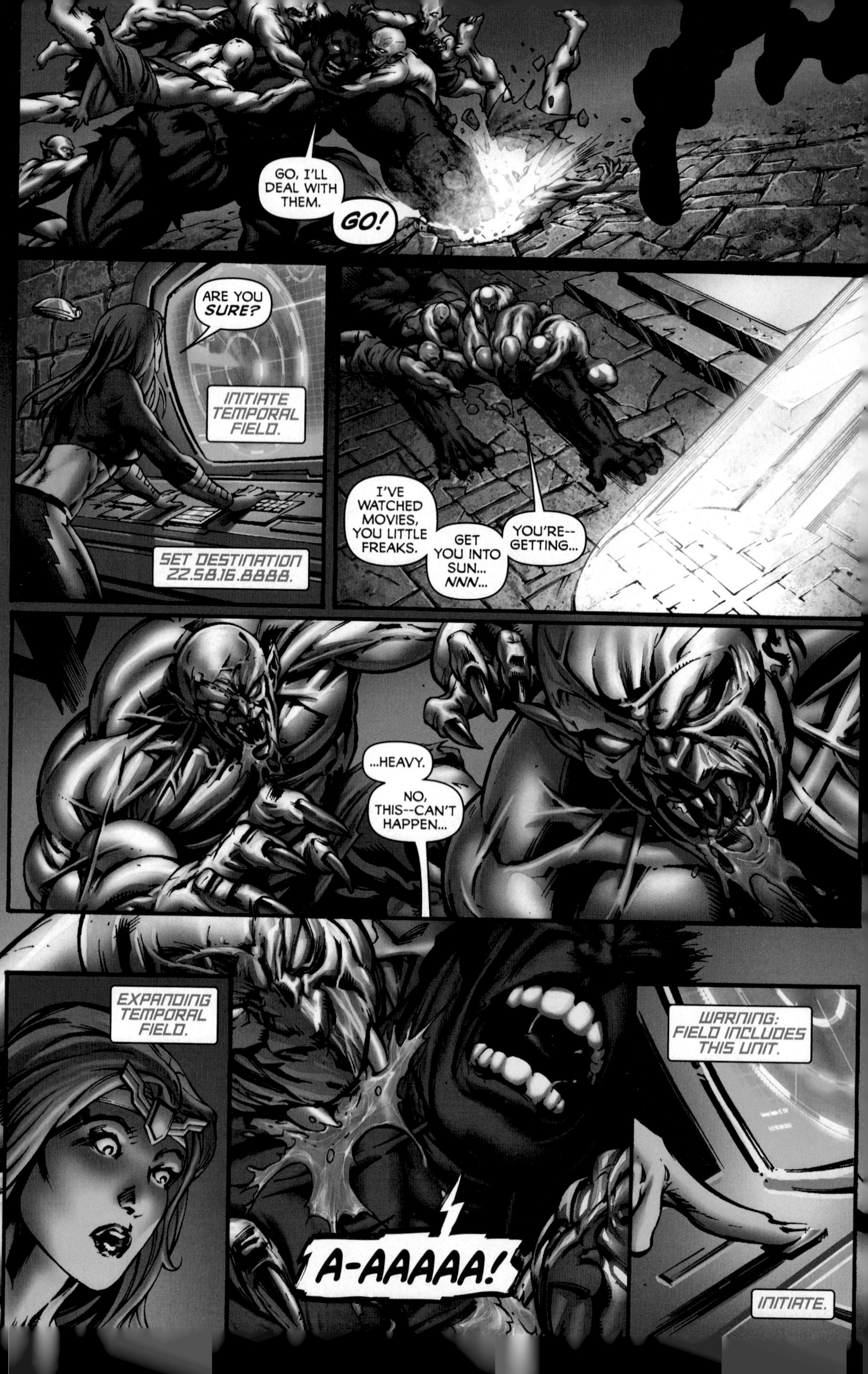
GO, I'LL DEAL WITH THEM.
GO!
ARE YOU SURE?
INITIATE TEMPORAL FIELD.
SET DESTINATION 22.58.16.8888.
I'VE WATCHED MOVIES, YOU LITTLE FREAKS.
GET YOU INTO SUN... NNN...
YOU'RE-- GETTING...
...HEAVY.
NO, THIS--CAN'T HAPPEN...
EXPANDING TEMPORAL FIELD.
A-AAAAA!
WARNING: FIELD INCLUDES THIS UNIT.
INITIATE.

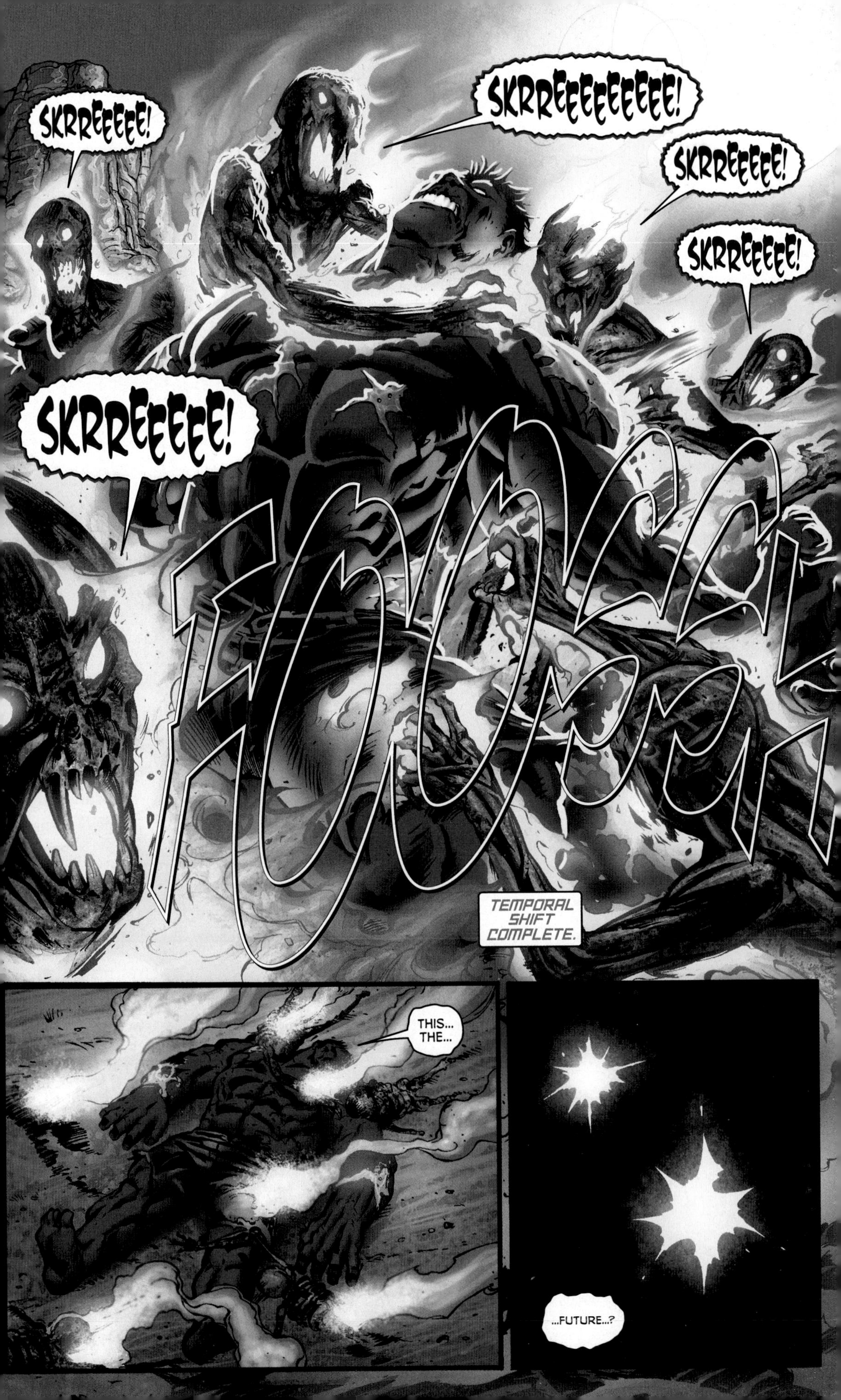
SKRREEEEE!
SKRREEEEEEEEEE!
SKRREEEEE!
SKRREEEEE!
SKRREEEEE!
TEMPORAL SHIFT COMPLETE.
THIS... THE...
...FUTURE...?

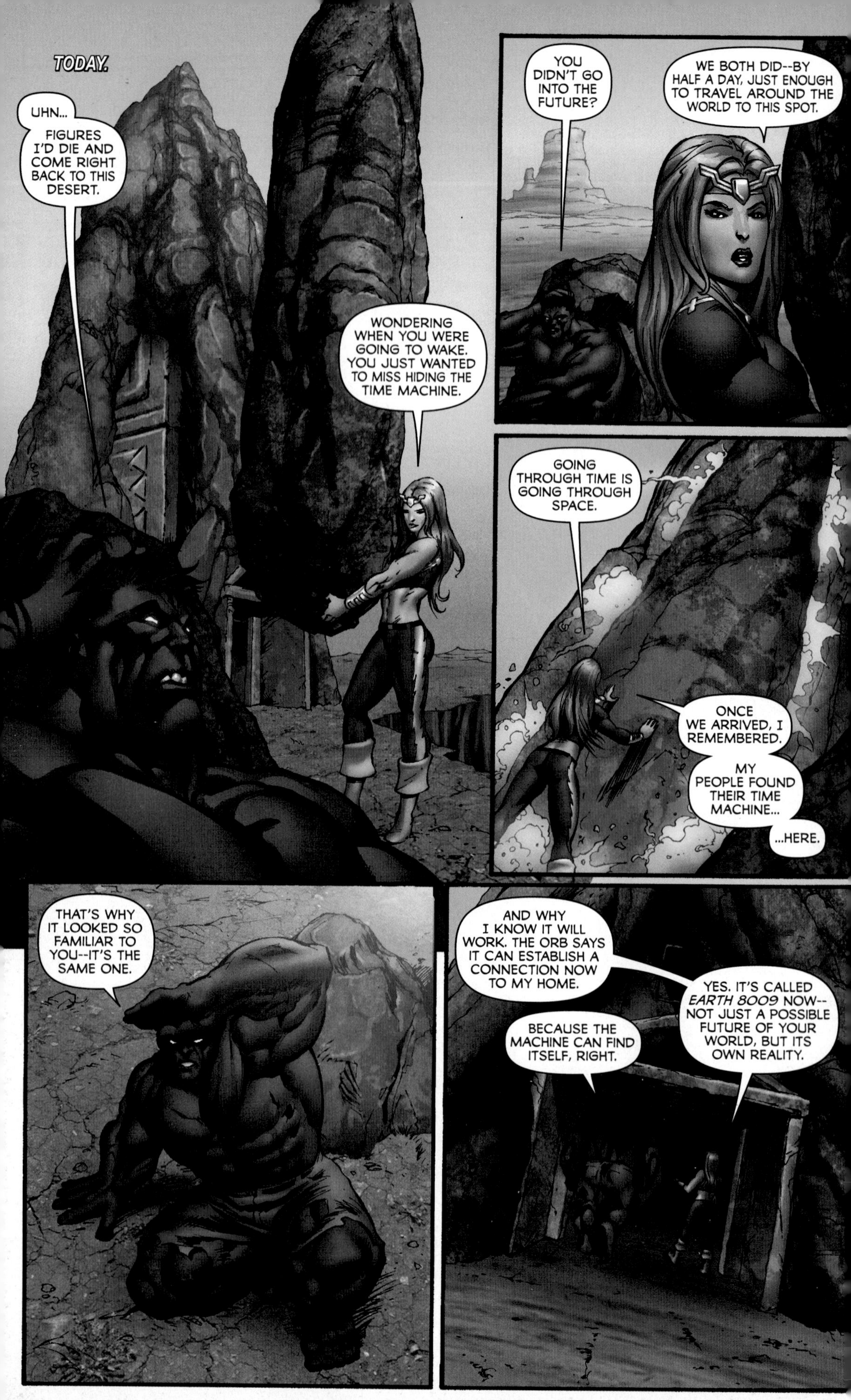
TODAY.
UHN... FIGURES I'D DIE AND COME RIGHT BACK TO THIS DESERT.
WONDERING WHEN YOU WERE GOING TO WAKE. YOU JUST WANTED TO MISS HIDING THE TIME MACHINE.
YOU DIDN'T GO INTO THE FUTURE?
WE BOTH DID--BY HALF A DAY, JUST ENOUGH TO TRAVEL AROUND THE WORLD TO THIS SPOT.
GOING THROUGH TIME IS GOING THROUGH SPACE.
ONCE WE ARRIVED, I REMEMBERED.
MY PEOPLE FOUND THEIR TIME MACHINE...
...HERE.
THAT'S WHY IT LOOKED SO FAMILIAR TO YOU--IT'S THE SAME ONE.
AND WHY I KNOW IT WILL WORK. THE ORB SAYS IT CAN ESTABLISH A CONNECTION NOW TO MY HOME.
BECAUSE THE MACHINE CAN FIND ITSELF, RIGHT.
YES. IT'S CALLED *EARTH 8009* NOW--NOT JUST A POSSIBLE FUTURE OF YOUR WORLD, BUT ITS OWN REALITY.

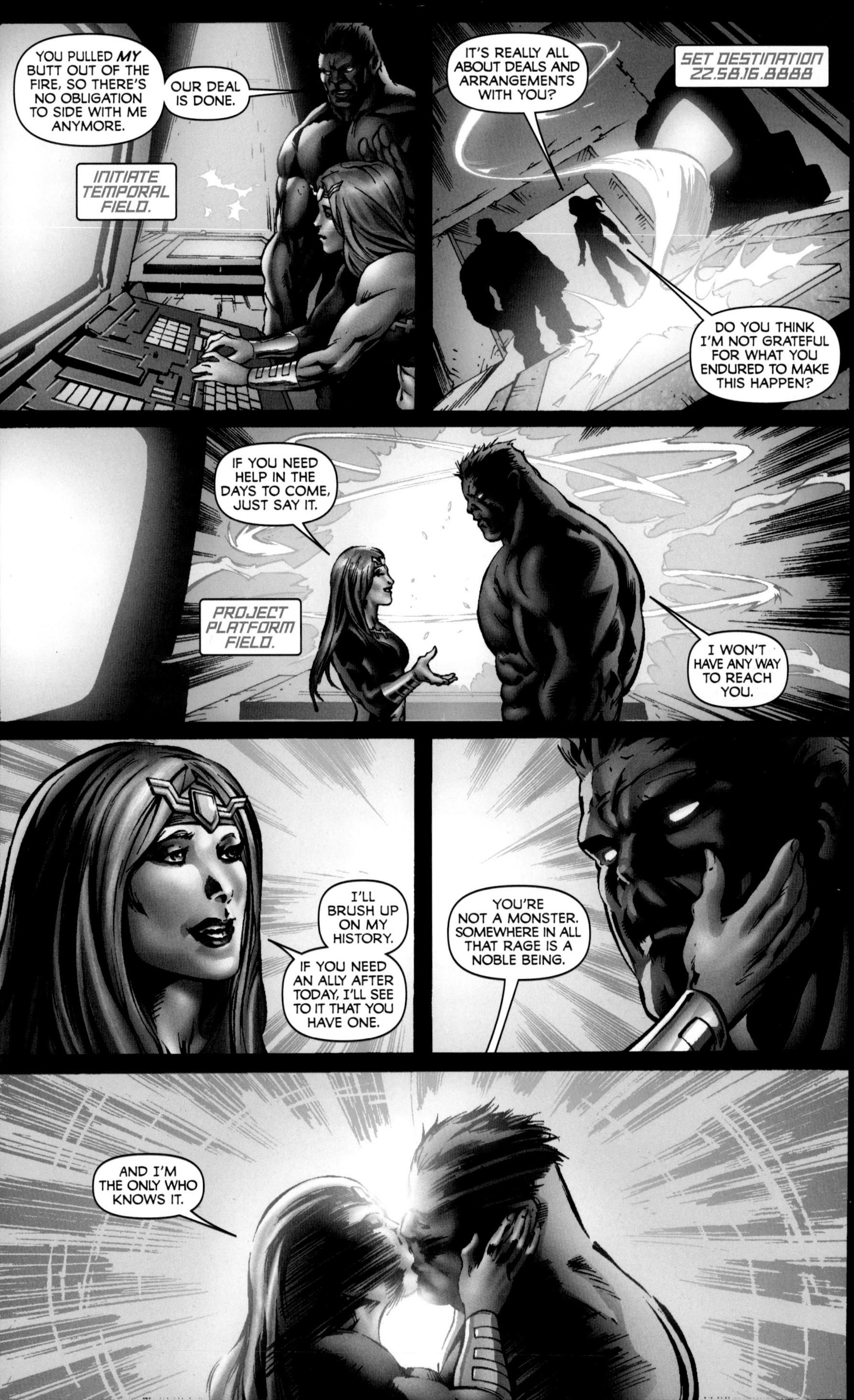
YOU PULLED MY BUTT OUT OF THE FIRE, SO THERE'S NO OBLIGATION TO SIDE WITH ME ANYMORE.
OUR DEAL IS DONE.
INITIATE TEMPORAL FIELD.
IT'S REALLY ALL ABOUT DEALS AND ARRANGEMENTS WITH YOU?
SET DESTINATION 22.58.16.8888
DO YOU THINK I'M NOT GRATEFUL FOR WHAT YOU ENDURED TO MAKE THIS HAPPEN?
IF YOU NEED HELP IN THE DAYS TO COME, JUST SAY IT.
PROJECT PLATFORM FIELD.
I WON'T HAVE ANY WAY TO REACH YOU.
I'LL BRUSH UP ON MY HISTORY.
IF YOU NEED AN ALLY AFTER TODAY, I'LL SEE TO IT THAT YOU HAVE ONE.
YOU'RE NOT A MONSTER. SOMEWHERE IN ALL THAT RAGE IS A NOBLE BEING.
AND I'M THE ONLY WHO KNOWS IT.

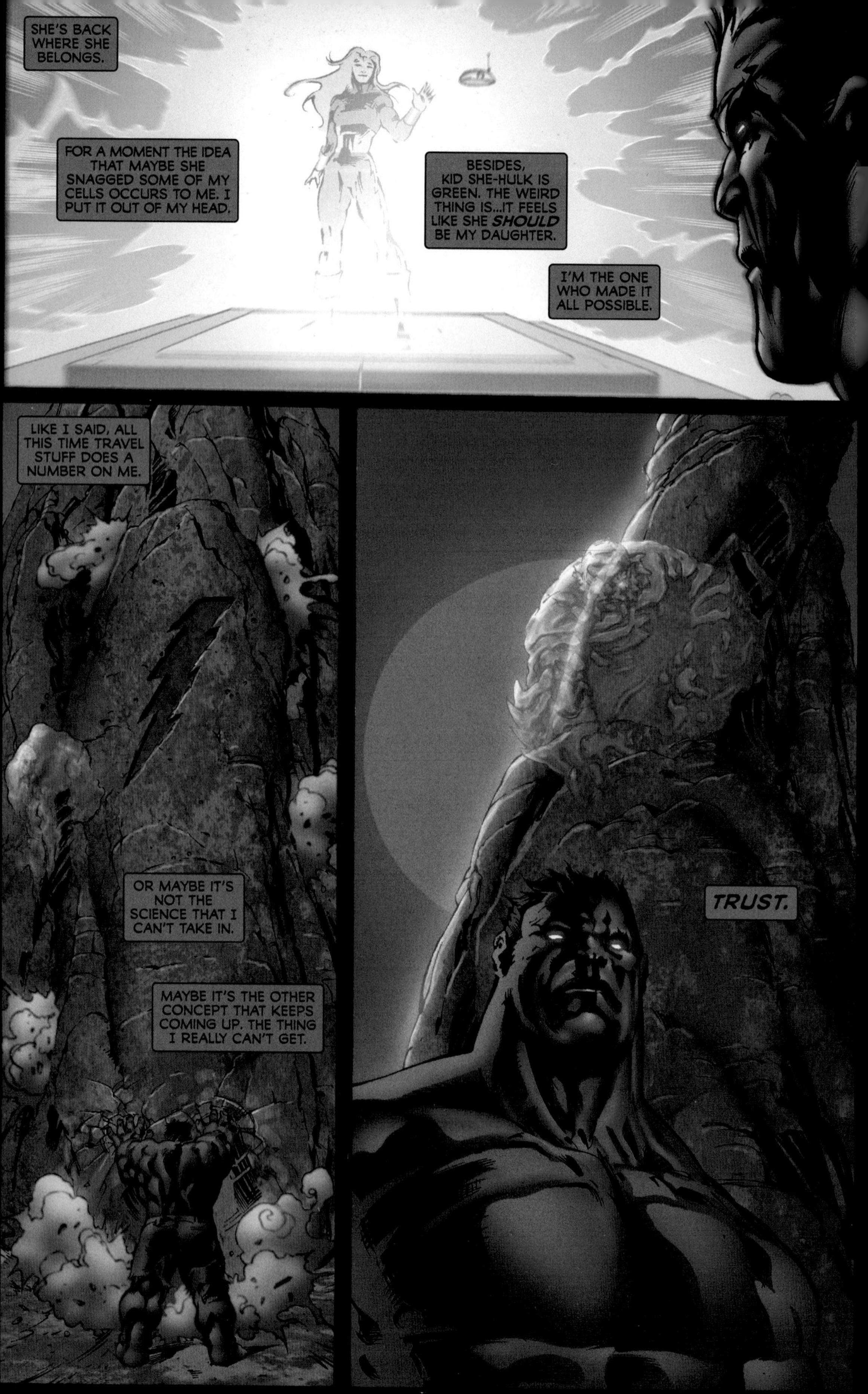
SHE'S BACK WHERE SHE BELONGS.
FOR A MOMENT THE IDEA THAT MAYBE SHE SNAGGED SOME OF MY CELLS OCCURS TO ME. I PUT IT OUT OF MY HEAD.
BESIDES, KID SHE-HULK IS GREEN. THE WEIRD THING IS...IT FEELS LIKE SHE SHOULD BE MY DAUGHTER.
I'M THE ONE WHO MADE IT ALL POSSIBLE.
LIKE I SAID, ALL THIS TIME TRAVEL STUFF DOES A NUMBER ON ME.
OR MAYBE IT'S NOT THE SCIENCE THAT I CAN'T TAKE IN.
MAYBE IT'S THE OTHER CONCEPT THAT KEEPS COMING UP. THE THING I REALLY CAN'T GET.
TRUST.

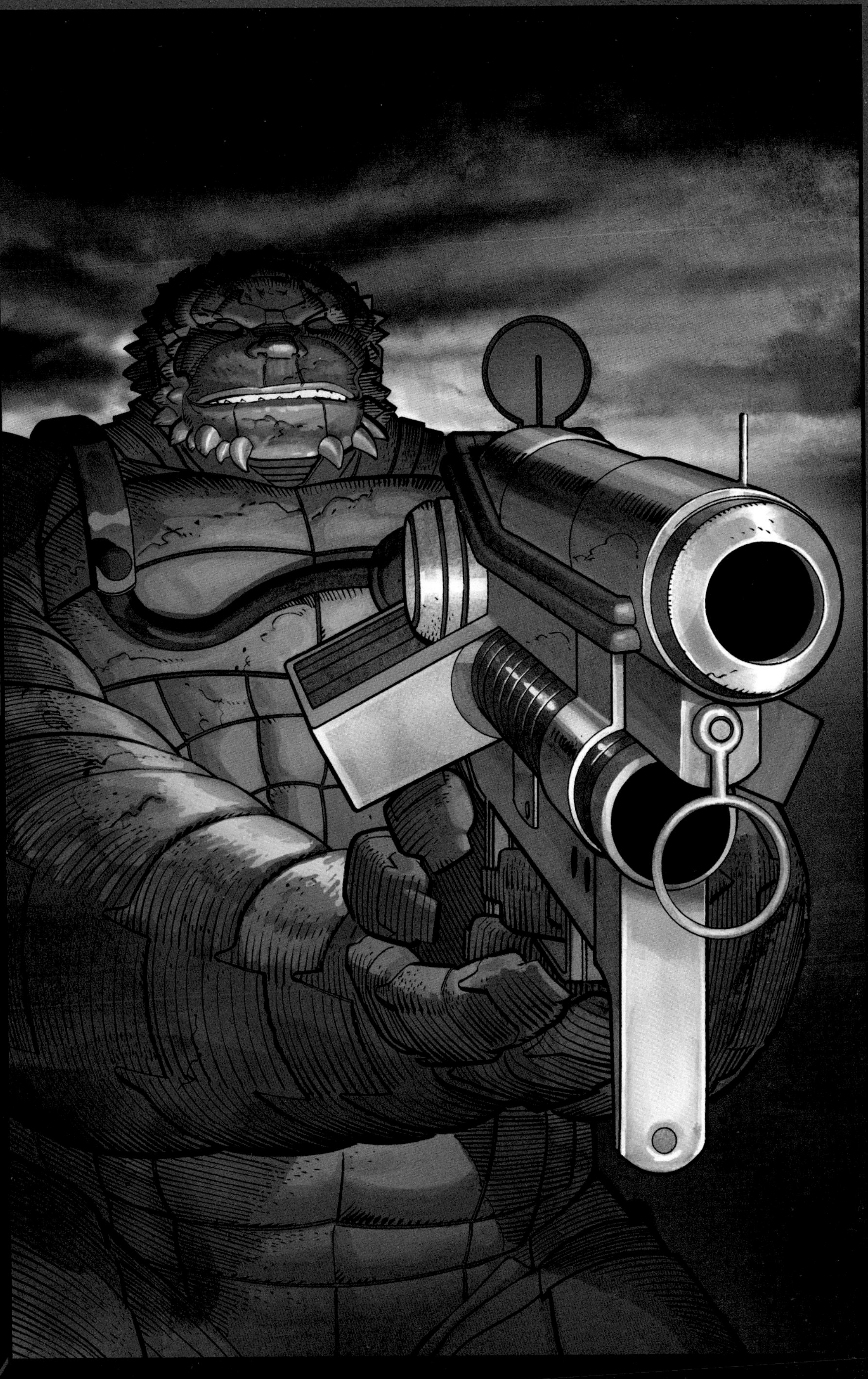

FALL OF THE HULKS: RED HULK #3

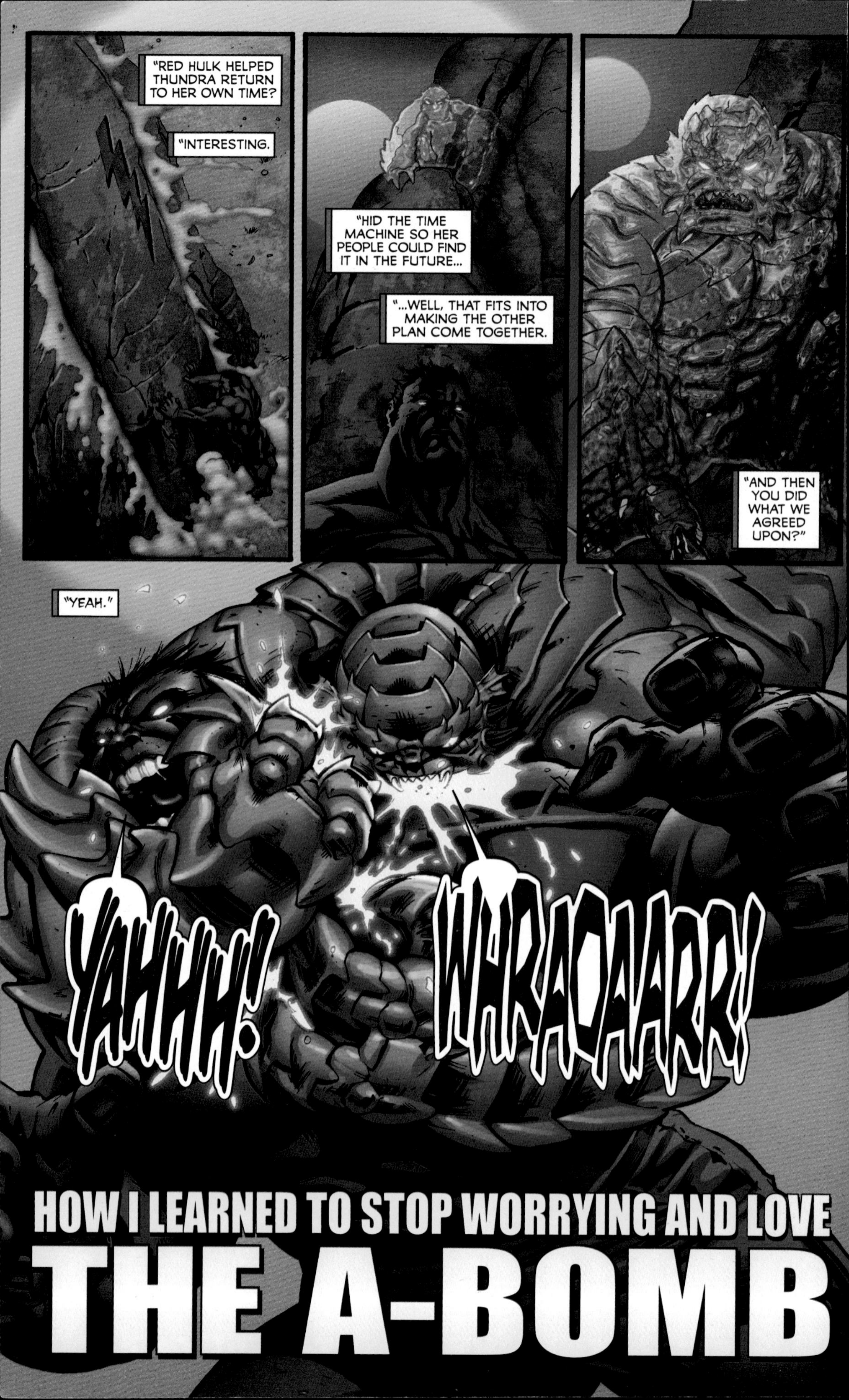

"RED HULK HELPED THUNDRA RETURN TO HER OWN TIME?
"INTERESTING.
"HID THE TIME MACHINE SO HER PEOPLE COULD FIND IT IN THE FUTURE...
"...WELL, THAT FITS INTO MAKING THE OTHER PLAN COME TOGETHER.
"AND THEN YOU DID WHAT WE AGREED UPON?"
"YEAH."
YAHHHH!
WHRAOAARR!
HOW I LEARNED TO STOP WORRYING AND LOVE
THE A-BOMB

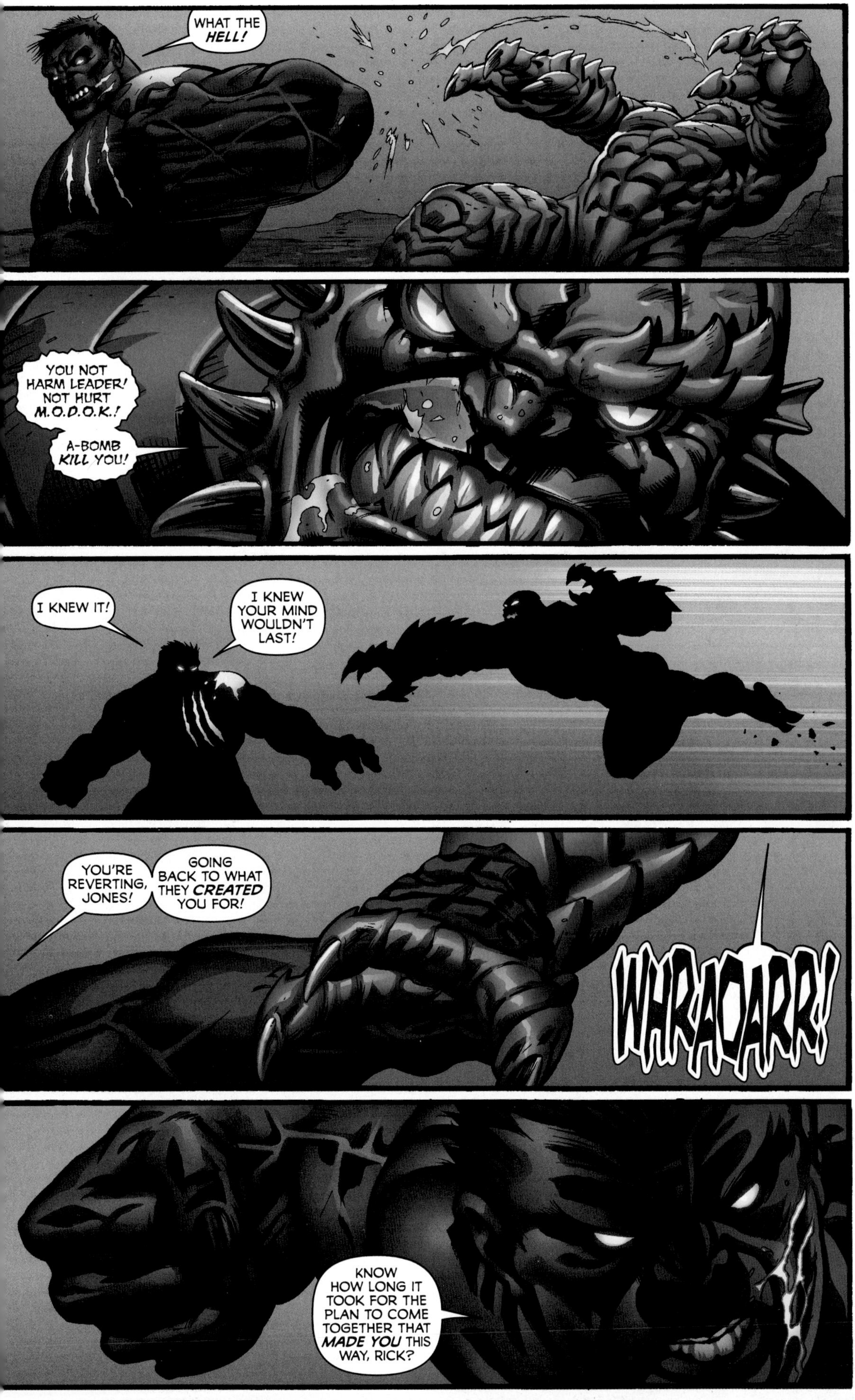
WHAT THE *HELL!*
YOU NOT HARM LEADER! NOT HURT *M.O.D.O.K.!*
A-BOMB *KILL* YOU!
I KNEW IT!
I KNEW YOUR MIND WOULDN'T LAST!
YOU'RE REVERTING, JONES!
GOING BACK TO WHAT THEY *CREATED* YOU FOR!
WHRAOARR!
KNOW HOW LONG IT TOOK FOR THE PLAN TO COME TOGETHER THAT *MADE YOU* THIS WAY, RICK?

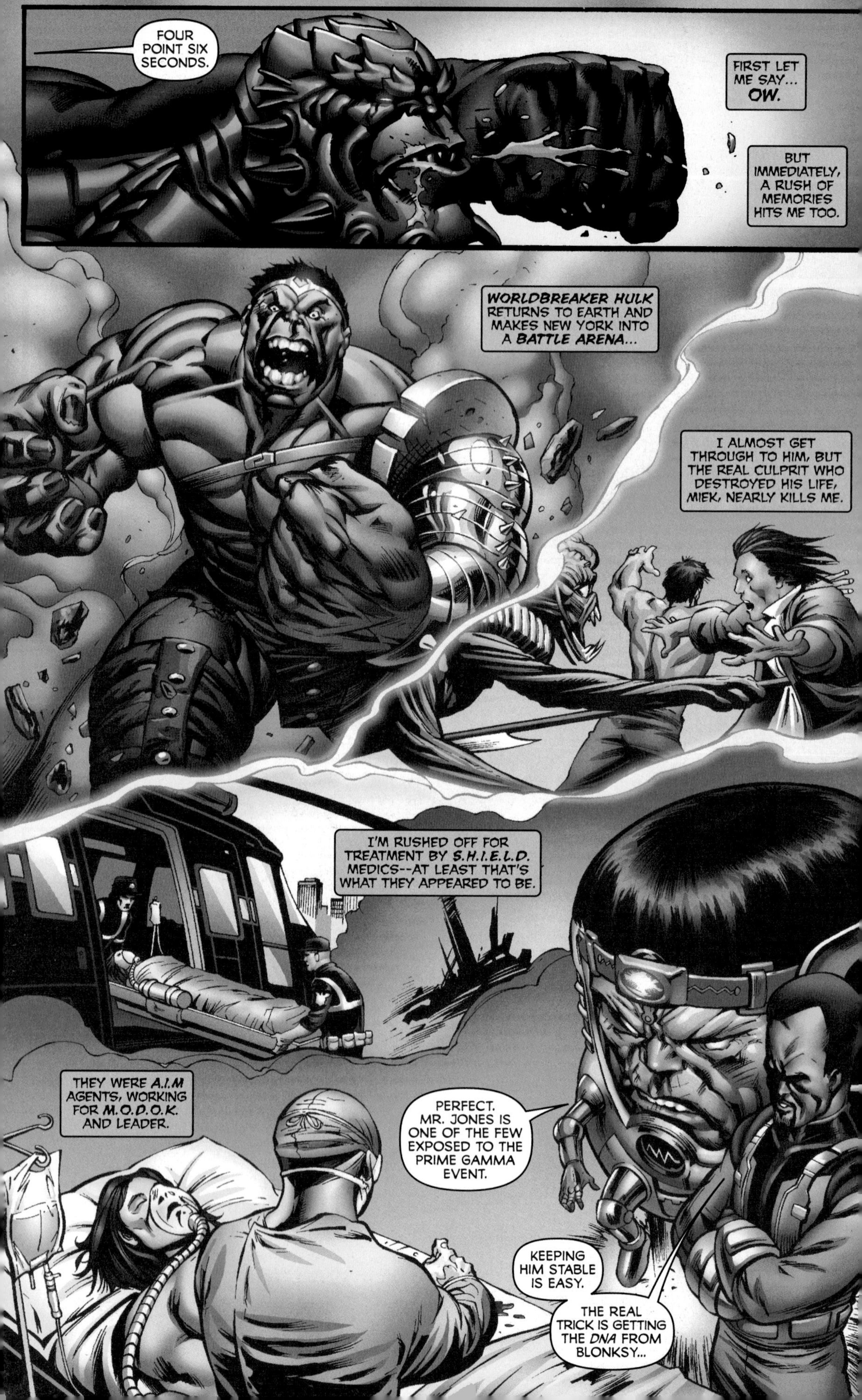

FOUR POINT SIX SECONDS.
FIRST LET ME SAY... OW.
BUT IMMEDIATELY, A RUSH OF MEMORIES HITS ME TOO.
WORLDBREAKER HULK RETURNS TO EARTH AND MAKES NEW YORK INTO A BATTLE ARENA...
I ALMOST GET THROUGH TO HIM, BUT THE REAL CULPRIT WHO DESTROYED HIS LIFE, MIEK, NEARLY KILLS ME.
I'M RUSHED OFF FOR TREATMENT BY S.H.I.E.L.D. MEDICS--AT LEAST THAT'S WHAT THEY APPEARED TO BE.
THEY WERE A.I.M AGENTS, WORKING FOR M.O.D.O.K. AND LEADER.
PERFECT. MR. JONES IS ONE OF THE FEW EXPOSED TO THE PRIME GAMMA EVENT.
KEEPING HIM STABLE IS EASY.
THE REAL TRICK IS GETTING THE DNA FROM BLONKSY...

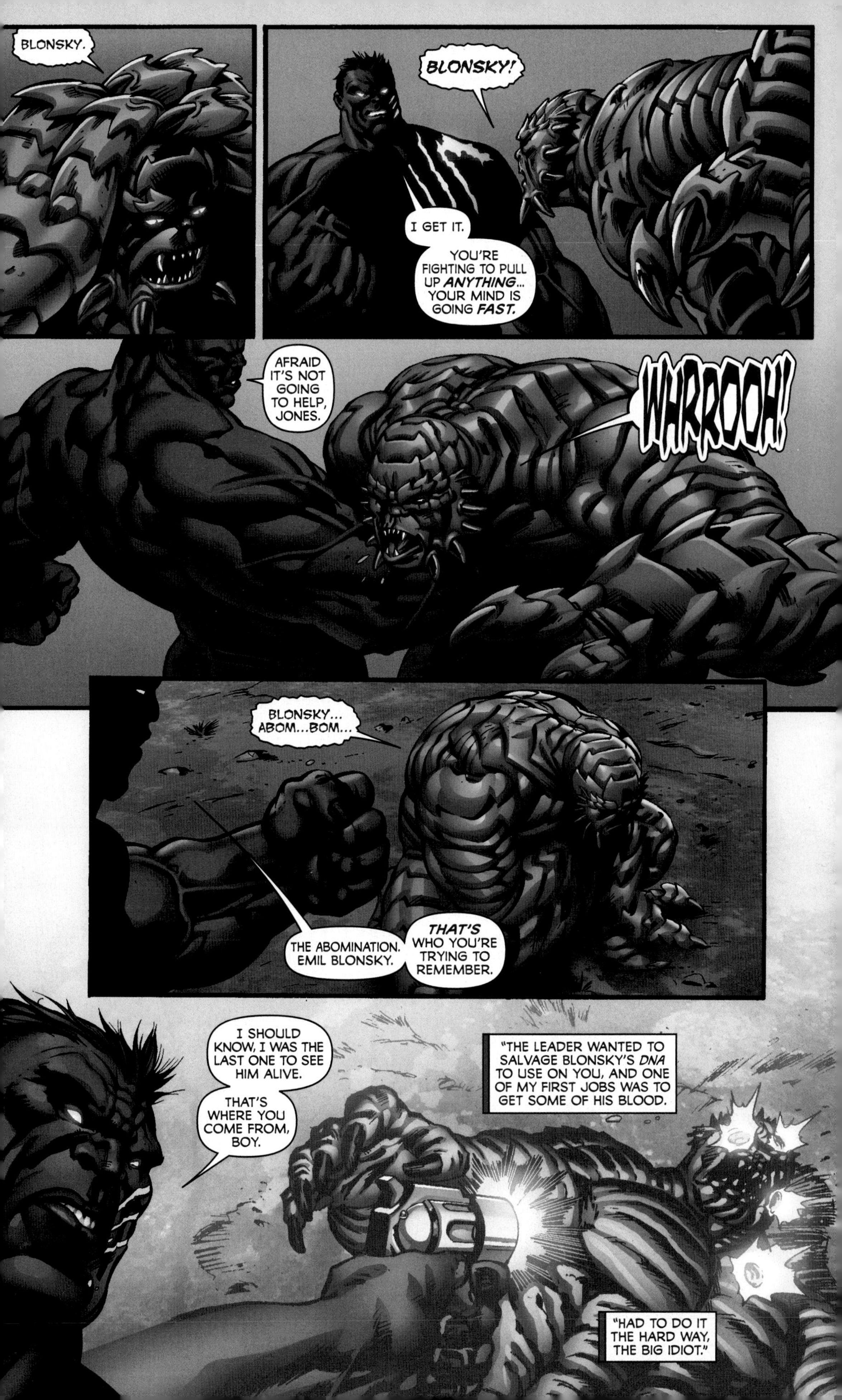
BLONSKY.
BLONSKY!
I GET IT.
YOU'RE FIGHTING TO PULL UP ANYTHING... YOUR MIND IS GOING FAST.
AFRAID IT'S NOT GOING TO HELP, JONES.
WHRROOH!
BLONSKY... ABOM...BOM...
THE ABOMINATION. EMIL BLONSKY.
THAT'S WHO YOU'RE TRYING TO REMEMBER.
I SHOULD KNOW, I WAS THE LAST ONE TO SEE HIM ALIVE.
THAT'S WHERE YOU COME FROM, BOY.
"THE LEADER WANTED TO SALVAGE BLONSKY'S DNA TO USE ON YOU, AND ONE OF MY FIRST JOBS WAS TO GET SOME OF HIS BLOOD.
"HAD TO DO IT THE HARD WAY, THE BIG IDIOT."

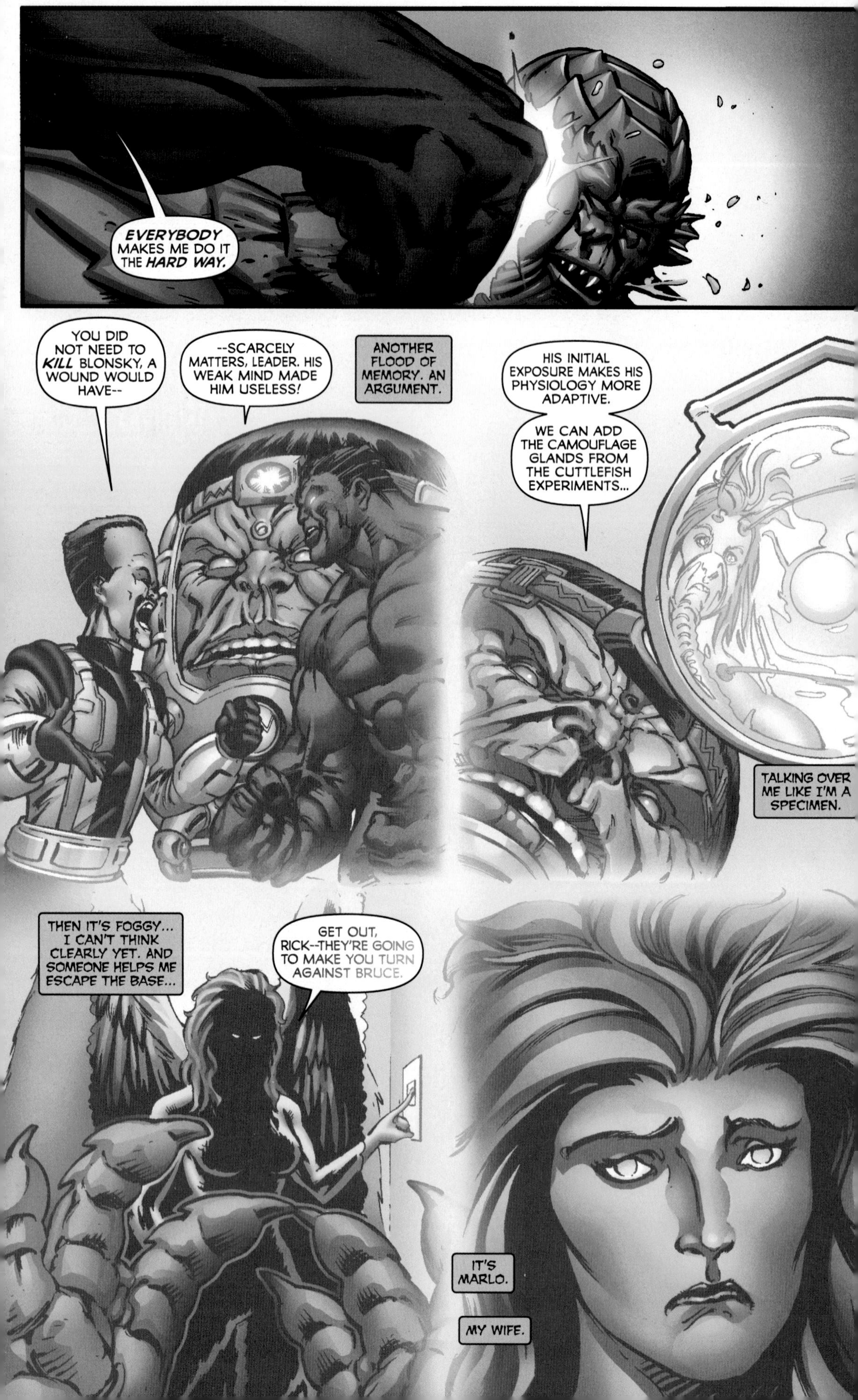
EVERYBODY MAKES ME DO IT THE HARD WAY.
YOU DID NOT NEED TO KILL BLONSKY, A WOUND WOULD HAVE--
--SCARCELY MATTERS, LEADER. HIS WEAK MIND MADE HIM USELESS!
ANOTHER FLOOD OF MEMORY. AN ARGUMENT.
HIS INITIAL EXPOSURE MAKES HIS PHYSIOLOGY MORE ADAPTIVE.
WE CAN ADD THE CAMOUFLAGE GLANDS FROM THE CUTTLEFISH EXPERIMENTS...
TALKING OVER ME LIKE I'M A SPECIMEN.
THEN IT'S FOGGY... I CAN'T THINK CLEARLY YET. AND SOMEONE HELPS ME ESCAPE THE BASE...
GET OUT, RICK--THEY'RE GOING TO MAKE YOU TURN AGAINST BRUCE.
IT'S MARLO.
MY WIFE.

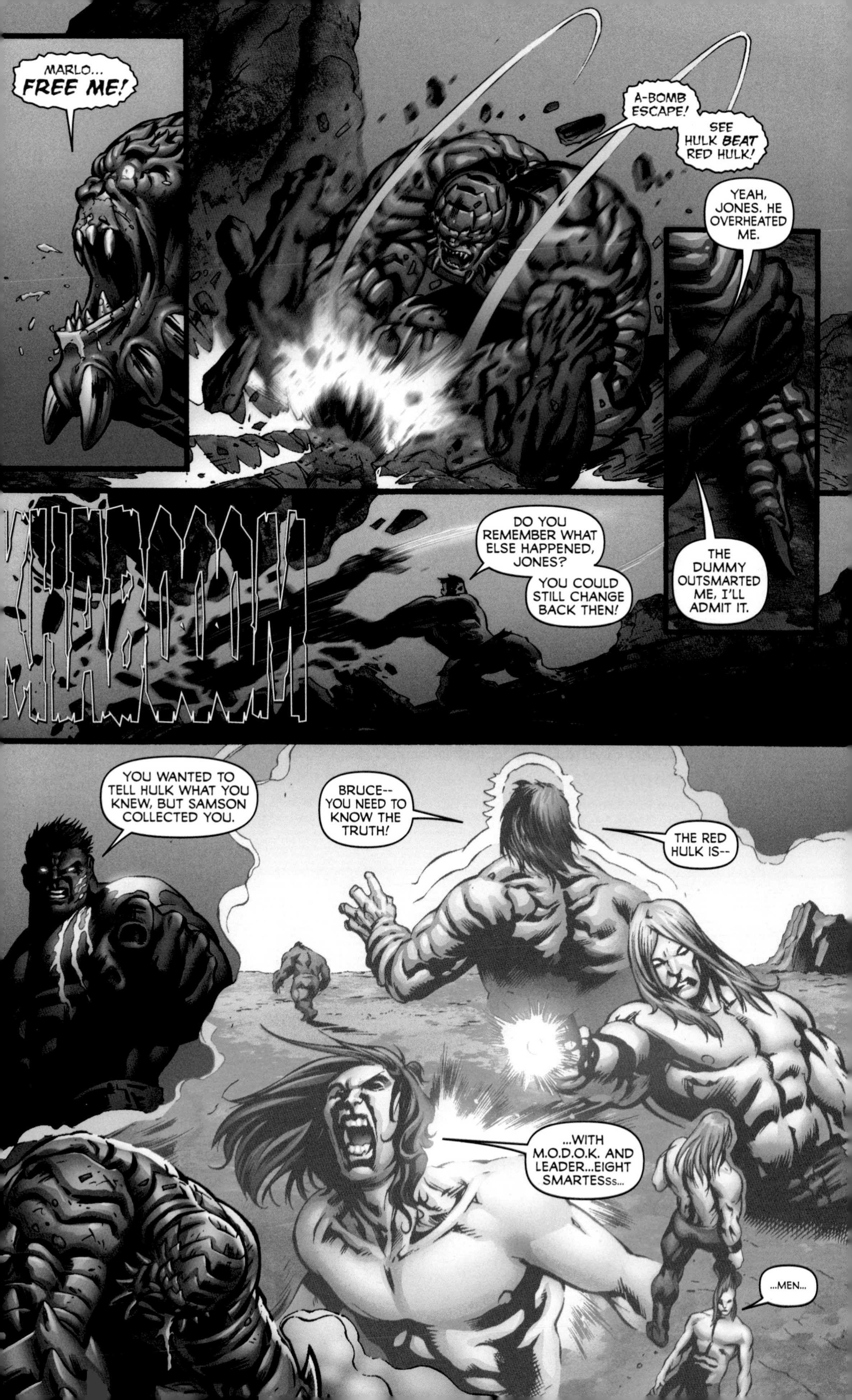
MARLO...
FREE ME!
A-BOMB ESCAPE!
SEE HULK BEAT RED HULK!
YEAH, JONES. HE OVERHEATED ME.
THE DUMMY OUTSMARTED ME, I'LL ADMIT IT.
DO YOU REMEMBER WHAT ELSE HAPPENED, JONES?
YOU COULD STILL CHANGE BACK THEN!
YOU WANTED TO TELL HULK WHAT YOU KNEW, BUT SAMSON COLLECTED YOU.
BRUCE-- YOU NEED TO KNOW THE TRUTH!
THE RED HULK IS--
...WITH M.O.D.O.K. AND LEADER...EIGHT SMARTESsS...
...MEN...

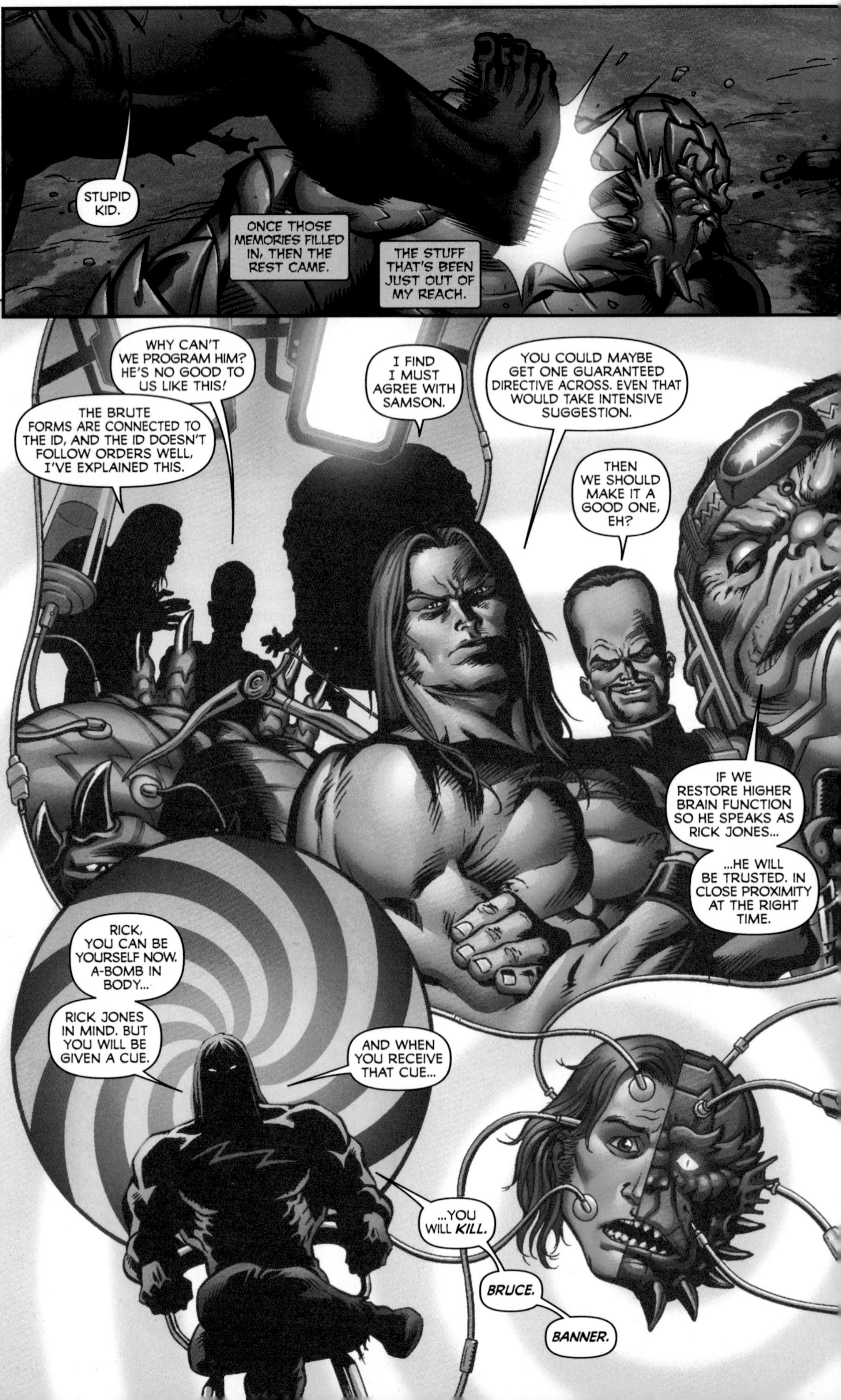

STUPID KID.
ONCE THOSE MEMORIES FILLED IN, THEN THE REST CAME.
THE STUFF THAT'S BEEN JUST OUT OF MY REACH.
WHY CAN'T WE PROGRAM HIM? HE'S NO GOOD TO US LIKE THIS!
THE BRUTE FORMS ARE CONNECTED TO THE ID, AND THE ID DOESN'T FOLLOW ORDERS WELL, I'VE EXPLAINED THIS.
I FIND I MUST AGREE WITH SAMSON.
YOU COULD MAYBE GET ONE GUARANTEED DIRECTIVE ACROSS. EVEN THAT WOULD TAKE INTENSIVE SUGGESTION.
THEN WE SHOULD MAKE IT A GOOD ONE, EH?
IF WE RESTORE HIGHER BRAIN FUNCTION SO HE SPEAKS AS RICK JONES...
...HE WILL BE TRUSTED. IN CLOSE PROXIMITY AT THE RIGHT TIME.
RICK, YOU CAN BE YOURSELF NOW. A-BOMB IN BODY...
RICK JONES IN MIND. BUT YOU WILL BE GIVEN A CUE.
AND WHEN YOU RECEIVE THAT CUE...
...YOU WILL *KILL.*
BRUCE.
BANNER.

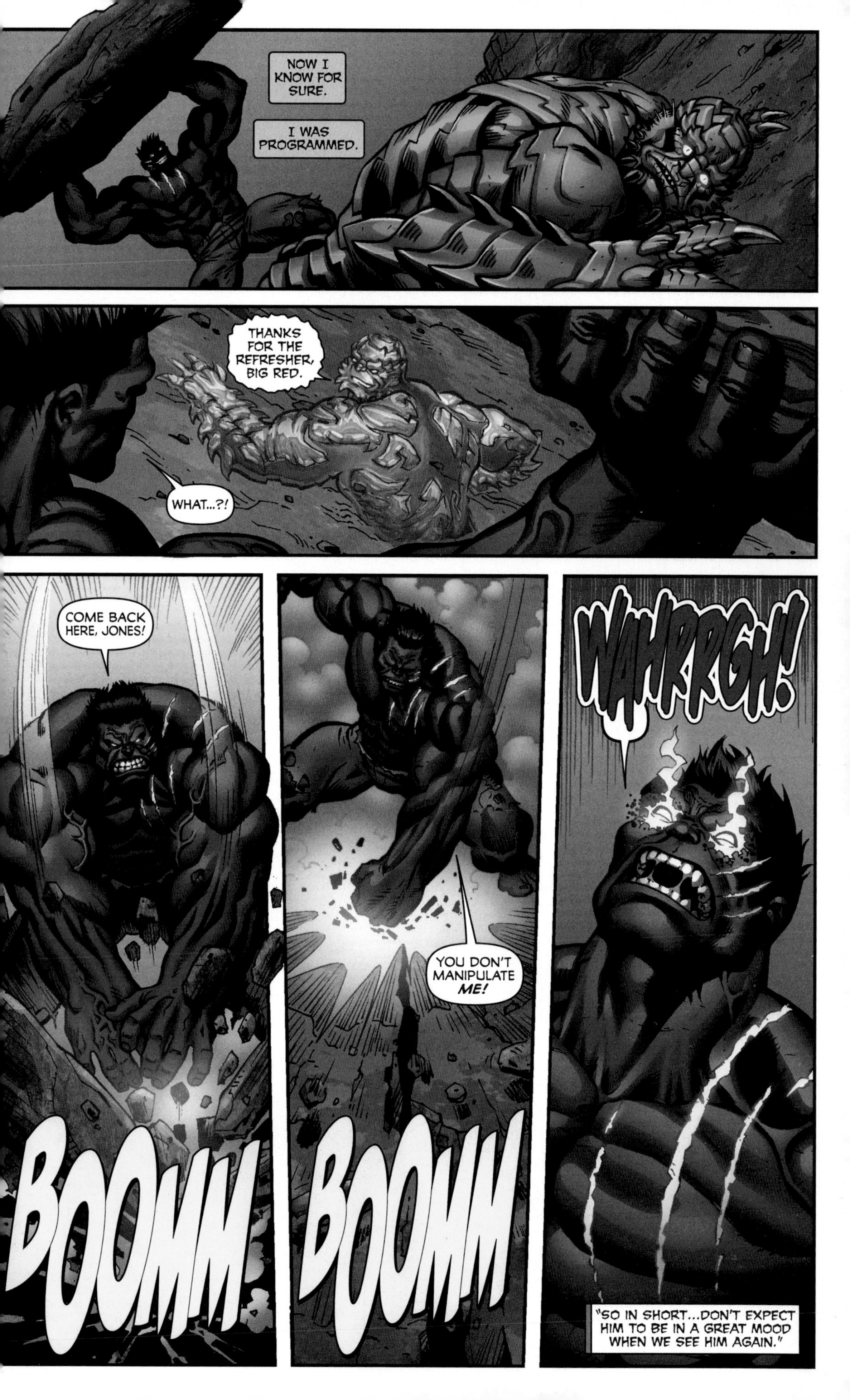
NOW I KNOW FOR SURE.
I WAS PROGRAMMED.
THANKS FOR THE REFRESHER, BIG RED.
WHAT...?!
COME BACK HERE, JONES!
BOOMM
YOU DON'T MANIPULATE *ME!*
BOOMM
WAHRRGH!
"SO IN SHORT...DON'T EXPECT HIM TO BE IN A GREAT MOOD WHEN WE SEE HIM AGAIN."

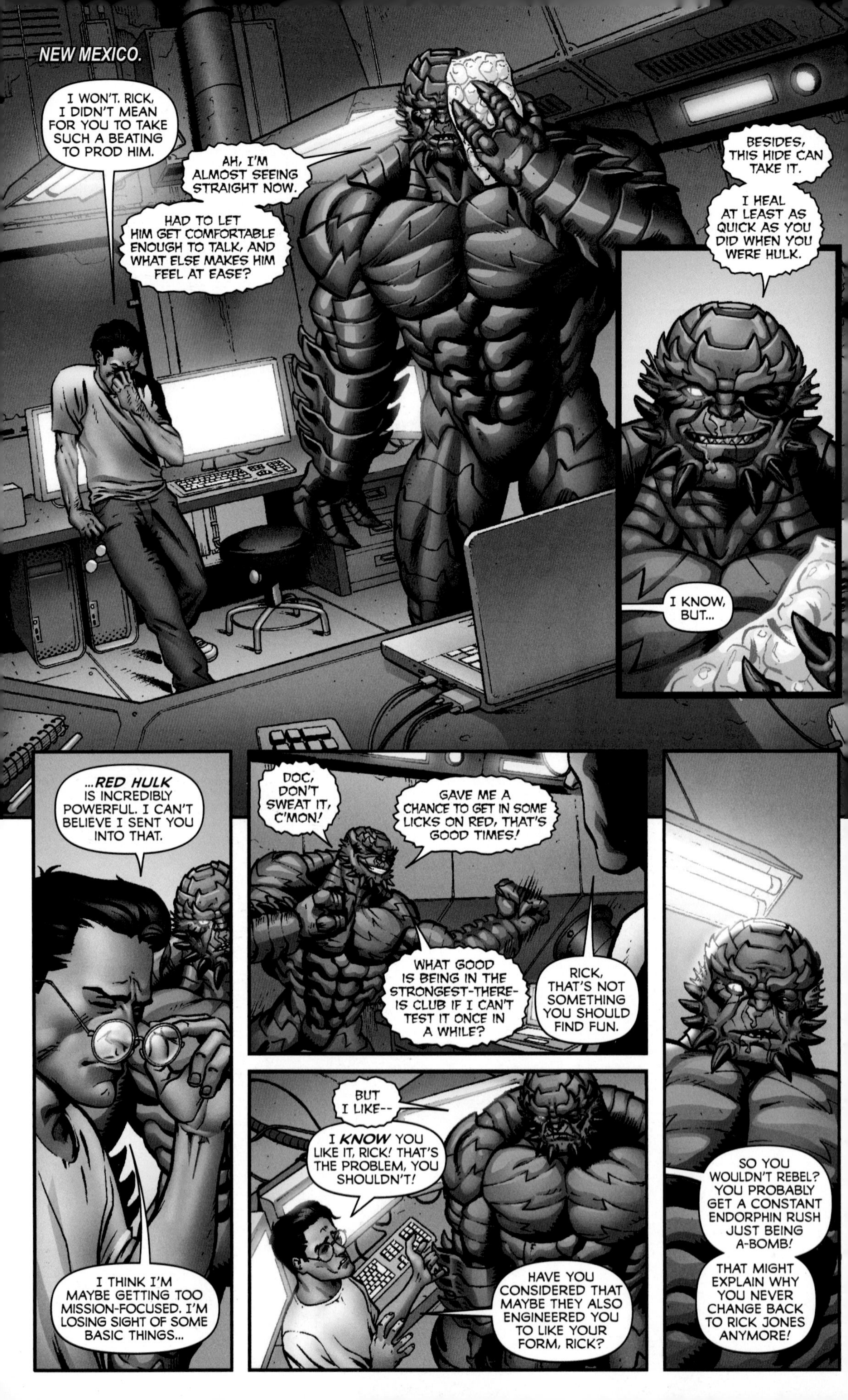
NEW MEXICO.
I WON'T. RICK, I DIDN'T MEAN FOR YOU TO TAKE SUCH A BEATING TO PROD HIM.
AH, I'M ALMOST SEEING STRAIGHT NOW.
HAD TO LET HIM GET COMFORTABLE ENOUGH TO TALK, AND WHAT ELSE MAKES HIM FEEL AT EASE?
BESIDES, THIS HIDE CAN TAKE IT.
I HEAL AT LEAST AS QUICK AS YOU DID WHEN YOU WERE HULK.
I KNOW, BUT...
...RED HULK IS INCREDIBLY POWERFUL. I CAN'T BELIEVE I SENT YOU INTO THAT.
I THINK I'M MAYBE GETTING TOO MISSION-FOCUSED. I'M LOSING SIGHT OF SOME BASIC THINGS...
DOC, DON'T SWEAT IT, C'MON!
GAVE ME A CHANCE TO GET IN SOME LICKS ON RED, THAT'S GOOD TIMES!
WHAT GOOD IS BEING IN THE STRONGEST-THERE-IS CLUB IF I CAN'T TEST IT ONCE IN A WHILE?
RICK, THAT'S NOT SOMETHING YOU SHOULD FIND FUN.
BUT I LIKE--
I KNOW YOU LIKE IT, RICK! THAT'S THE PROBLEM, YOU SHOULDN'T!
HAVE YOU CONSIDERED THAT MAYBE THEY ALSO ENGINEERED YOU TO LIKE YOUR FORM, RICK?
SO YOU WOULDN'T REBEL? YOU PROBABLY GET A CONSTANT ENDORPHIN RUSH JUST BEING A-BOMB!
THAT MIGHT EXPLAIN WHY YOU NEVER CHANGE BACK TO RICK JONES ANYMORE!

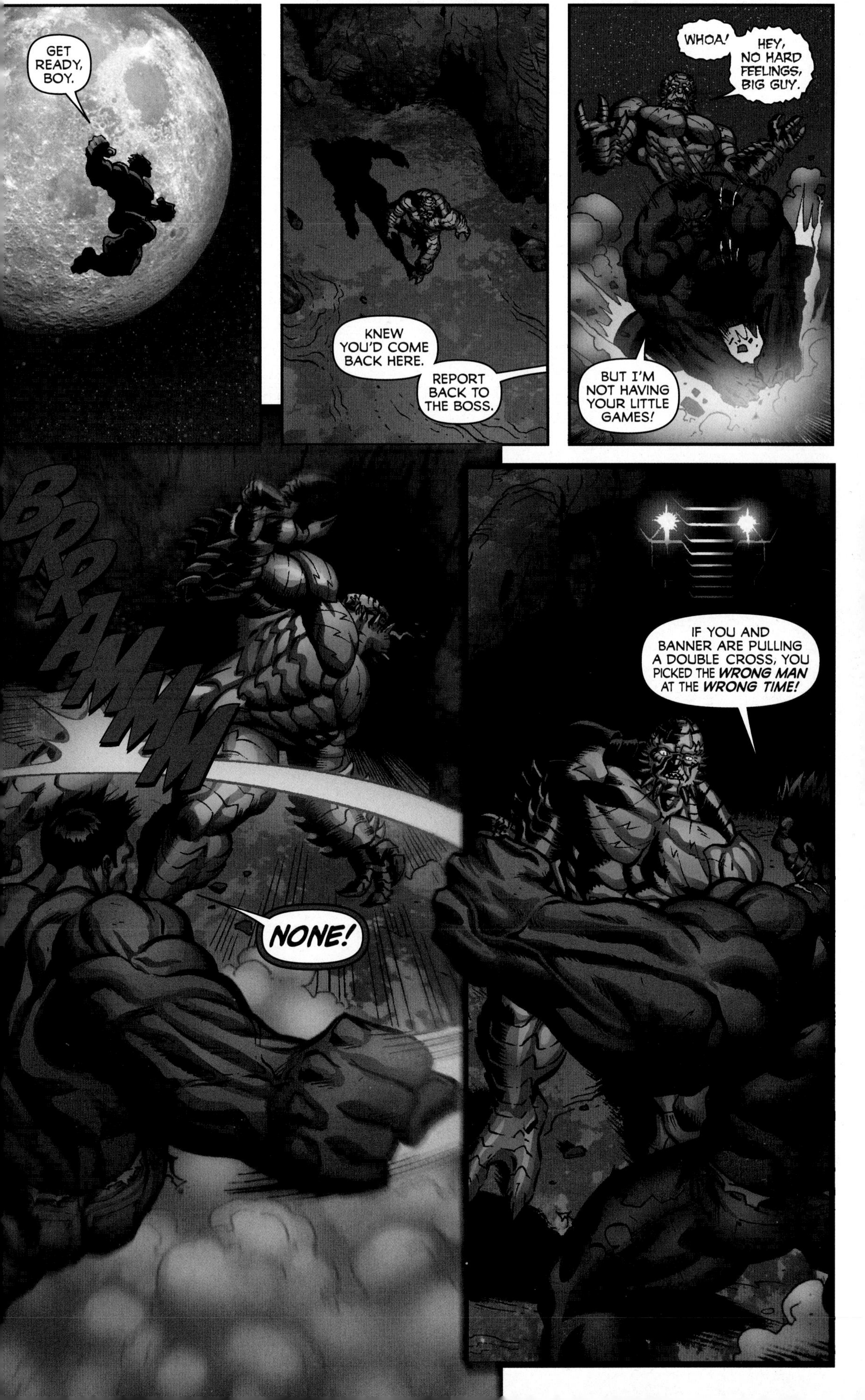
GET READY, BOY.
KNEW YOU'D COME BACK HERE.
REPORT BACK TO THE BOSS.
WHOA!
HEY, NO HARD FEELINGS, BIG GUY.
BUT I'M NOT HAVING YOUR LITTLE GAMES!
BRRAMMM
NONE!
IF YOU AND BANNER ARE PULLING A DOUBLE CROSS, YOU PICKED THE WRONG MAN AT THE WRONG TIME!

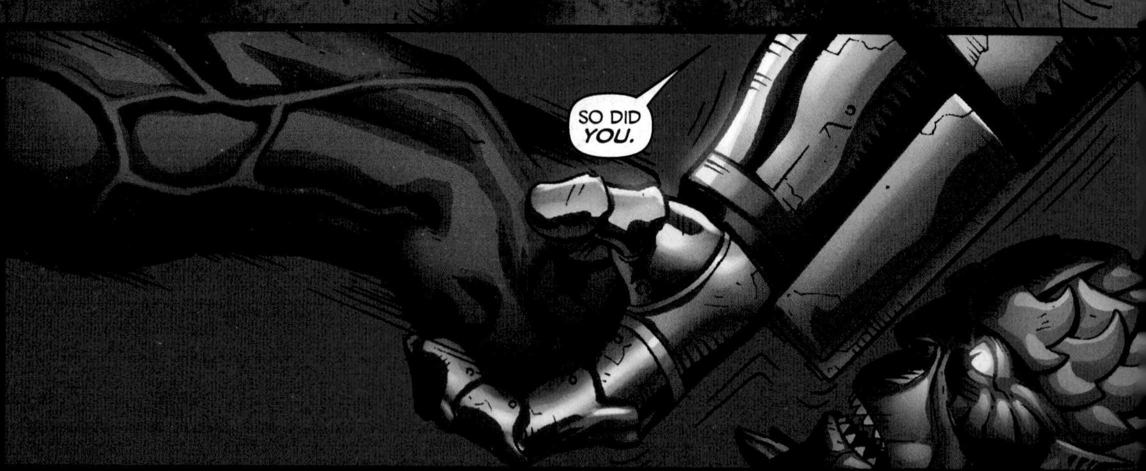
SO DID YOU.
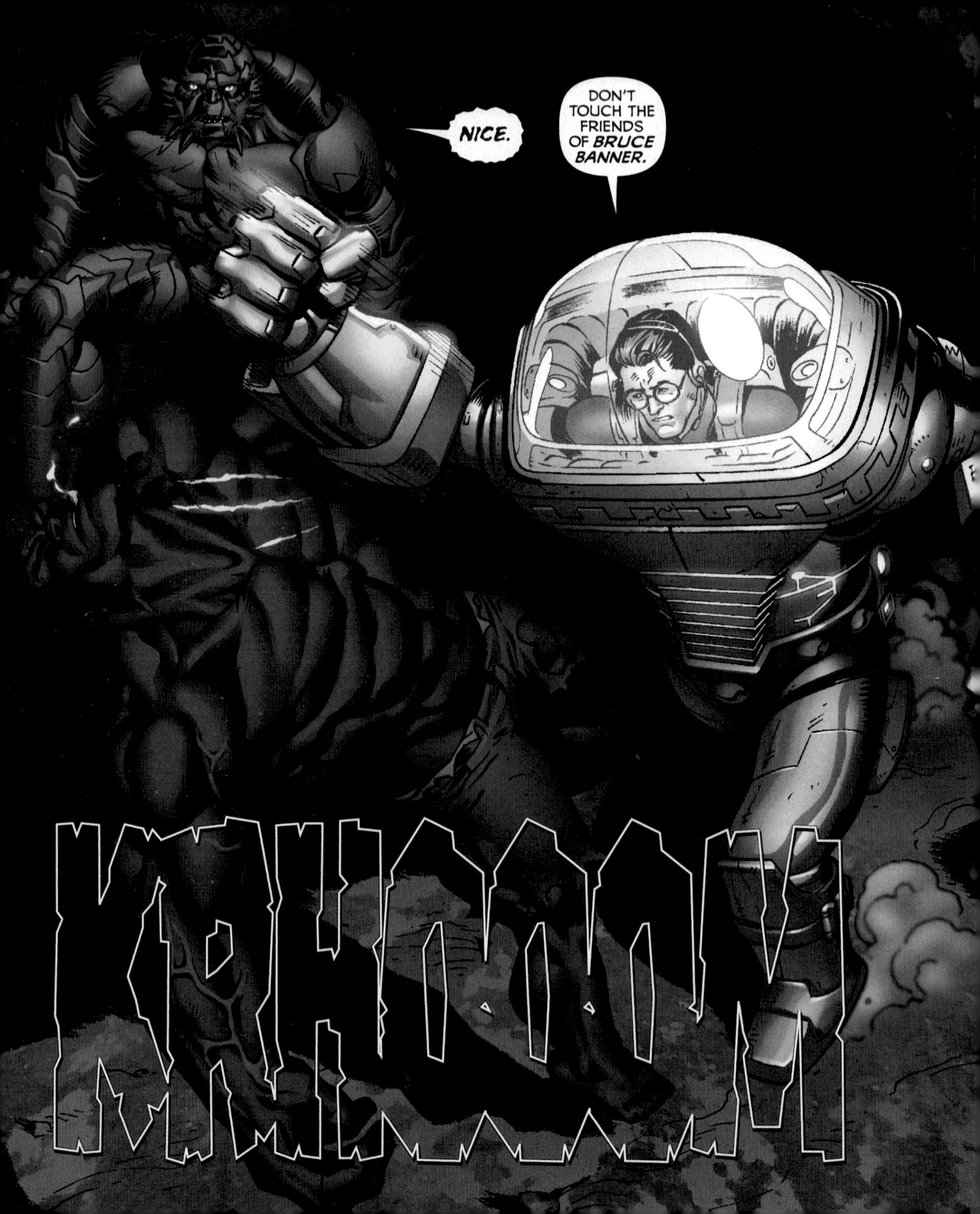
NICE.
DON'T TOUCH THE FRIENDS OF BRUCE BANNER.
KRHOOOM

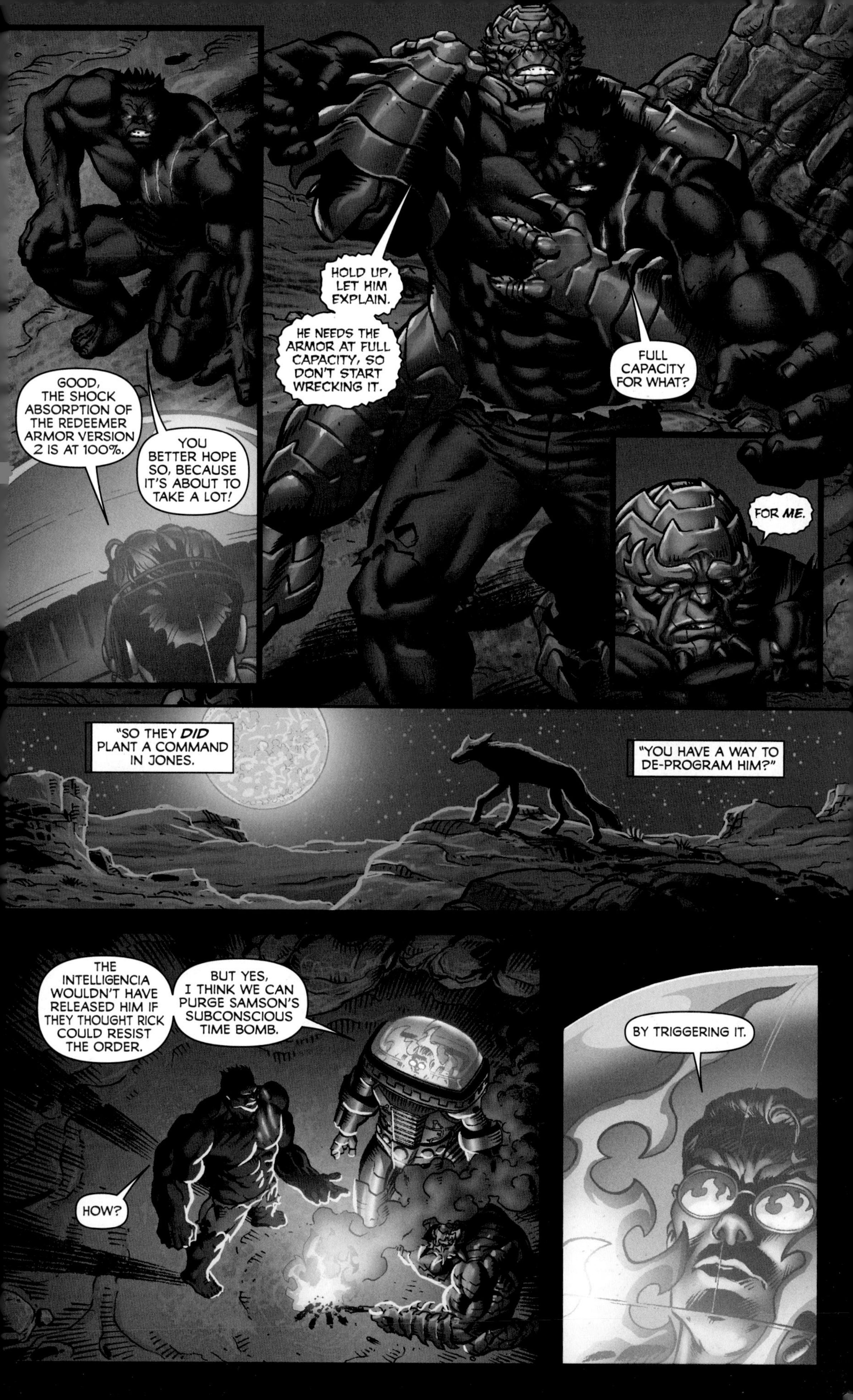
GOOD, THE SHOCK ABSORPTION OF THE REDEEMER ARMOR VERSION 2 IS AT 100%.
YOU BETTER HOPE SO, BECAUSE IT'S ABOUT TO TAKE A LOT!
HOLD UP, LET HIM EXPLAIN.
HE NEEDS THE ARMOR AT FULL CAPACITY, SO DON'T START WRECKING IT.
FULL CAPACITY FOR WHAT?
FOR *ME*.
"SO THEY *DID* PLANT A COMMAND IN JONES.
"YOU HAVE A WAY TO DE-PROGRAM HIM?"
THE INTELLIGENCIA WOULDN'T HAVE RELEASED HIM IF THEY THOUGHT RICK COULD RESIST THE ORDER.
BUT YES, I THINK WE CAN PURGE SAMSON'S SUBCONSCIOUS TIME BOMB.
HOW?
BY TRIGGERING IT.

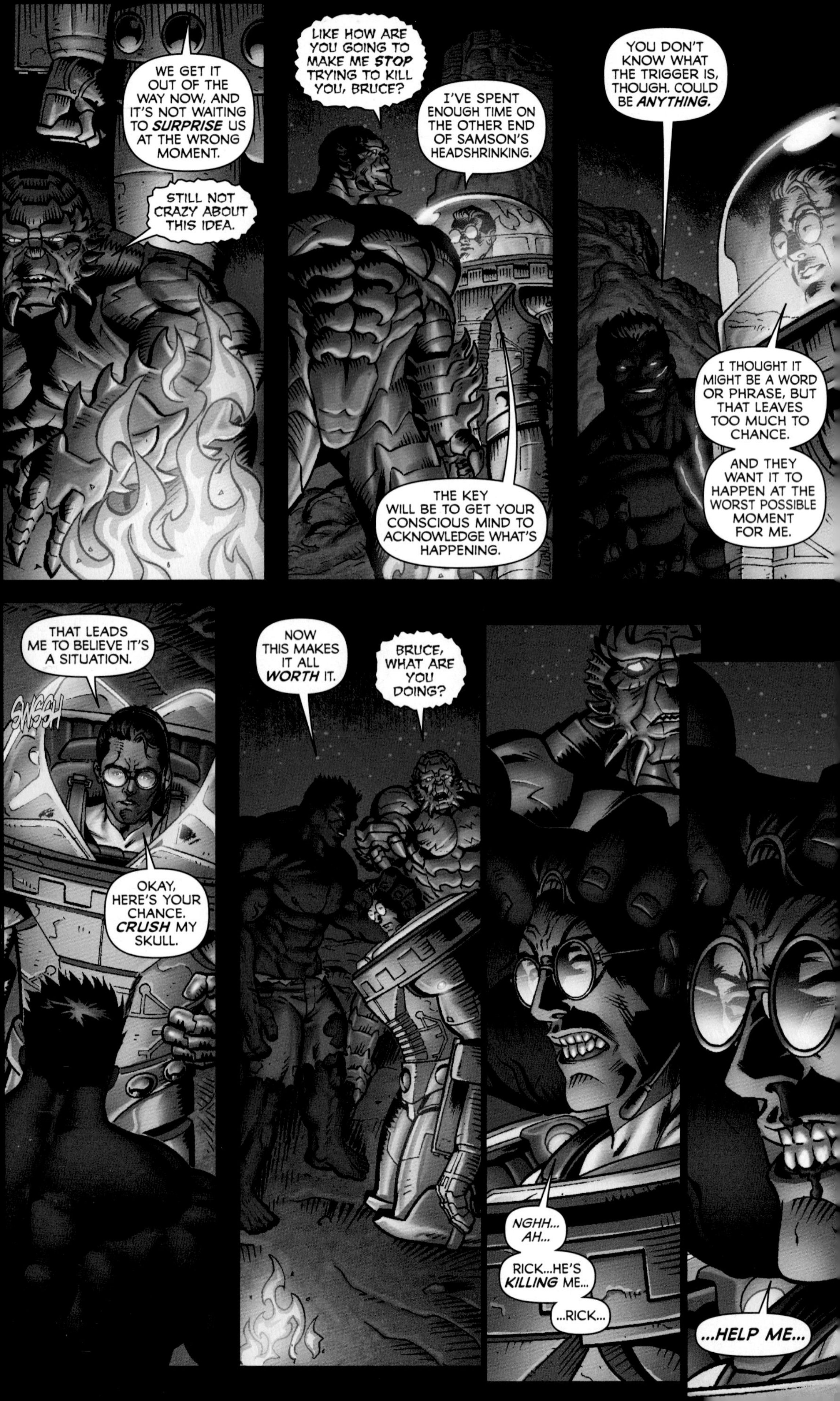
WE GET IT OUT OF THE WAY NOW, AND IT'S NOT WAITING TO SURPRISE US AT THE WRONG MOMENT.
STILL NOT CRAZY ABOUT THIS IDEA.
LIKE HOW ARE YOU GOING TO MAKE ME STOP TRYING TO KILL YOU, BRUCE?
I'VE SPENT ENOUGH TIME ON THE OTHER END OF SAMSON'S HEADSHRINKING.
THE KEY WILL BE TO GET YOUR CONSCIOUS MIND TO ACKNOWLEDGE WHAT'S HAPPENING.
YOU DON'T KNOW WHAT THE TRIGGER IS, THOUGH. COULD BE ANYTHING.
I THOUGHT IT MIGHT BE A WORD OR PHRASE, BUT THAT LEAVES TOO MUCH TO CHANCE.
AND THEY WANT IT TO HAPPEN AT THE WORST POSSIBLE MOMENT FOR ME.
THAT LEADS ME TO BELIEVE IT'S A SITUATION.
SWSSH
OKAY, HERE'S YOUR CHANCE. CRUSH MY SKULL.
NOW THIS MAKES IT ALL WORTH IT.
BRUCE, WHAT ARE YOU DOING?
NGHH... AH...
RICK...HE'S KILLING ME...
...RICK...
...HELP ME...

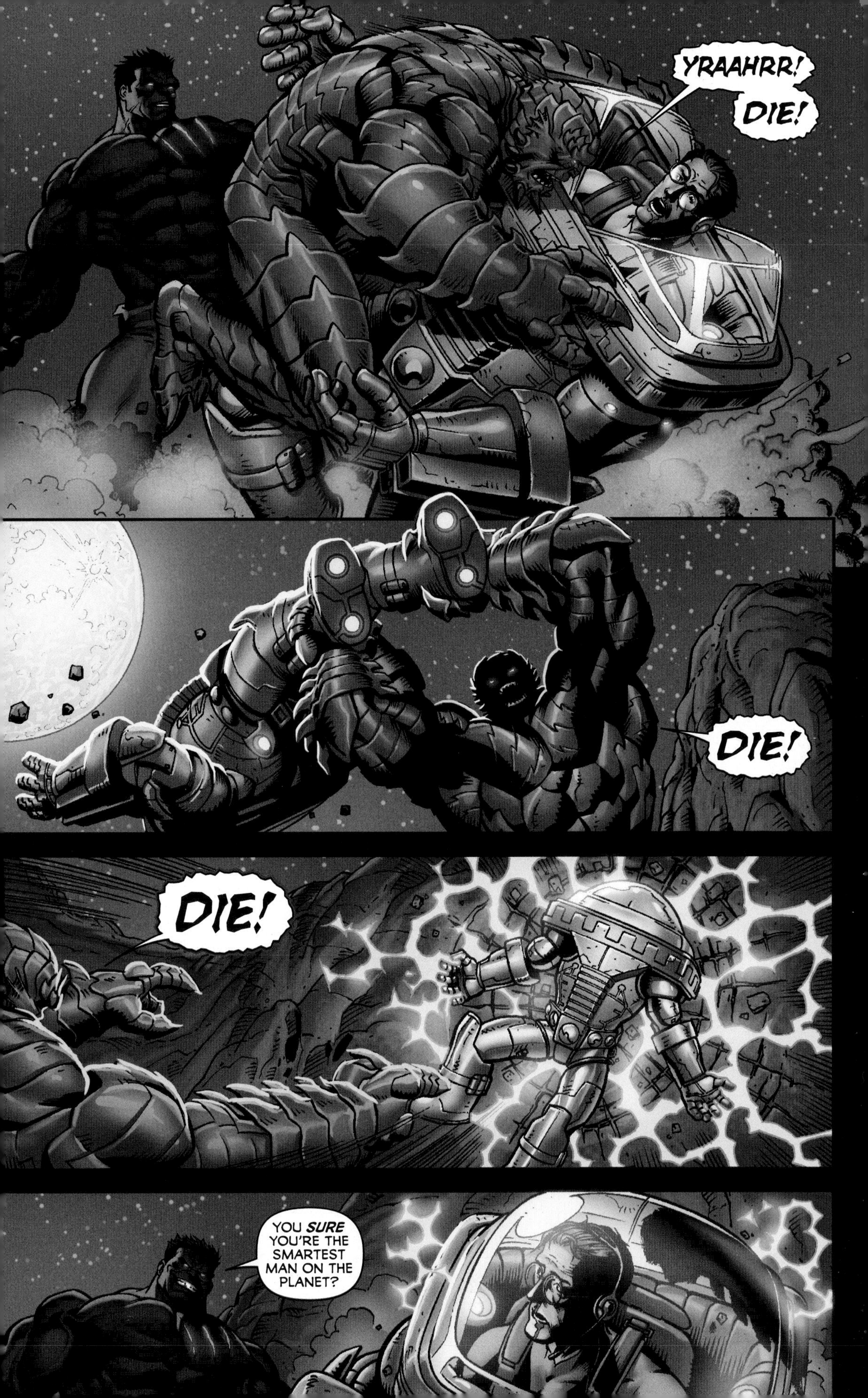
YRAAHRR! DIE!
DIE!
DIE!
YOU SURE YOU'RE THE SMARTEST MAN ON THE PLANET?

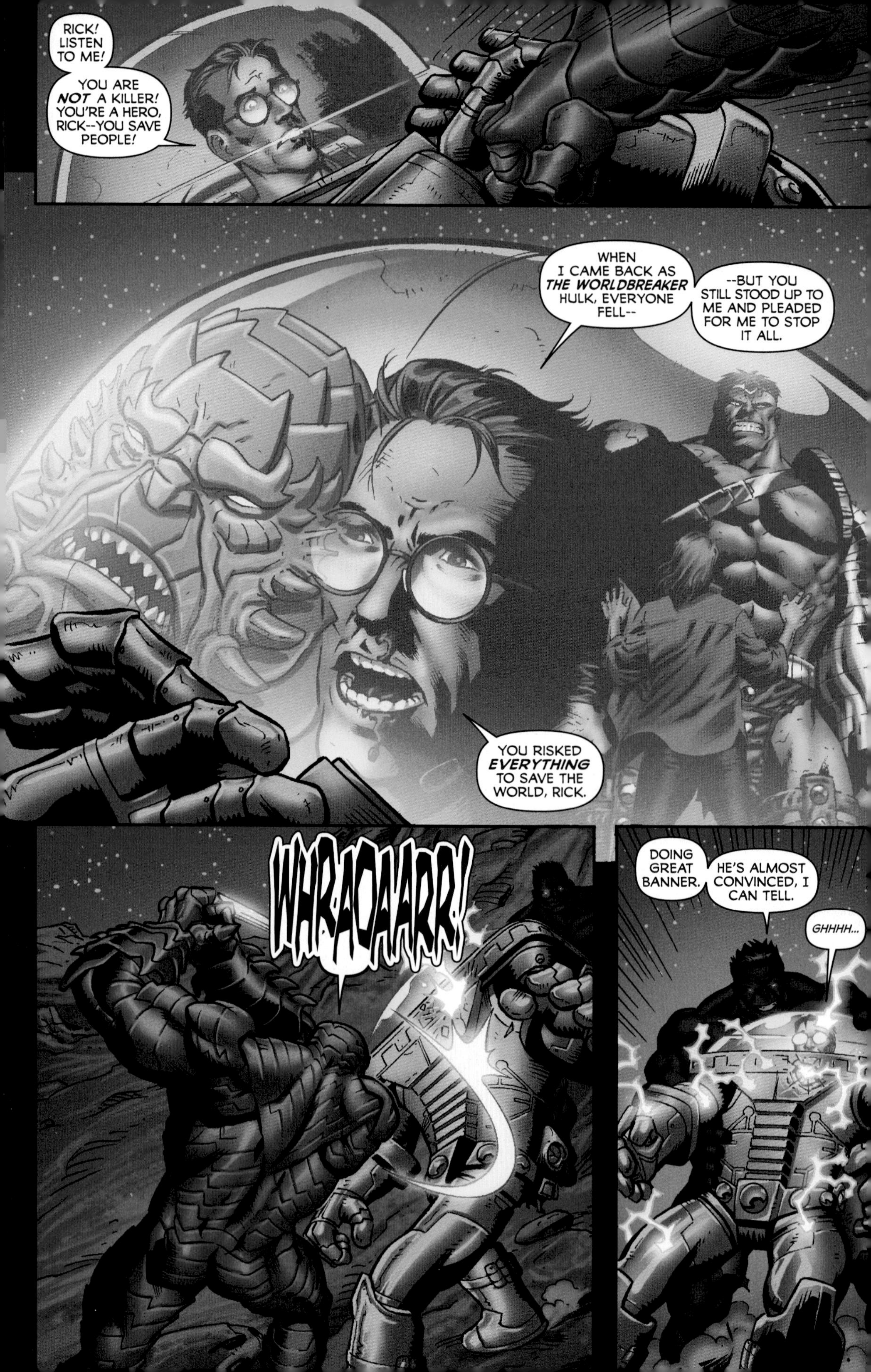
RICK! LISTEN TO ME!
YOU ARE *NOT* A KILLER! YOU'RE A HERO, RICK--YOU SAVE PEOPLE!
WHEN I CAME BACK AS *THE WORLDBREAKER* HULK, EVERYONE FELL--
--BUT YOU STILL STOOD UP TO ME AND PLEADED FOR ME TO STOP IT ALL.
YOU RISKED *EVERYTHING* TO SAVE THE WORLD, RICK.
WHRAOAARR!
DOING GREAT BANNER.
HE'S ALMOST CONVINCED, I CAN TELL.
GHHHH...

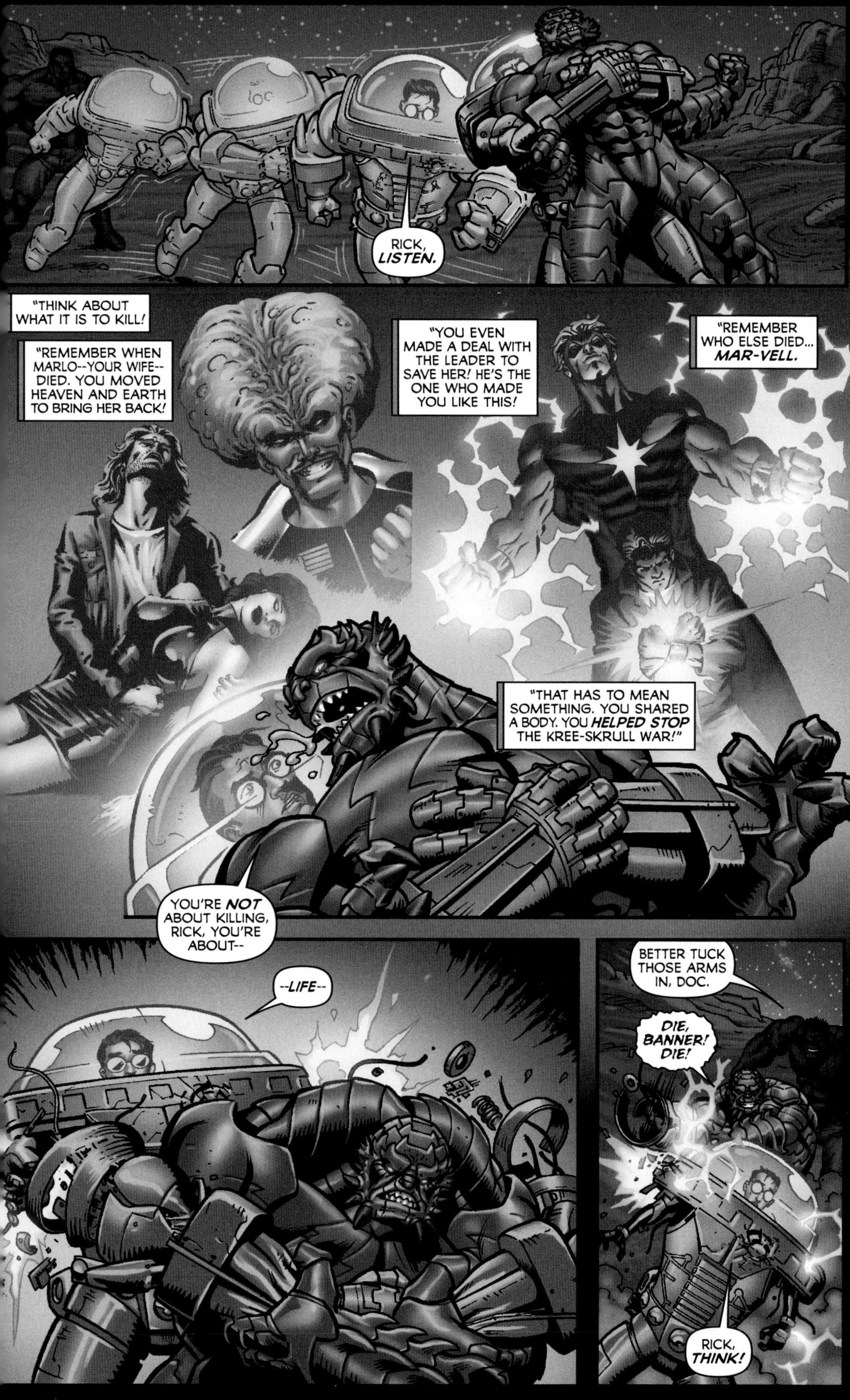

RICK, LISTEN.
"THINK ABOUT WHAT IT IS TO KILL!
"REMEMBER WHEN MARLO--YOUR WIFE--DIED. YOU MOVED HEAVEN AND EARTH TO BRING HER BACK!
"YOU EVEN MADE A DEAL WITH THE LEADER TO SAVE HER! HE'S THE ONE WHO MADE YOU LIKE THIS!
"REMEMBER WHO ELSE DIED... MAR-VELL.
"THAT HAS TO MEAN SOMETHING. YOU SHARED A BODY. YOU HELPED STOP THE KREE-SKRULL WAR!"
YOU'RE NOT ABOUT KILLING, RICK, YOU'RE ABOUT--
--LIFE--
BETTER TUCK THOSE ARMS IN, DOC.
DIE, BANNER! DIE!
RICK, THINK!

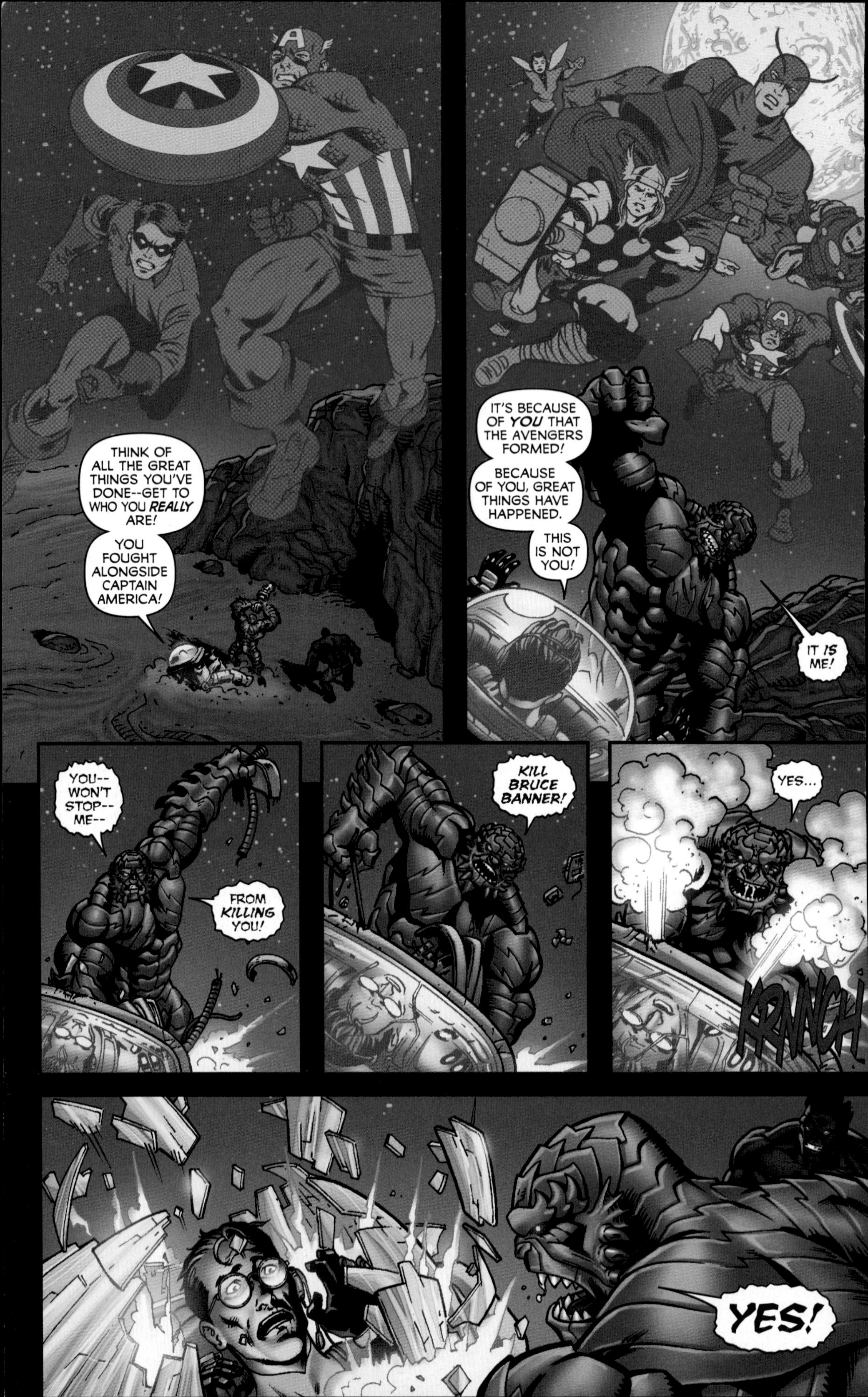
THINK OF ALL THE GREAT THINGS YOU'VE DONE--GET TO WHO YOU *REALLY* ARE!
YOU FOUGHT ALONGSIDE CAPTAIN AMERICA!
IT'S BECAUSE OF *YOU* THAT THE AVENGERS FORMED!
BECAUSE OF YOU, GREAT THINGS HAVE HAPPENED.
THIS IS NOT YOU!
IT *IS* ME!
YOU-- WON'T STOP-- ME--
FROM *KILLING* YOU!
KILL BRUCE BANNER!
YES...
KRNNCH
YES!

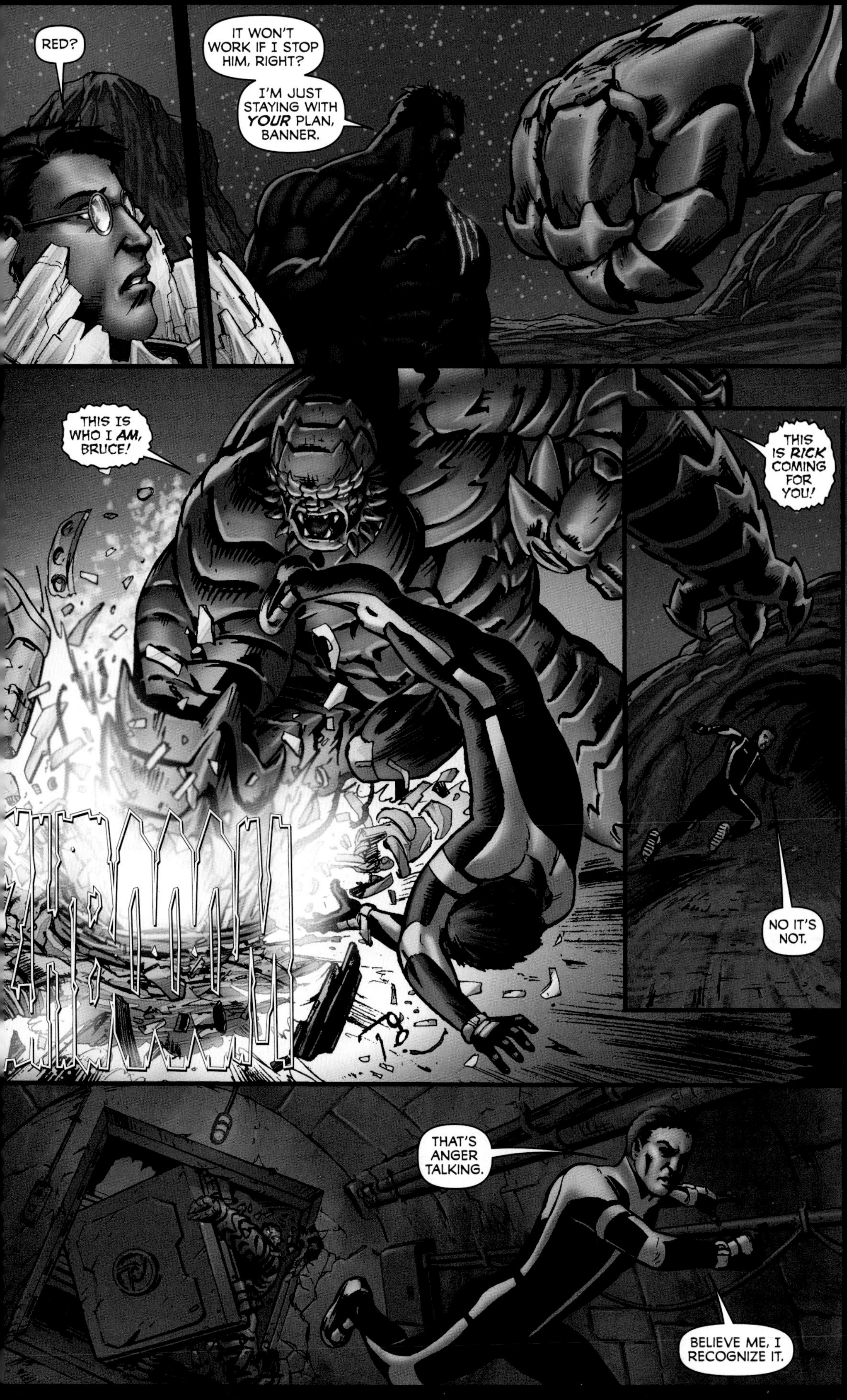
RED?
IT WON'T WORK IF I STOP HIM, RIGHT?
I'M JUST STAYING WITH *YOUR* PLAN, BANNER.
THIS IS WHO I *AM*, BRUCE!
THIS IS *RICK* COMING FOR YOU!
NO IT'S NOT.
THAT'S ANGER TALKING.
BELIEVE ME, I RECOGNIZE IT.

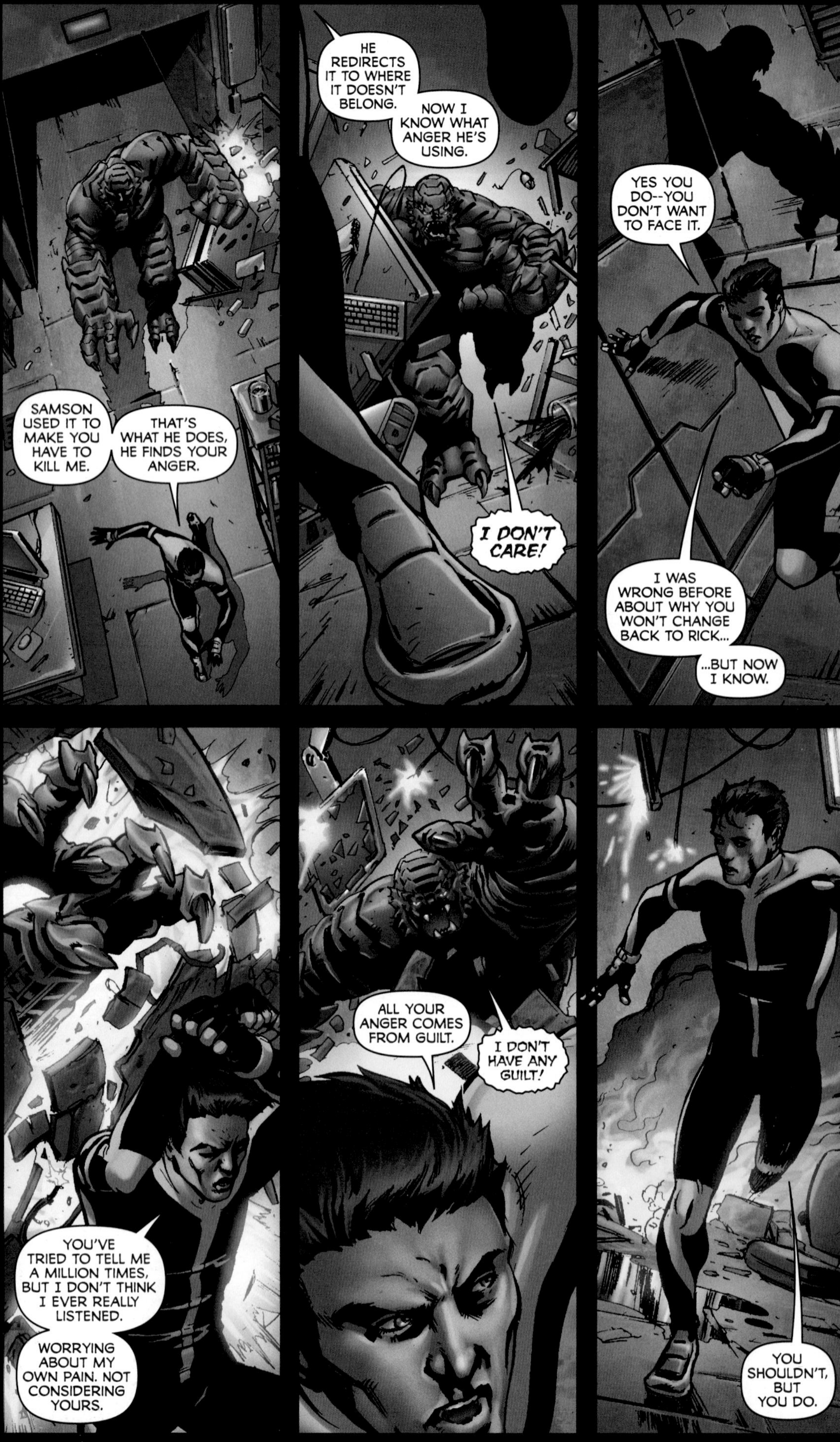

SAMSON USED IT TO MAKE YOU HAVE TO KILL ME.
THAT'S WHAT HE DOES, HE FINDS YOUR ANGER.
HE REDIRECTS IT TO WHERE IT DOESN'T BELONG.
NOW I KNOW WHAT ANGER HE'S USING.
I DON'T CARE!
YES YOU DO--YOU DON'T WANT TO FACE IT.
I WAS WRONG BEFORE ABOUT WHY YOU WON'T CHANGE BACK TO RICK...
...BUT NOW I KNOW.
YOU'VE TRIED TO TELL ME A MILLION TIMES, BUT I DON'T THINK I EVER REALLY LISTENED.
WORRYING ABOUT MY OWN PAIN. NOT CONSIDERING YOURS.
ALL YOUR ANGER COMES FROM GUILT.
I DON'T HAVE ANY GUILT!
YOU SHOULDN'T, BUT YOU DO.

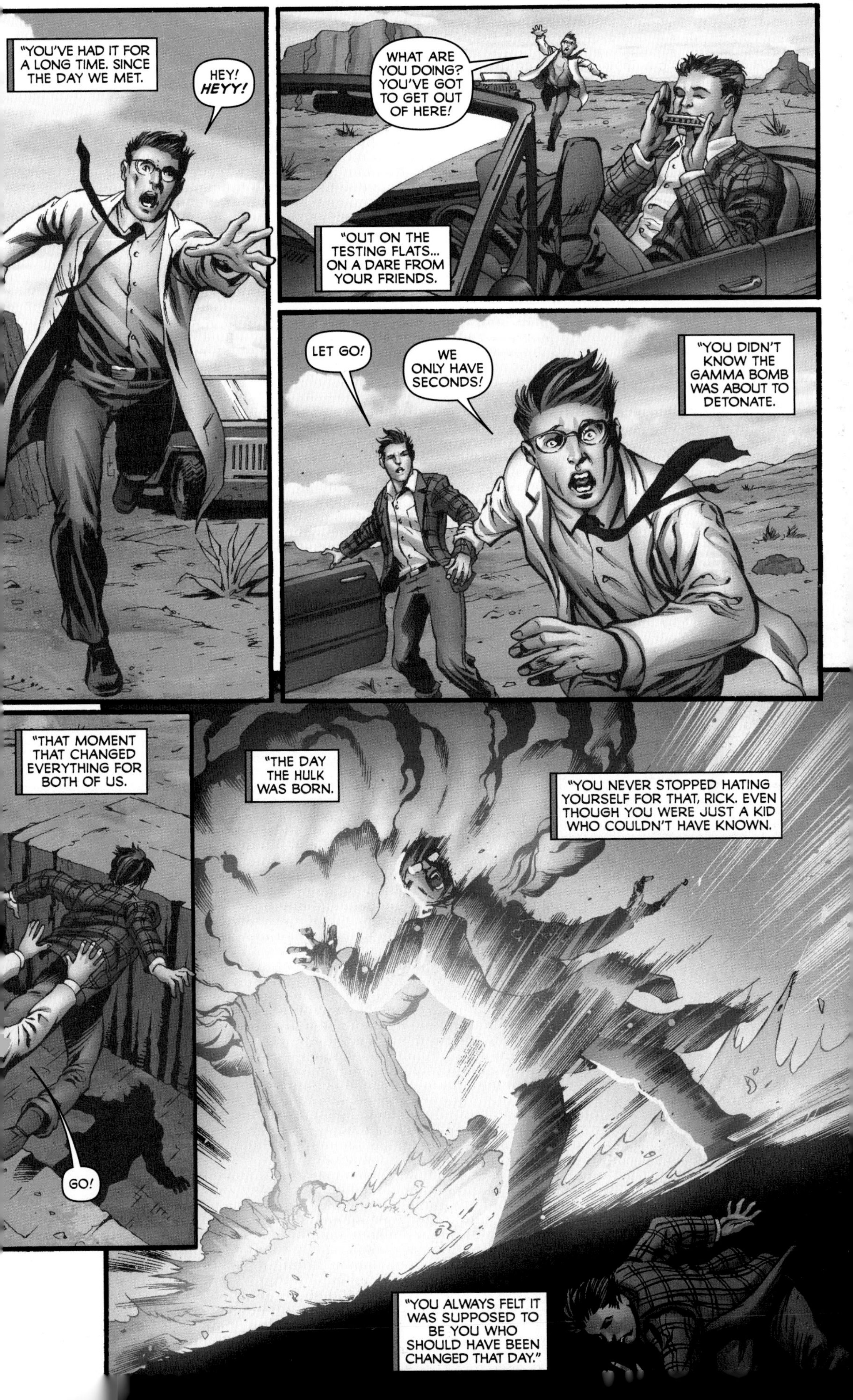
"YOU'VE HAD IT FOR A LONG TIME. SINCE THE DAY WE MET.
HEY! HEYY!
WHAT ARE YOU DOING? YOU'VE GOT TO GET OUT OF HERE!
"OUT ON THE TESTING FLATS... ON A DARE FROM YOUR FRIENDS.
LET GO!
WE ONLY HAVE SECONDS!
"YOU DIDN'T KNOW THE GAMMA BOMB WAS ABOUT TO DETONATE.
"THAT MOMENT THAT CHANGED EVERYTHING FOR BOTH OF US.
GO!
"THE DAY THE HULK WAS BORN.
"YOU NEVER STOPPED HATING YOURSELF FOR THAT, RICK. EVEN THOUGH YOU WERE JUST A KID WHO COULDN'T HAVE KNOWN.
"YOU ALWAYS FELT IT WAS SUPPOSED TO BE YOU WHO SHOULD HAVE BEEN CHANGED THAT DAY."

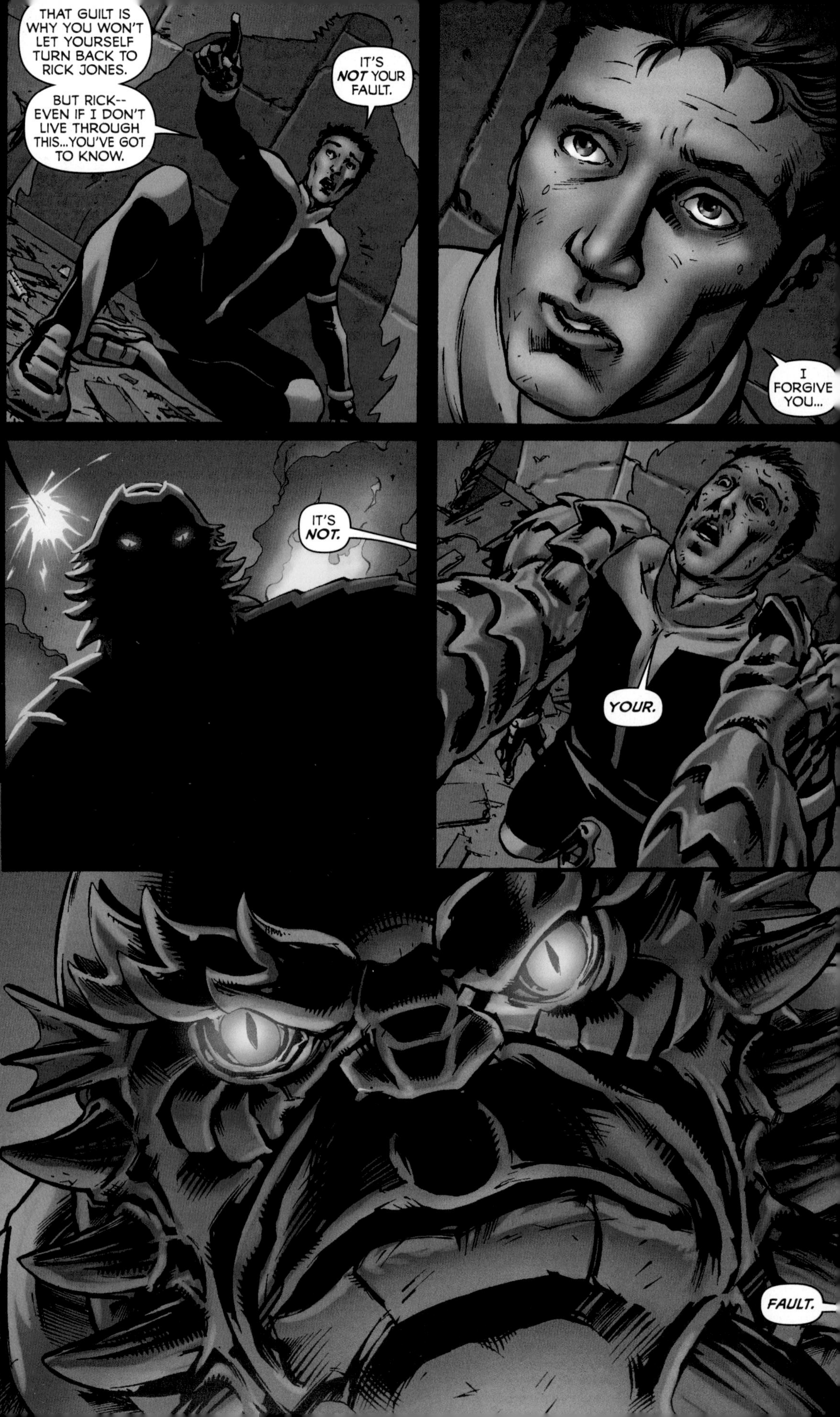
THAT GUILT IS WHY YOU WON'T LET YOURSELF TURN BACK TO RICK JONES.
BUT RICK-- EVEN IF I DON'T LIVE THROUGH THIS...YOU'VE GOT TO KNOW.
IT'S **NOT** YOUR FAULT.
I FORGIVE YOU...
IT'S **NOT.**
YOUR.
FAULT.

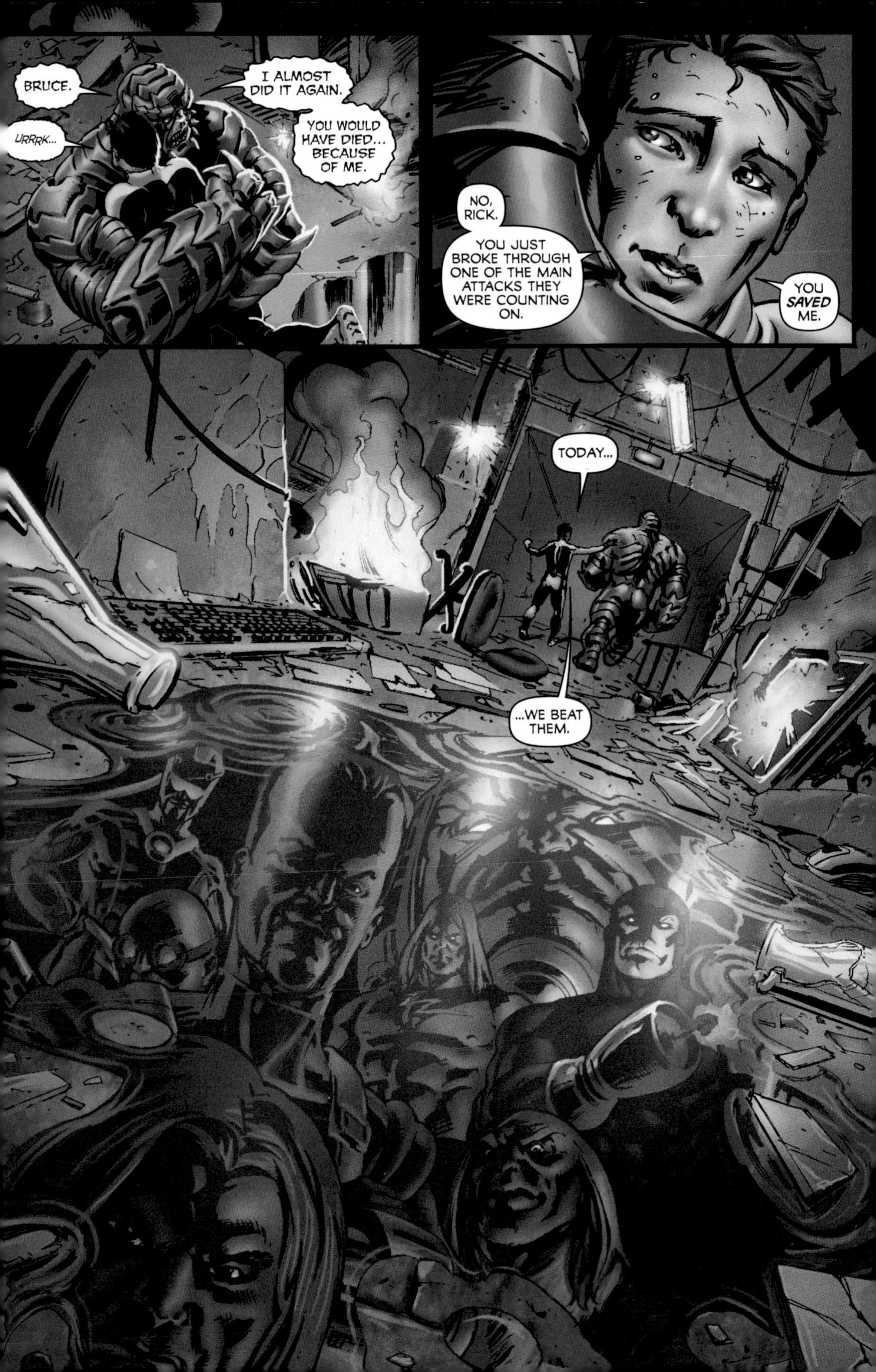

BRUCE.
URRRK...
I ALMOST DID IT AGAIN.
YOU WOULD HAVE DIED... BECAUSE OF ME.
NO, RICK.
YOU JUST BROKE THROUGH ONE OF THE MAIN ATTACKS THEY WERE COUNTING ON.
YOU *SAVED* ME.
TODAY...
...WE BEAT THEM.

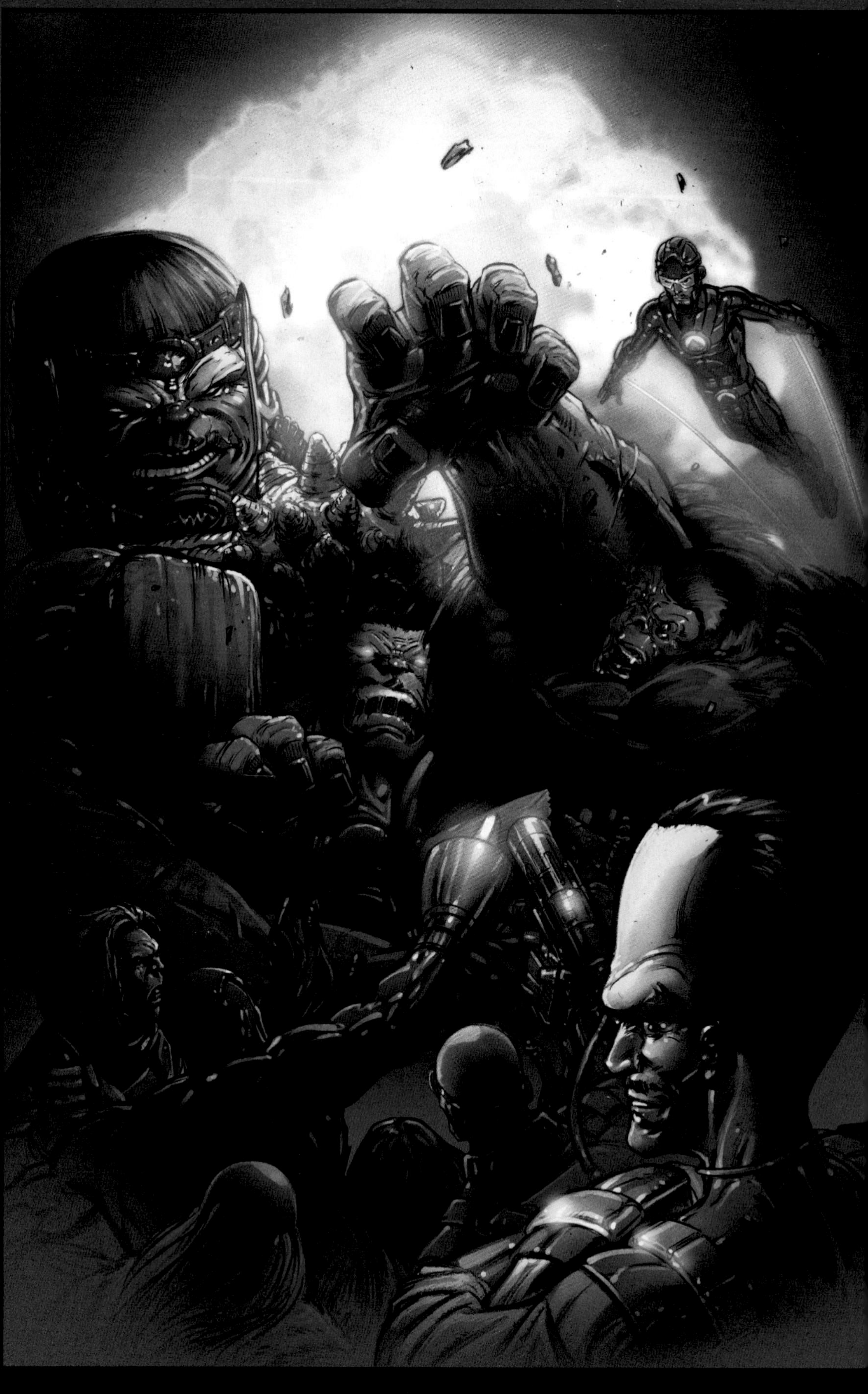

FALL OF THE HULKS: RED HULK #4

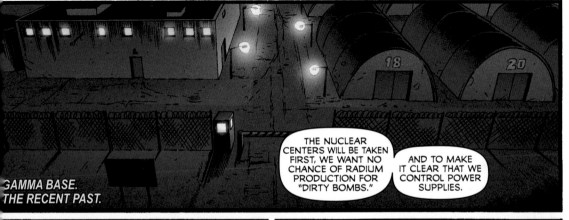

GAMMA BASE.
THE RECENT PAST.

THE NUCLEAR CENTERS WILL BE TAKEN FIRST, WE WANT NO CHANCE OF RADIUM PRODUCTION FOR "DIRTY BOMBS."

AND TO MAKE IT CLEAR THAT WE CONTROL POWER SUPPLIES.

WE'LL INTRODUCE M.O.D.O.K.'S INHIBITOR SUPPLEMENTS WITH CROP DUSTING AS WELL AS THE WATER SUPPLIES.

I ESTIMATE STILL 14% OF THEIR POPULATIONS CAN AVOID TREATMENT BY INDIVIDUAL FARMING.

ONLY .04% OF THOSE WOULD BE IN MANAGEMENT OR GOVERNMENTAL AUTHORITY. THREAT LEVEL POSED IS MINIMAL.

MOST CONSUME PROCESSED FOODS, EASY TO MANIPULATE.

YOU ARE NOT ACCOUNTING FOR THE SHEER LANDMASS OF THE SOVIET STATES.

FORMER SOVIET STATES, GHOST.

IT WILL REQUIRE SUBCONSCIOUS FREQUENCY INFLUENCE AS WELL AS CHEMICAL.

YOU CAME IN LATE, WE WILL ALREADY BE DOING THAT.

WE CAN COMMANDEER 93% OF ALL BROADCAST SATELLITES TO THAT END.

LOOK AT THIS.

YET ANOTHER WAR ROOM FULL OF BIG THINKERS, CARVING UP THE WORLD LIKE IT'S A BOARD GAME.

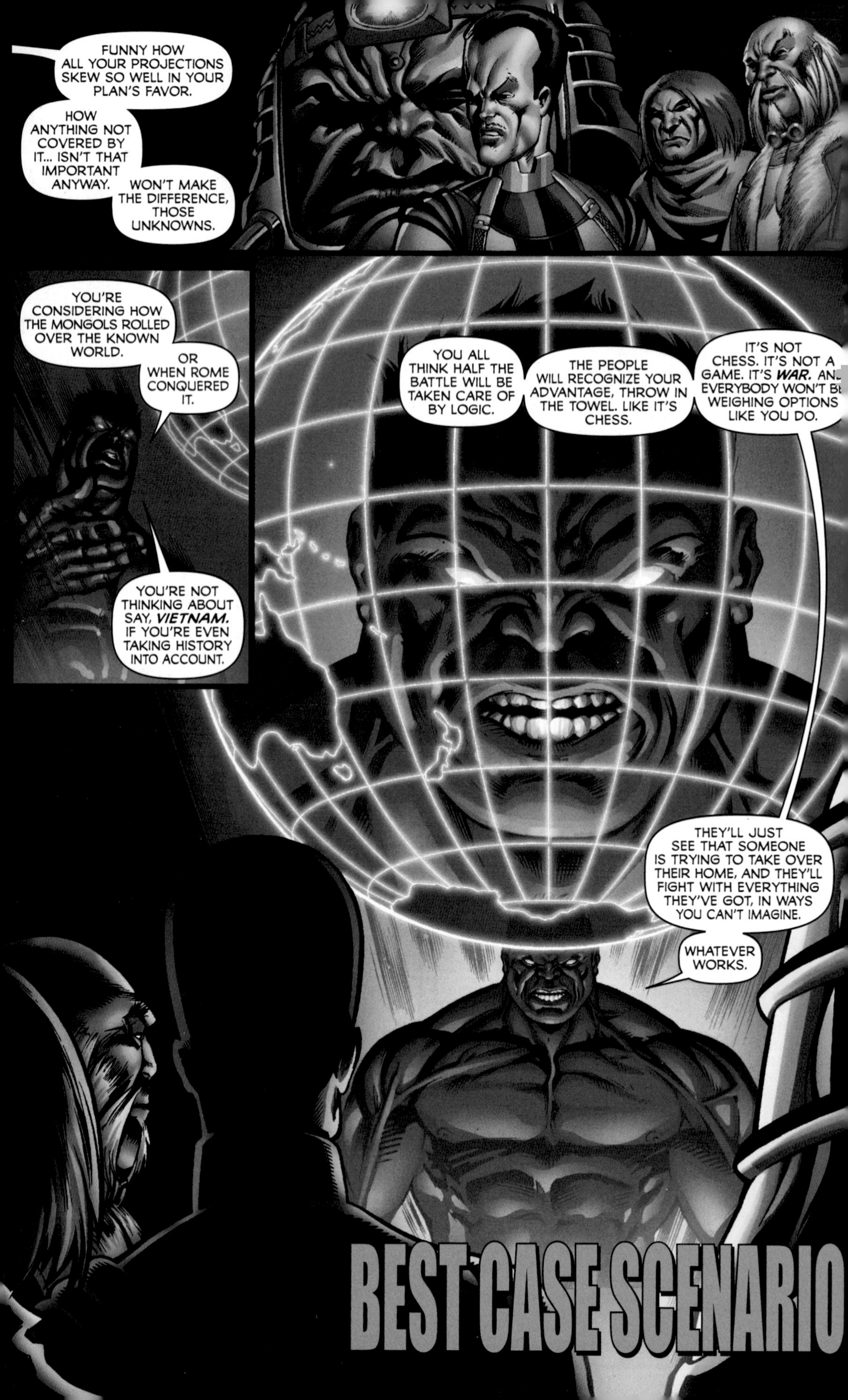
FUNNY HOW ALL YOUR PROJECTIONS SKEW SO WELL IN YOUR PLAN'S FAVOR.
HOW ANYTHING NOT COVERED BY IT... ISN'T THAT IMPORTANT ANYWAY.
WON'T MAKE THE DIFFERENCE, THOSE UNKNOWNS.
YOU'RE CONSIDERING HOW THE MONGOLS ROLLED OVER THE KNOWN WORLD.
OR WHEN ROME CONQUERED IT.
YOU'RE NOT THINKING ABOUT SAY, *VIETNAM.* IF YOU'RE EVEN TAKING HISTORY INTO ACCOUNT.
YOU ALL THINK HALF THE BATTLE WILL BE TAKEN CARE OF BY LOGIC.
THE PEOPLE WILL RECOGNIZE YOUR ADVANTAGE, THROW IN THE TOWEL. LIKE IT'S CHESS.
IT'S NOT CHESS. IT'S NOT A GAME. IT'S *WAR.*
THEY'LL JUST SEE THAT SOMEONE IS TRYING TO TAKE OVER THEIR HOME, AND THEY'LL FIGHT WITH EVERYTHING THEY'VE GOT, IN WAYS YOU CAN'T IMAGINE.
WHATEVER WORKS.
BEST CASE SCENARIO

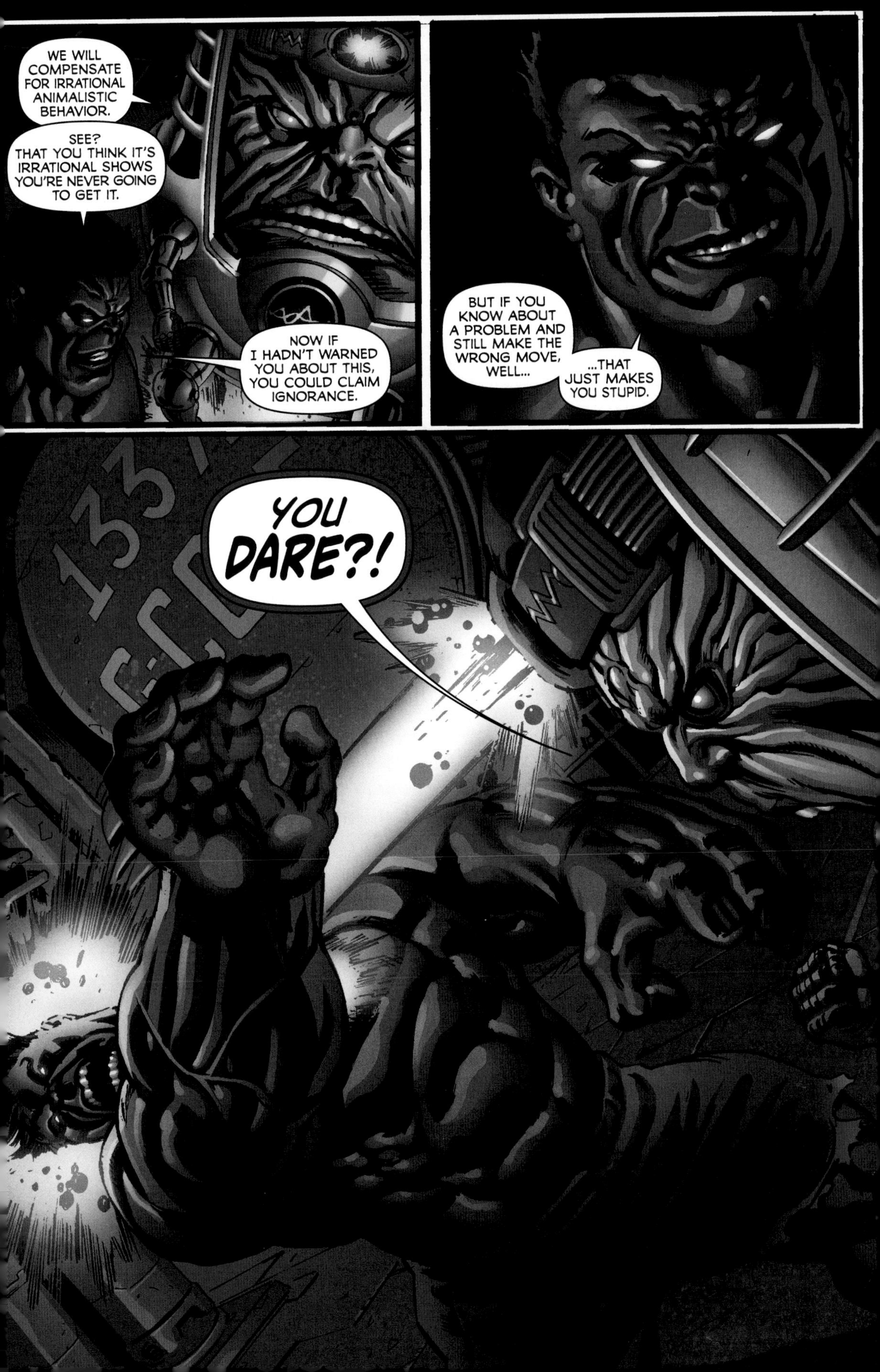
WE WILL COMPENSATE FOR IRRATIONAL ANIMALISTIC BEHAVIOR.
SEE? THAT YOU THINK IT'S IRRATIONAL SHOWS YOU'RE NEVER GOING TO GET IT.
NOW IF I HADN'T WARNED YOU ABOUT THIS, YOU COULD CLAIM IGNORANCE.
BUT IF YOU KNOW ABOUT A PROBLEM AND STILL MAKE THE WRONG MOVE, WELL...
...THAT JUST MAKES YOU STUPID.
YOU DARE?!

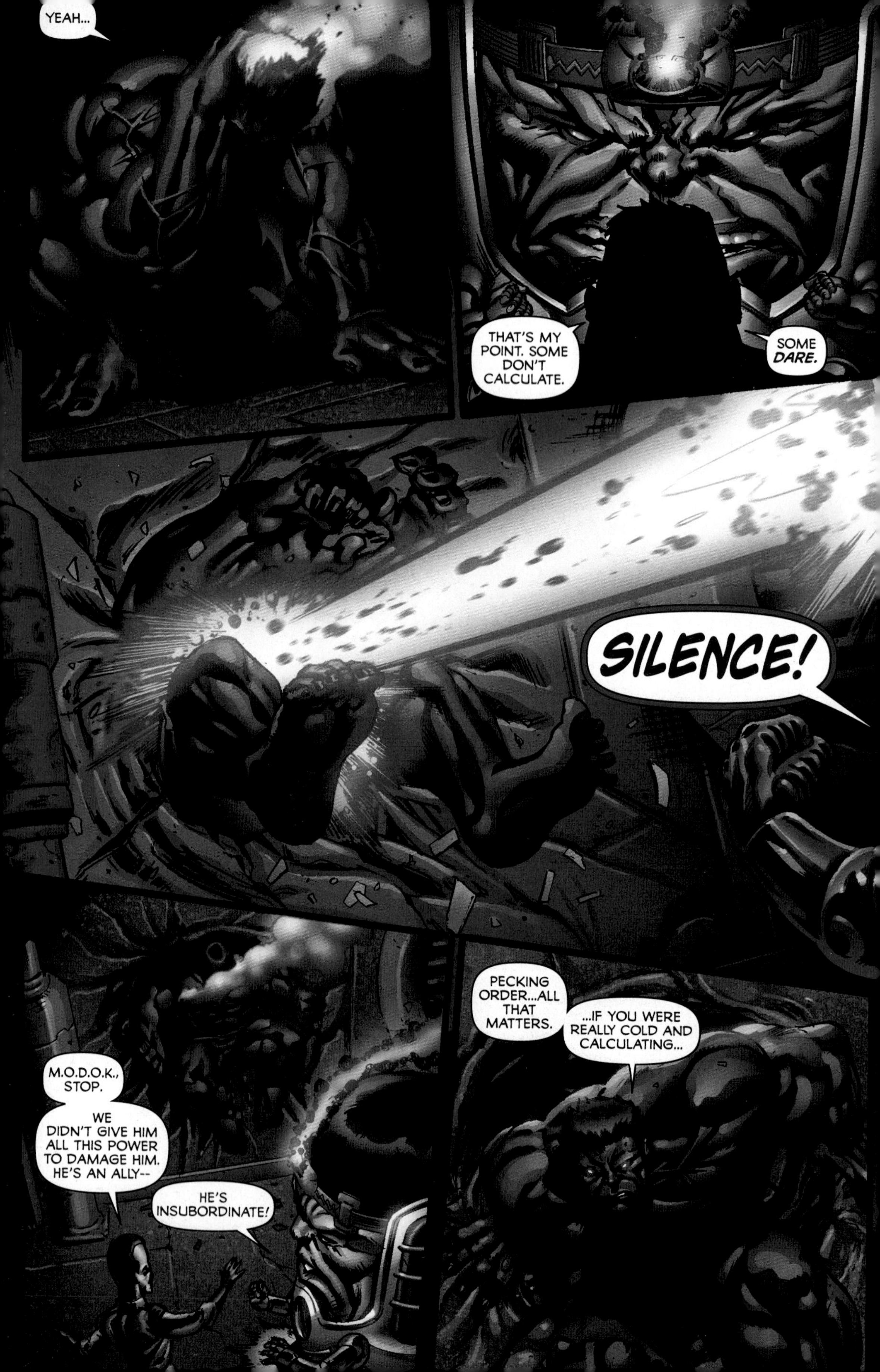
YEAH...
THAT'S MY POINT. SOME DON'T CALCULATE.
SOME DARE.
SILENCE!
M.O.D.O.K., STOP.
WE DIDN'T GIVE HIM ALL THIS POWER TO DAMAGE HIM. HE'S AN ALLY--
HE'S INSUBORDINATE!
PECKING ORDER...ALL THAT MATTERS.
...IF YOU WERE REALLY COLD AND CALCULATING...

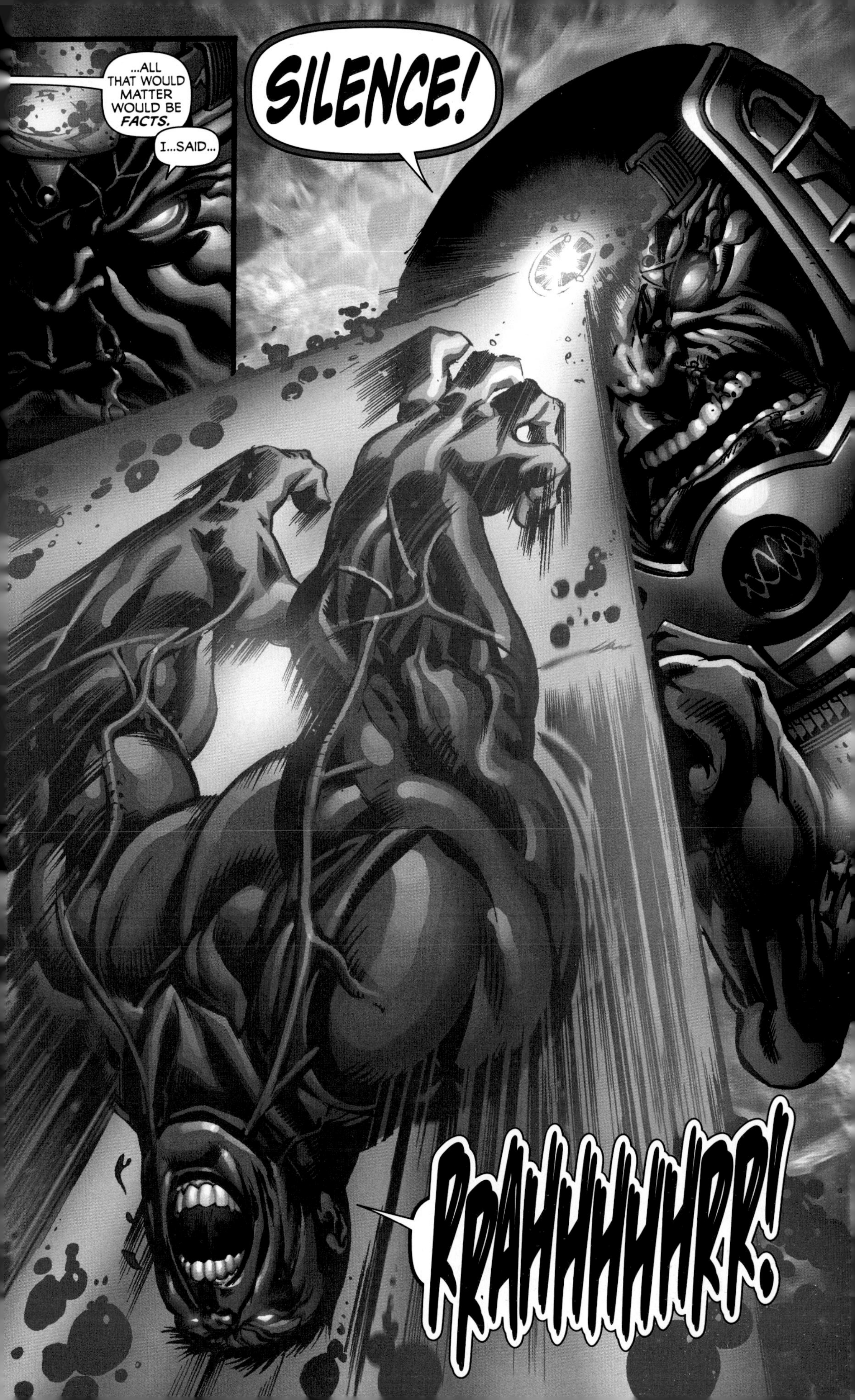
...ALL THAT WOULD MATTER WOULD BE *FACTS.*
I...SAID...
SILENCE!
RRAHHHHHRR!

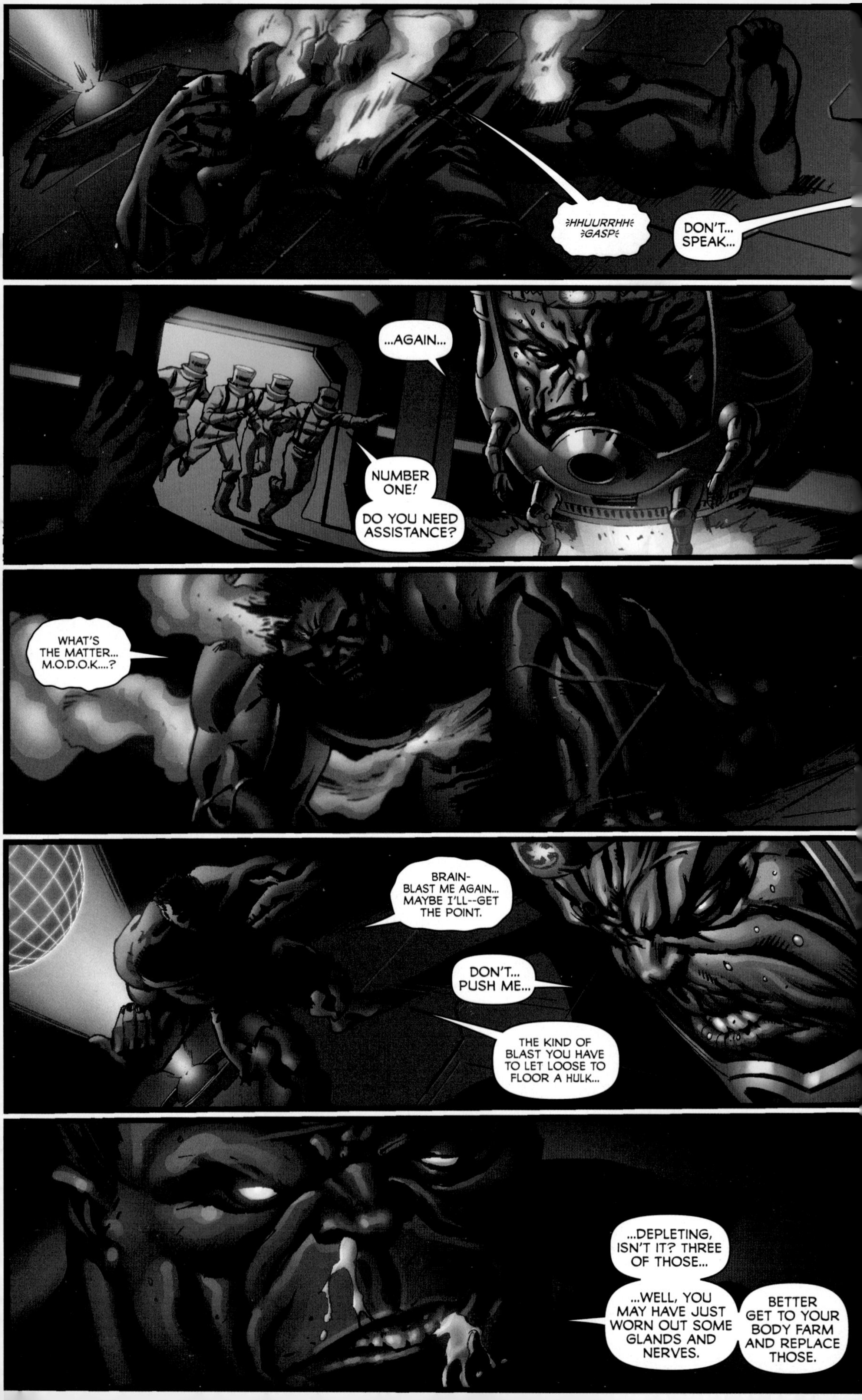

HHUURRHH GASP
DON'T... SPEAK...
...AGAIN...
NUMBER ONE!
DO YOU NEED ASSISTANCE?
WHAT'S THE MATTER... M.O.D.O.K....?
BRAIN-BLAST ME AGAIN... MAYBE I'LL--GET THE POINT.
DON'T... PUSH ME...
THE KIND OF BLAST YOU HAVE TO LET LOOSE TO FLOOR A HULK...
...DEPLETING, ISN'T IT? THREE OF THOSE...
...WELL, YOU MAY HAVE JUST WORN OUT SOME GLANDS AND NERVES.
BETTER GET TO YOUR BODY FARM AND REPLACE THOSE.

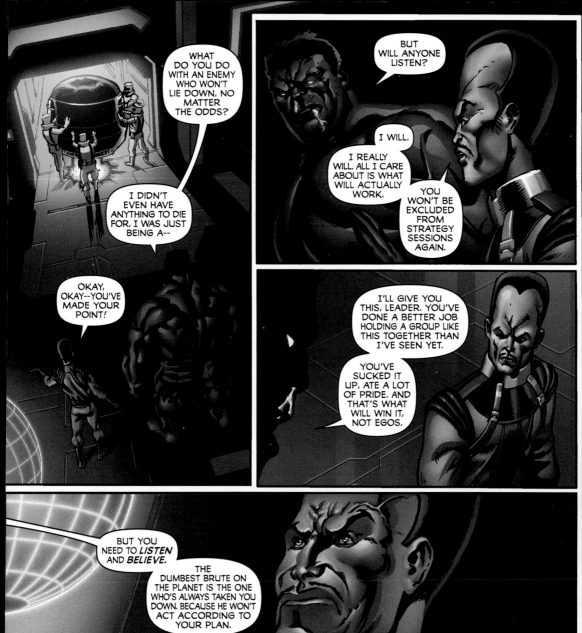

WHAT DO YOU DO WITH AN ENEMY WHO WON'T LIE DOWN, NO MATTER THE ODDS?

I DIDN'T EVEN HAVE ANYTHING TO DIE FOR, I WAS JUST BEING A--

OKAY, OKAY--YOU'VE MADE YOUR POINT!

BUT WILL ANYONE LISTEN?

I WILL. I REALLY WILL. ALL I CARE ABOUT IS WHAT WILL ACTUALLY WORK.

YOU WON'T BE EXCLUDED FROM STRATEGY SESSIONS AGAIN.

I'LL GIVE YOU THIS, LEADER. YOU'VE DONE A BETTER JOB HOLDING A GROUP LIKE THIS TOGETHER THAN I'VE SEEN YET.

YOU'VE SUCKED IT UP, ATE A LOT OF PRIDE. AND THAT'S WHAT WILL WIN IT, NOT EGOS.

BUT YOU NEED TO LISTEN AND BELIEVE.

THE DUMBEST BRUTE ON THE PLANET IS THE ONE WHO'S ALWAYS TAKEN YOU DOWN. BECAUSE HE WON'T ACT ACCORDING TO YOUR PLAN.

I'LL HELP YOU FIGURE OUT THAT CAMPAIGN, HOW TO DEFEAT REAL PEOPLE.

BUT IF YOU DON'T GO AHEAD AND FACTOR HULK INTO IT...

...YOU MIGHT AS WELL THROW UP THE WHITE FLAG NOW.

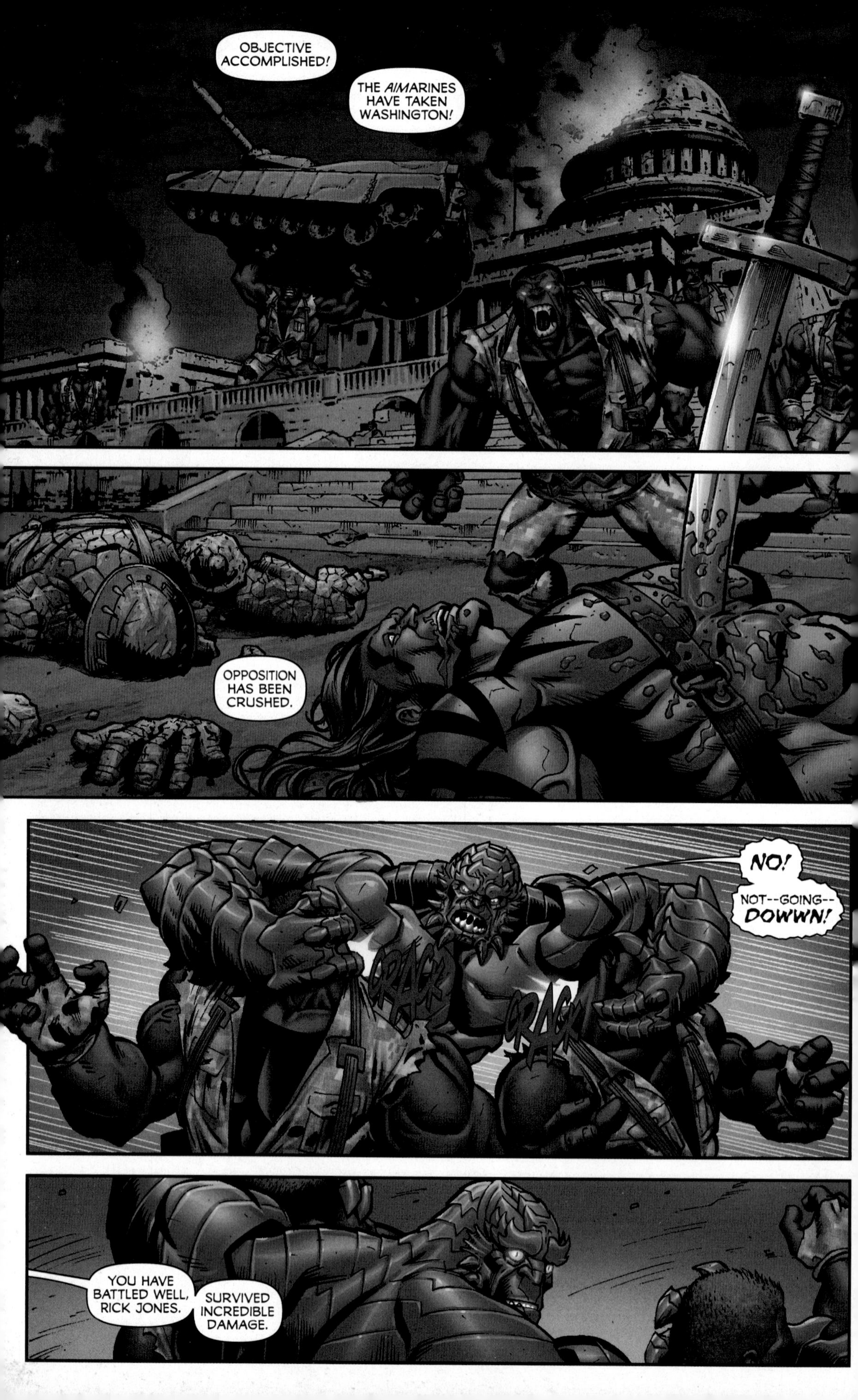
OBJECTIVE ACCOMPLISHED!
THE AIMARINES HAVE TAKEN WASHINGTON!
OPPOSITION HAS BEEN CRUSHED.
CRACK
CRACK
NO!
NOT--GOING-- DOWWN!
YOU HAVE BATTLED WELL, RICK JONES.
SURVIVED INCREDIBLE DAMAGE.

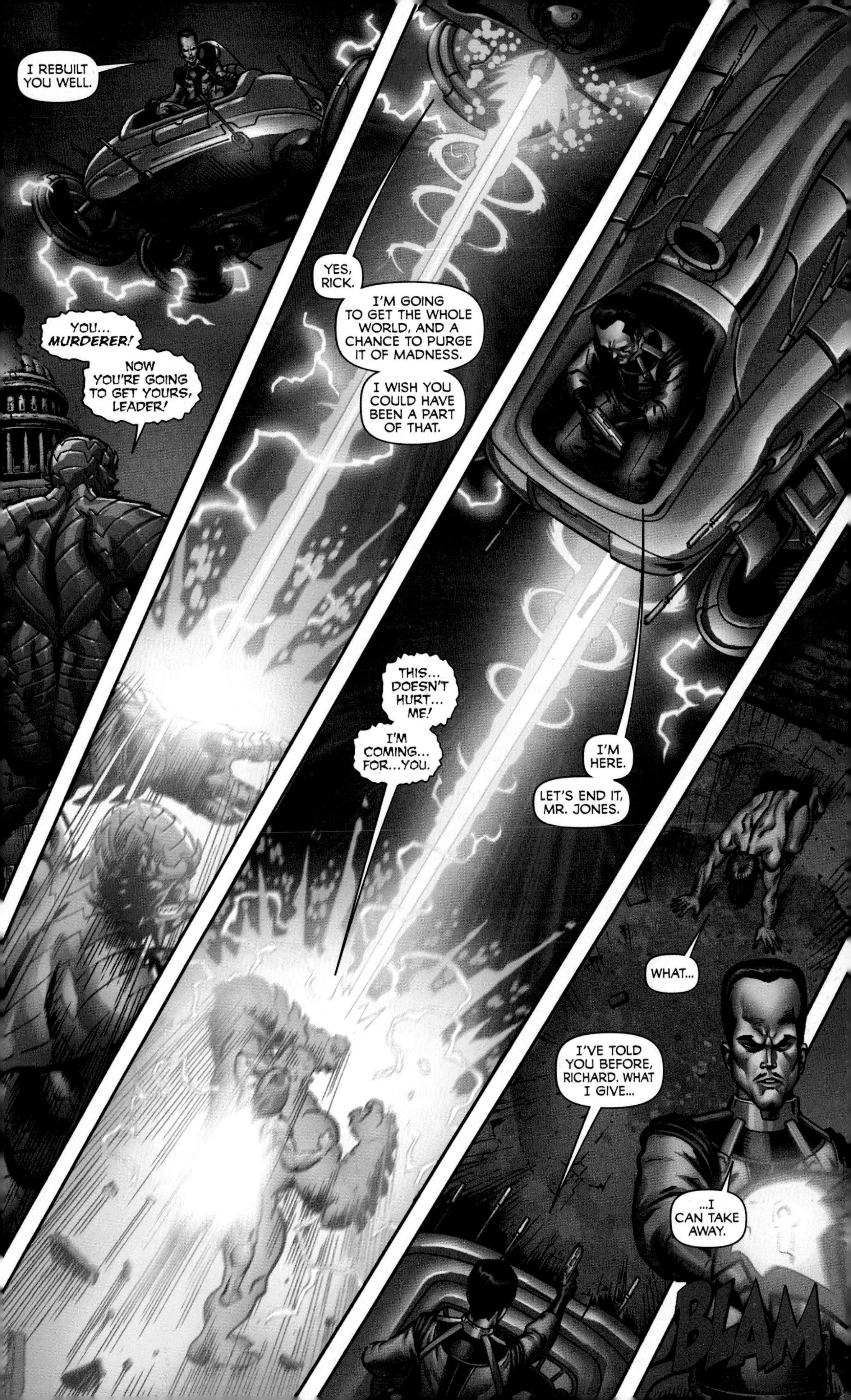
I REBUILT YOU WELL.
YOU... *MURDERER!*
NOW YOU'RE GOING TO GET YOURS, LEADER!
YES, RICK.
I'M GOING TO GET THE WHOLE WORLD, AND A CHANCE TO PURGE IT OF MADNESS.
I WISH YOU COULD HAVE BEEN A PART OF THAT.
THIS... DOESN'T HURT... ME!
I'M COMING... FOR...YOU.
I'M HERE.
LET'S END IT, MR. JONES.
WHAT...
I'VE TOLD YOU BEFORE, RICHARD. WHAT I GIVE...
...I CAN TAKE AWAY.
BLAM

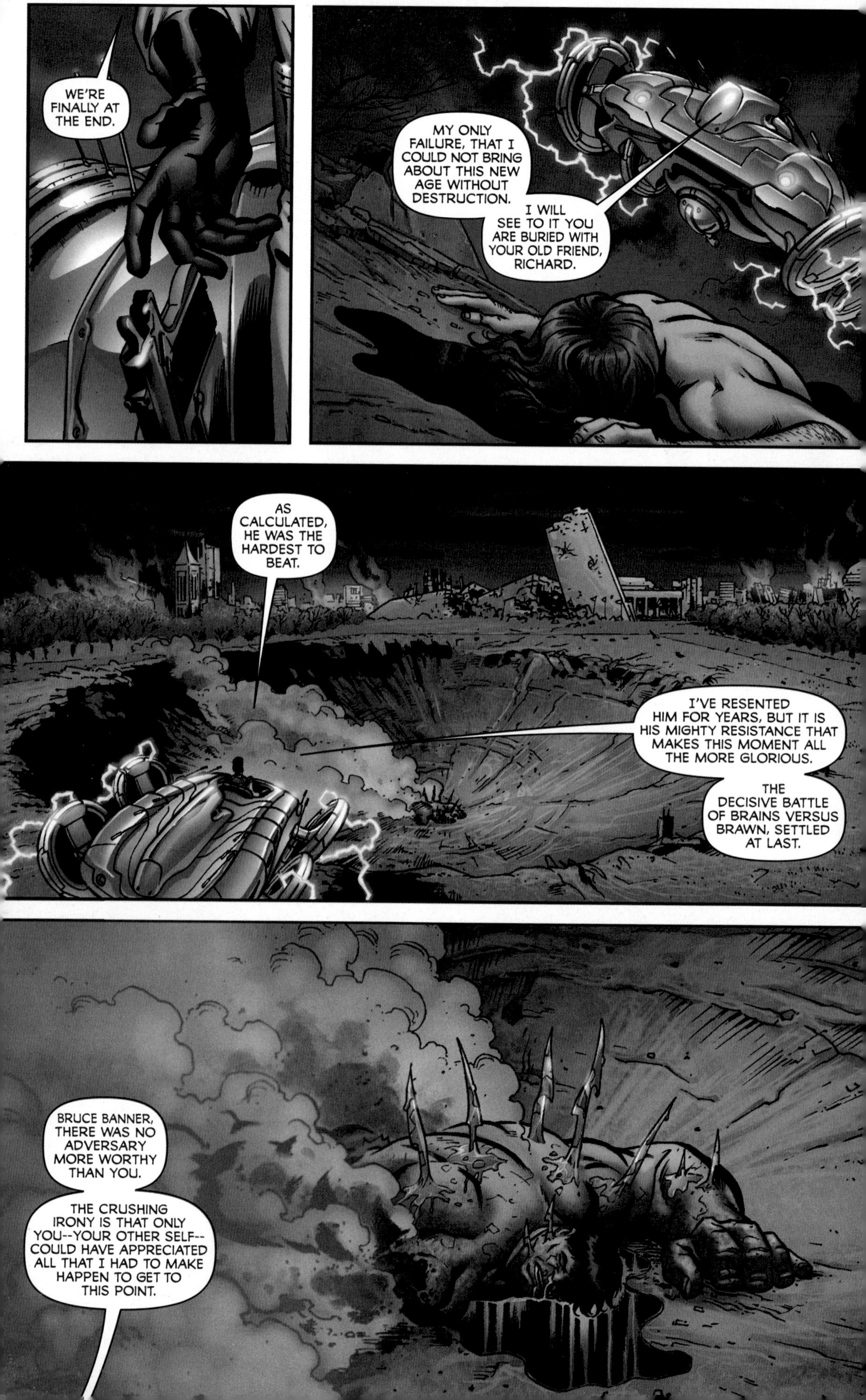
WE'RE FINALLY AT THE END.
MY ONLY FAILURE, THAT I COULD NOT BRING ABOUT THIS NEW AGE WITHOUT DESTRUCTION.
I WILL SEE TO IT YOU ARE BURIED WITH YOUR OLD FRIEND, RICHARD.
AS CALCULATED, HE WAS THE HARDEST TO BEAT.
I'VE RESENTED HIM FOR YEARS, BUT IT IS HIS MIGHTY RESISTANCE THAT MAKES THIS MOMENT ALL THE MORE GLORIOUS.
THE DECISIVE BATTLE OF BRAINS VERSUS BRAWN, SETTLED AT LAST.
BRUCE BANNER, THERE WAS NO ADVERSARY MORE WORTHY THAN YOU.
THE CRUSHING IRONY IS THAT ONLY YOU--YOUR OTHER SELF--COULD HAVE APPRECIATED ALL THAT I HAD TO MAKE HAPPEN TO GET TO THIS POINT.

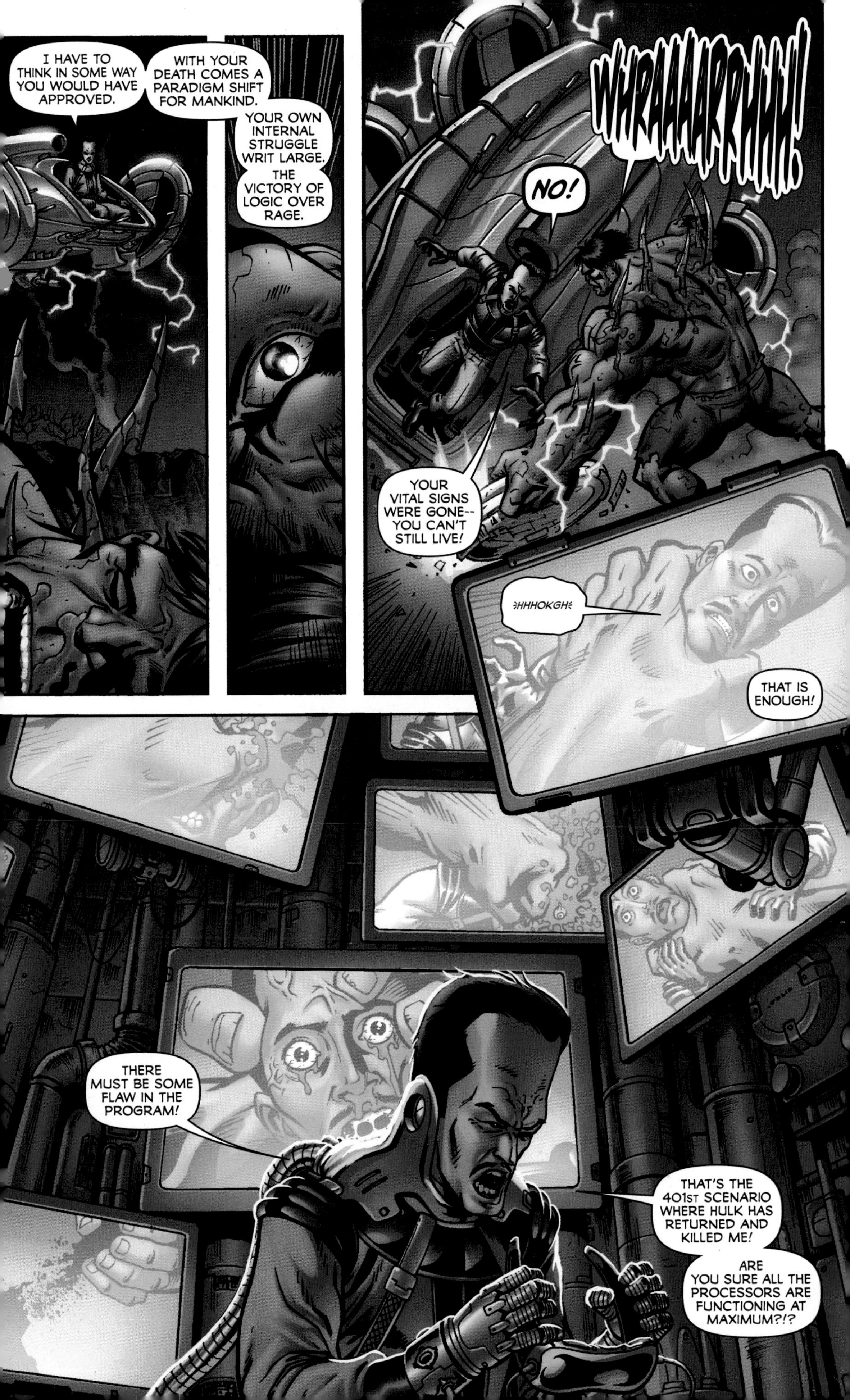
I HAVE TO THINK IN SOME WAY YOU WOULD HAVE APPROVED.
WITH YOUR DEATH COMES A PARADIGM SHIFT FOR MANKIND.
YOUR OWN INTERNAL STRUGGLE WRIT LARGE.
THE VICTORY OF LOGIC OVER RAGE.
WHRAAAARRHHH!
NO!
YOUR VITAL SIGNS WERE GONE-- YOU CAN'T STILL LIVE!
HHHOKGH
THAT IS ENOUGH!
THERE MUST BE SOME FLAW IN THE PROGRAM!
THAT'S THE 401ST SCENARIO WHERE HULK HAS RETURNED AND KILLED ME!
ARE YOU SURE ALL THE PROCESSORS ARE FUNCTIONING AT MAXIMUM?!?

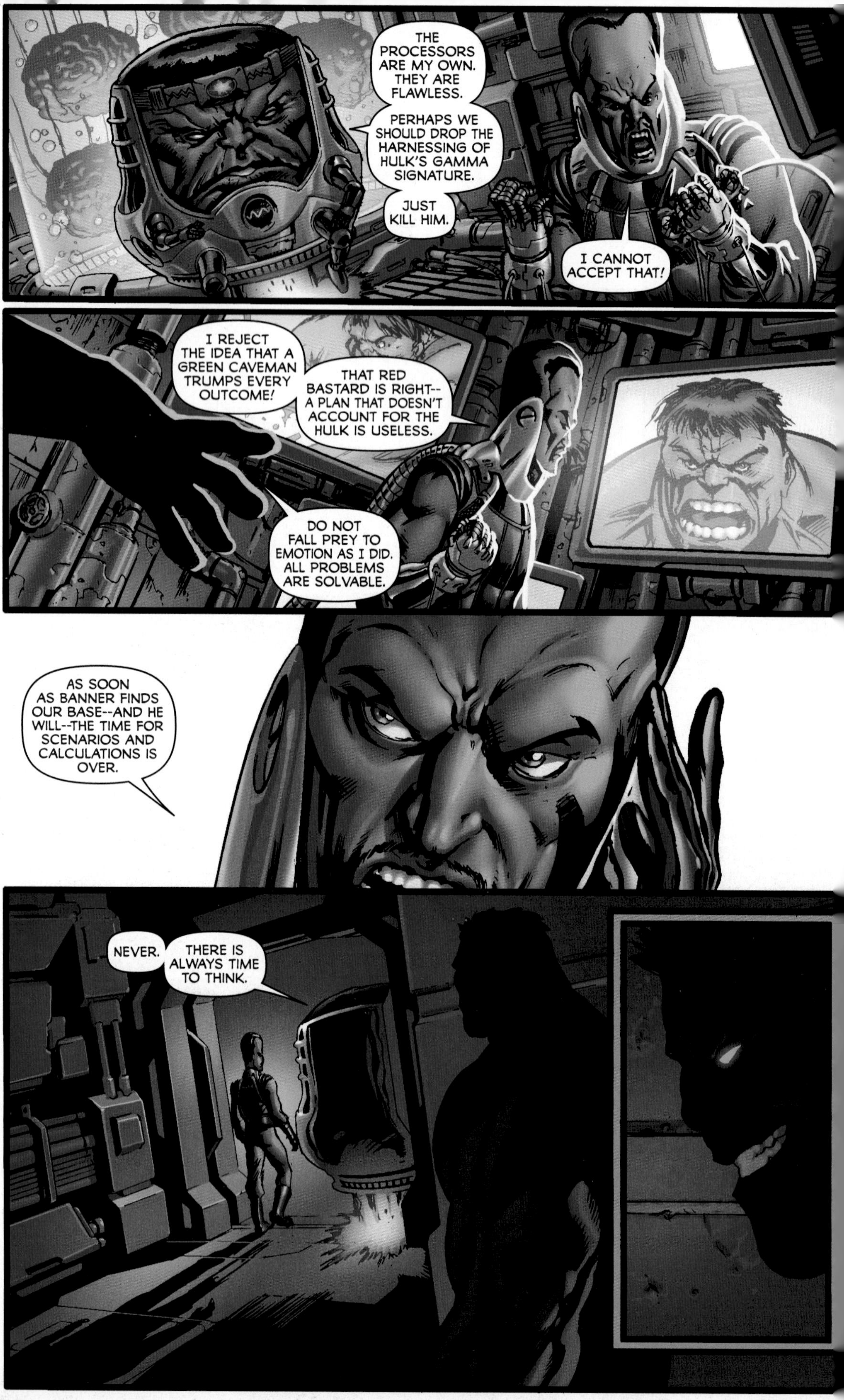
THE PROCESSORS ARE MY OWN. THEY ARE FLAWLESS.
PERHAPS WE SHOULD DROP THE HARNESSING OF HULK'S GAMMA SIGNATURE.
JUST KILL HIM.
I CANNOT ACCEPT THAT!
I REJECT THE IDEA THAT A GREEN CAVEMAN TRUMPS EVERY OUTCOME!
THAT RED BASTARD IS RIGHT-- A PLAN THAT DOESN'T ACCOUNT FOR THE HULK IS USELESS.
DO NOT FALL PREY TO EMOTION AS I DID. ALL PROBLEMS ARE SOLVABLE.
AS SOON AS BANNER FINDS OUR BASE--AND HE WILL--THE TIME FOR SCENARIOS AND CALCULATIONS IS OVER.
NEVER.
THERE IS ALWAYS TIME TO THINK.

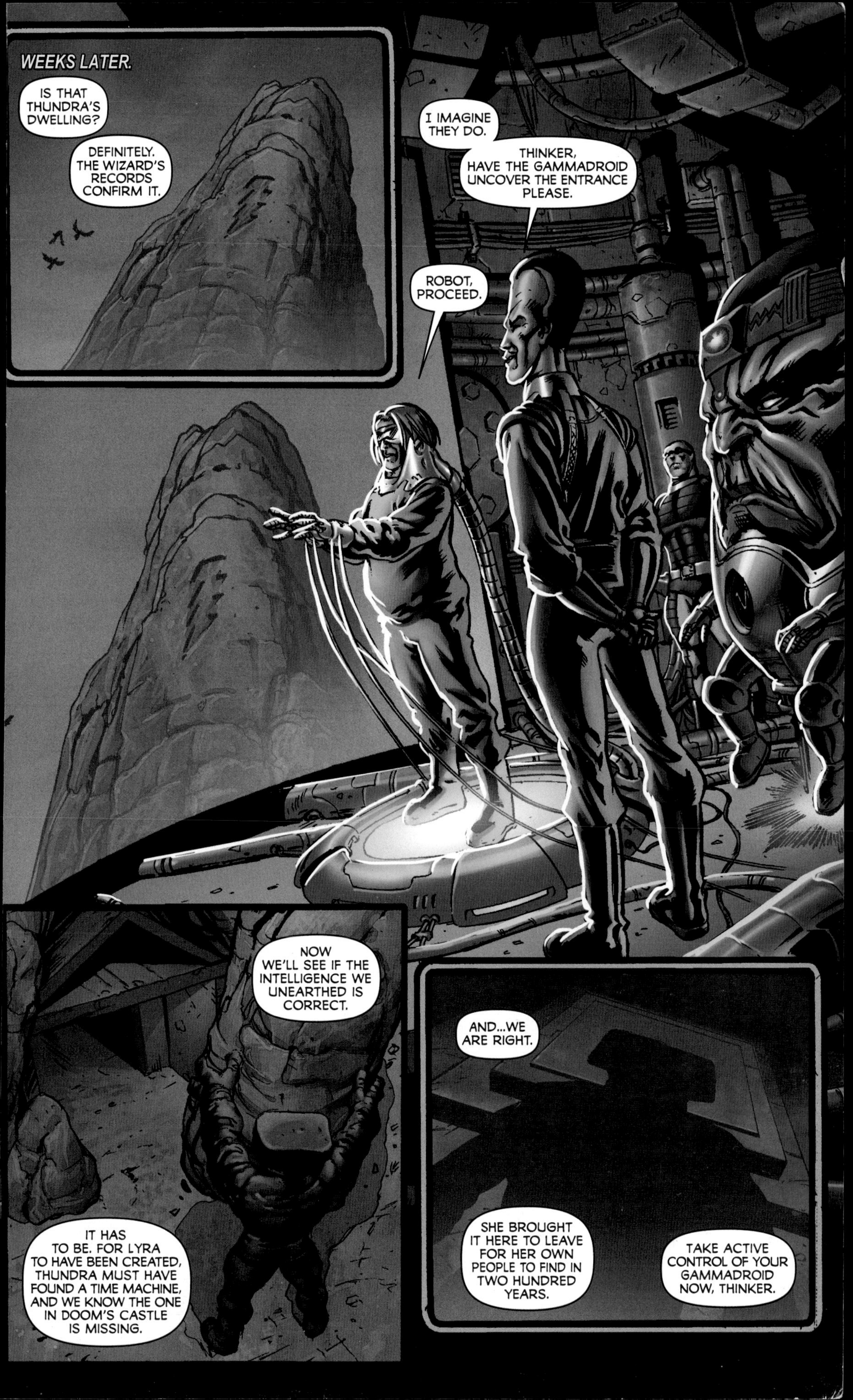

WEEKS LATER.
IS THAT THUNDRA'S DWELLING?
DEFINITELY. THE WIZARD'S RECORDS CONFIRM IT.
I IMAGINE THEY DO.
THINKER, HAVE THE GAMMADROID UNCOVER THE ENTRANCE PLEASE.
ROBOT, PROCEED.
NOW WE'LL SEE IF THE INTELLIGENCE WE UNEARTHED IS CORRECT.
IT HAS TO BE. FOR LYRA TO HAVE BEEN CREATED, THUNDRA MUST HAVE FOUND A TIME MACHINE, AND WE KNOW THE ONE IN DOOM'S CASTLE IS MISSING.
AND...WE ARE RIGHT.
SHE BROUGHT IT HERE TO LEAVE FOR HER OWN PEOPLE TO FIND IN TWO HUNDRED YEARS.
TAKE ACTIVE CONTROL OF YOUR GAMMADROID NOW, THINKER.

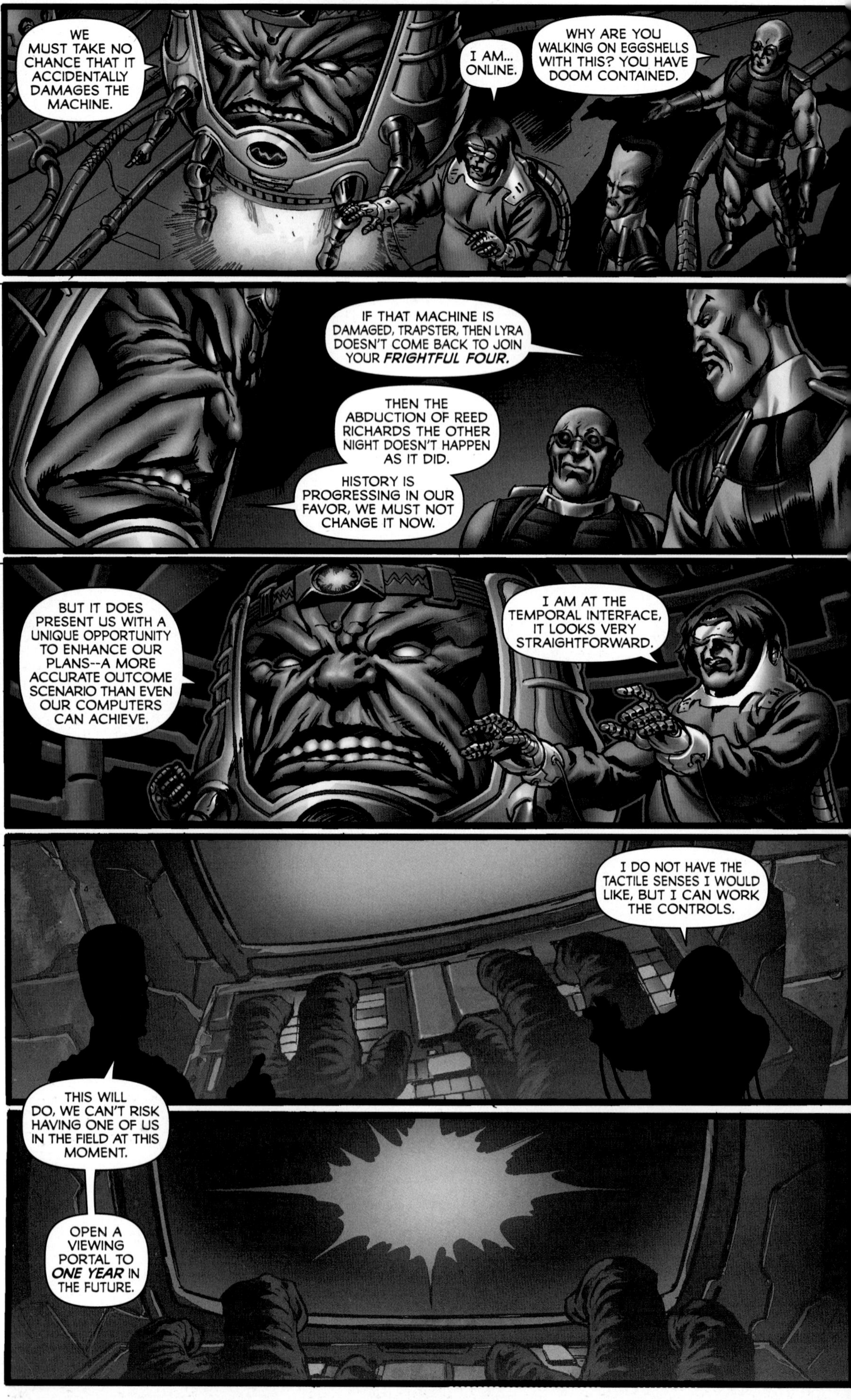
WE MUST TAKE NO CHANCE THAT IT ACCIDENTALLY DAMAGES THE MACHINE.
I AM... ONLINE.
WHY ARE YOU WALKING ON EGGSHELLS WITH THIS? YOU HAVE DOOM CONTAINED.
IF THAT MACHINE IS DAMAGED, TRAPSTER, THEN LYRA DOESN'T COME BACK TO JOIN YOUR *FRIGHTFUL FOUR.*
THEN THE ABDUCTION OF REED RICHARDS THE OTHER NIGHT DOESN'T HAPPEN AS IT DID.
HISTORY IS PROGRESSING IN OUR FAVOR, WE MUST NOT CHANGE IT NOW.
BUT IT DOES PRESENT US WITH A UNIQUE OPPORTUNITY TO ENHANCE OUR PLANS--A MORE ACCURATE OUTCOME SCENARIO THAN EVEN OUR COMPUTERS CAN ACHIEVE.
I AM AT THE TEMPORAL INTERFACE, IT LOOKS VERY STRAIGHTFORWARD.
I DO NOT HAVE THE TACTILE SENSES I WOULD LIKE, BUT I CAN WORK THE CONTROLS.
THIS WILL DO, WE CAN'T RISK HAVING ONE OF US IN THE FIELD AT THIS MOMENT.
OPEN A VIEWING PORTAL TO *ONE YEAR* IN THE FUTURE.

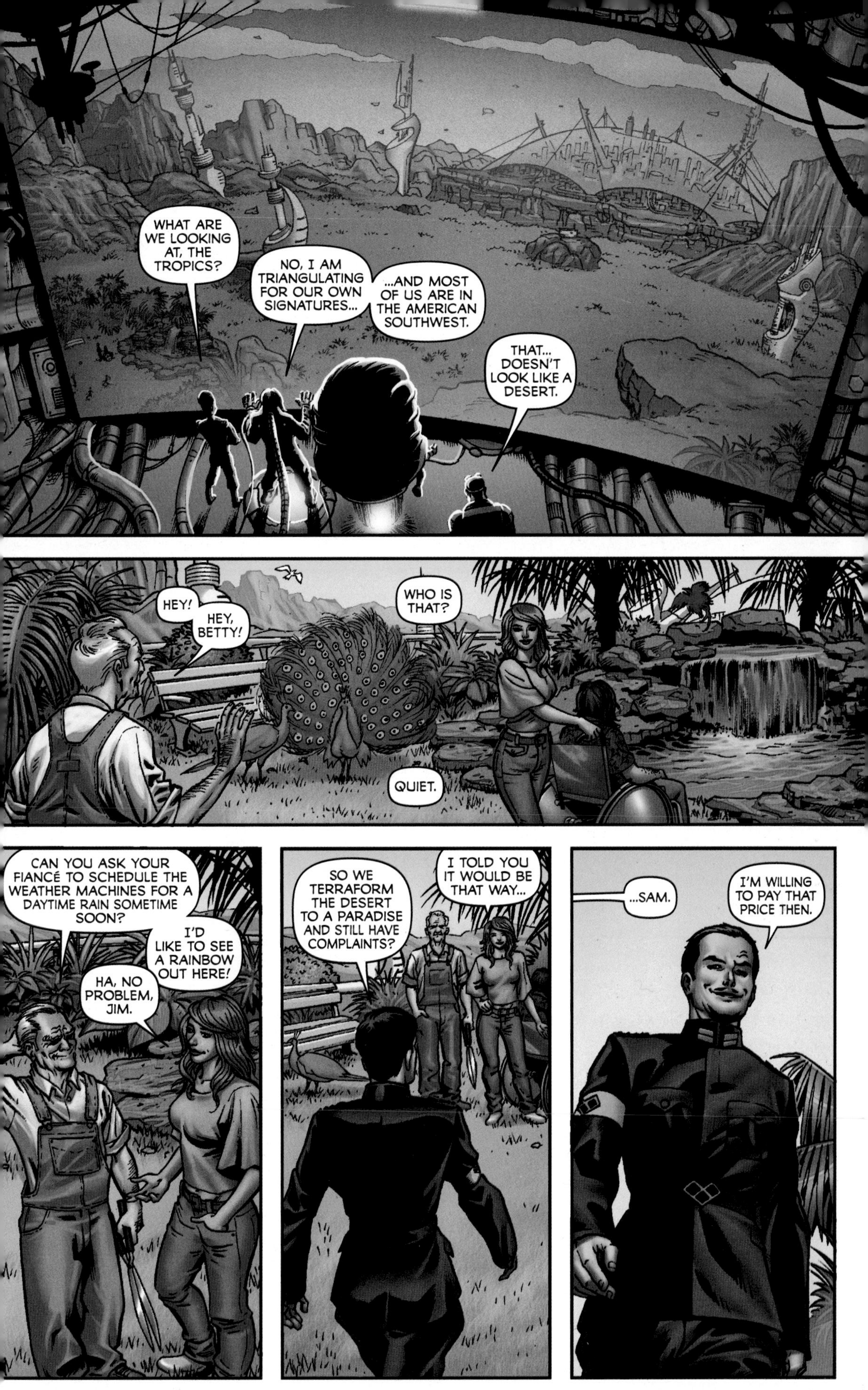
WHAT ARE WE LOOKING AT, THE TROPICS?
NO, I AM TRIANGULATING FOR OUR OWN SIGNATURES...
...AND MOST OF US ARE IN THE AMERICAN SOUTHWEST.
THAT... DOESN'T LOOK LIKE A DESERT.
HEY!
HEY, BETTY!
WHO IS THAT?
QUIET.
CAN YOU ASK YOUR FIANCÉ TO SCHEDULE THE WEATHER MACHINES FOR A DAYTIME RAIN SOMETIME SOON?
I'D LIKE TO SEE A RAINBOW OUT HERE!
HA, NO PROBLEM, JIM.
SO WE TERRAFORM THE DESERT TO A PARADISE AND STILL HAVE COMPLAINTS?
I TOLD YOU IT WOULD BE THAT WAY...
...SAM.
I'M WILLING TO PAY THAT PRICE THEN.

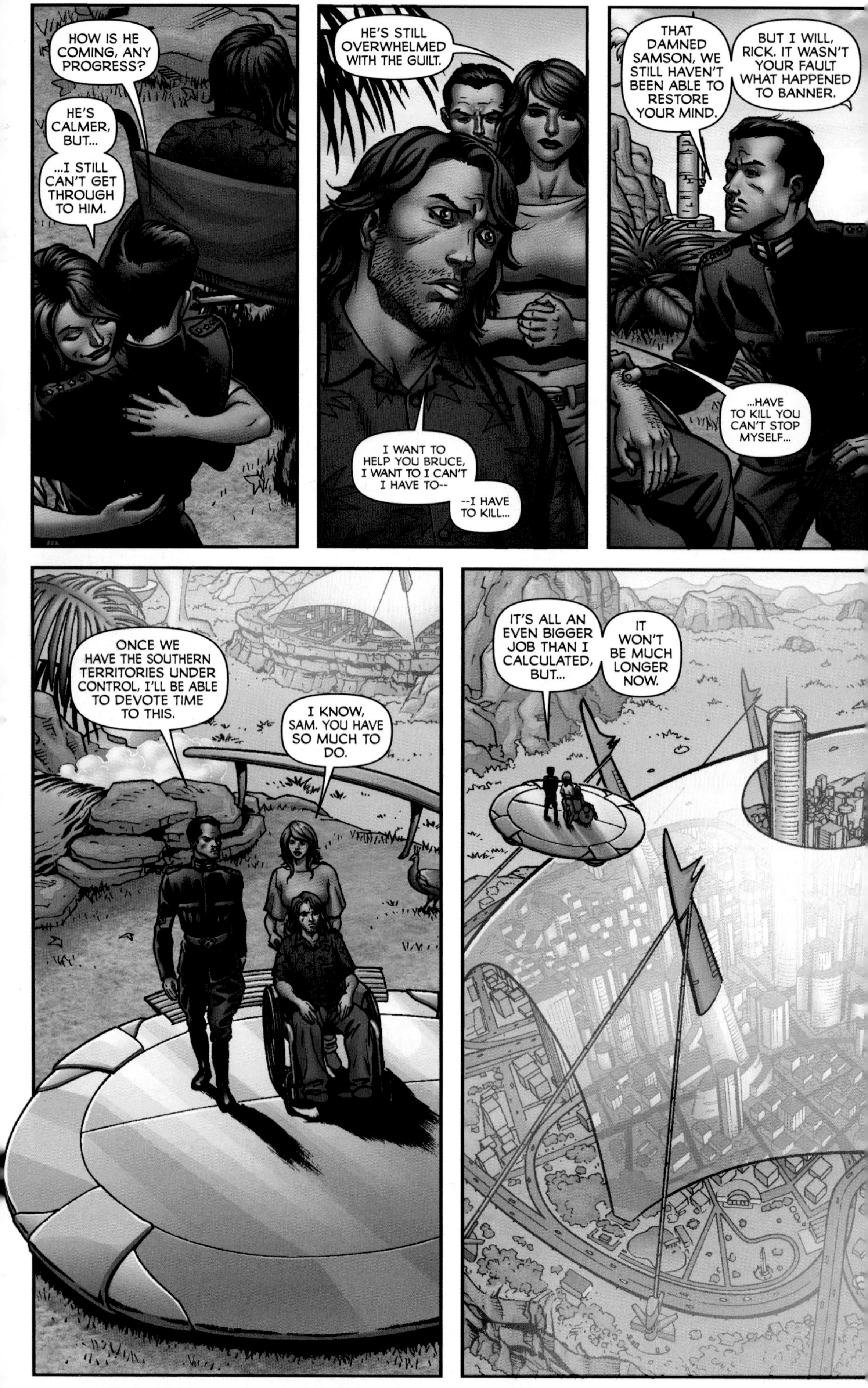

HOW IS HE COMING, ANY PROGRESS?
HE'S CALMER, BUT...
...I STILL CAN'T GET THROUGH TO HIM.
HE'S STILL OVERWHELMED WITH THE GUILT.
I WANT TO HELP YOU BRUCE, I WANT TO I CAN'T I HAVE TO--
--I HAVE TO KILL...
THAT DAMNED SAMSON, WE STILL HAVEN'T BEEN ABLE TO RESTORE YOUR MIND.
BUT I WILL, RICK. IT WASN'T YOUR FAULT WHAT HAPPENED TO BANNER.
...HAVE TO KILL YOU CAN'T STOP MYSELF...
ONCE WE HAVE THE SOUTHERN TERRITORIES UNDER CONTROL, I'LL BE ABLE TO DEVOTE TIME TO THIS.
I KNOW, SAM. YOU HAVE SO MUCH TO DO.
IT'S ALL AN EVEN BIGGER JOB THAN I CALCULATED, BUT...
IT WON'T BE MUCH LONGER NOW.

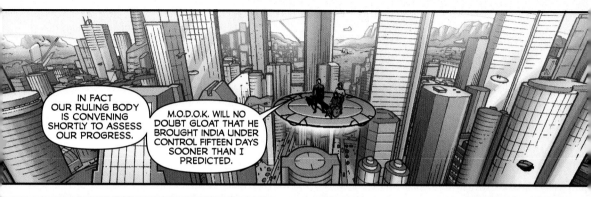

IN FACT OUR RULING BODY IS CONVENING SHORTLY TO ASSESS OUR PROGRESS.

M.O.D.O.K. WILL NO DOUBT GLOAT THAT HE BROUGHT INDIA UNDER CONTROL FIFTEEN DAYS SOONER THAN I PREDICTED.

BUT FAIR ENOUGH, HE WON THE BET.

RICK, YOU'LL GO WITH THE PHYSICAL THERAPISTS NOW.

ALL HAIL THE PROTECTOR OF THE WESTERN HEMISPHERE, *SUPREME LEADER STERNS!*

PLEASE, GUARD, SAVE ALL THE POMP FOR CEREMONIES.

YES, SIR!

I'M STILL UNCOMFORTABLE WITH ALL OF THIS FORMALITY.

ALL THE RESEARCH SHOWS THAT IT MAKES THE PEOPLE FEEL SAFE THOUGH, RIGHT?

THAT THERE IS ORDER IN PLACE AND AN UNDERLYING LOGIC TO LIFE--JUST WHAT EVERYONE DESIRES.

EVEN IF THEY THINK THEY DO NOT.

HOW'S YOUR NEWS, IGOR?

HOW'S YOUR NEWS, LEADER. YOU ARE JUST IN TIME.

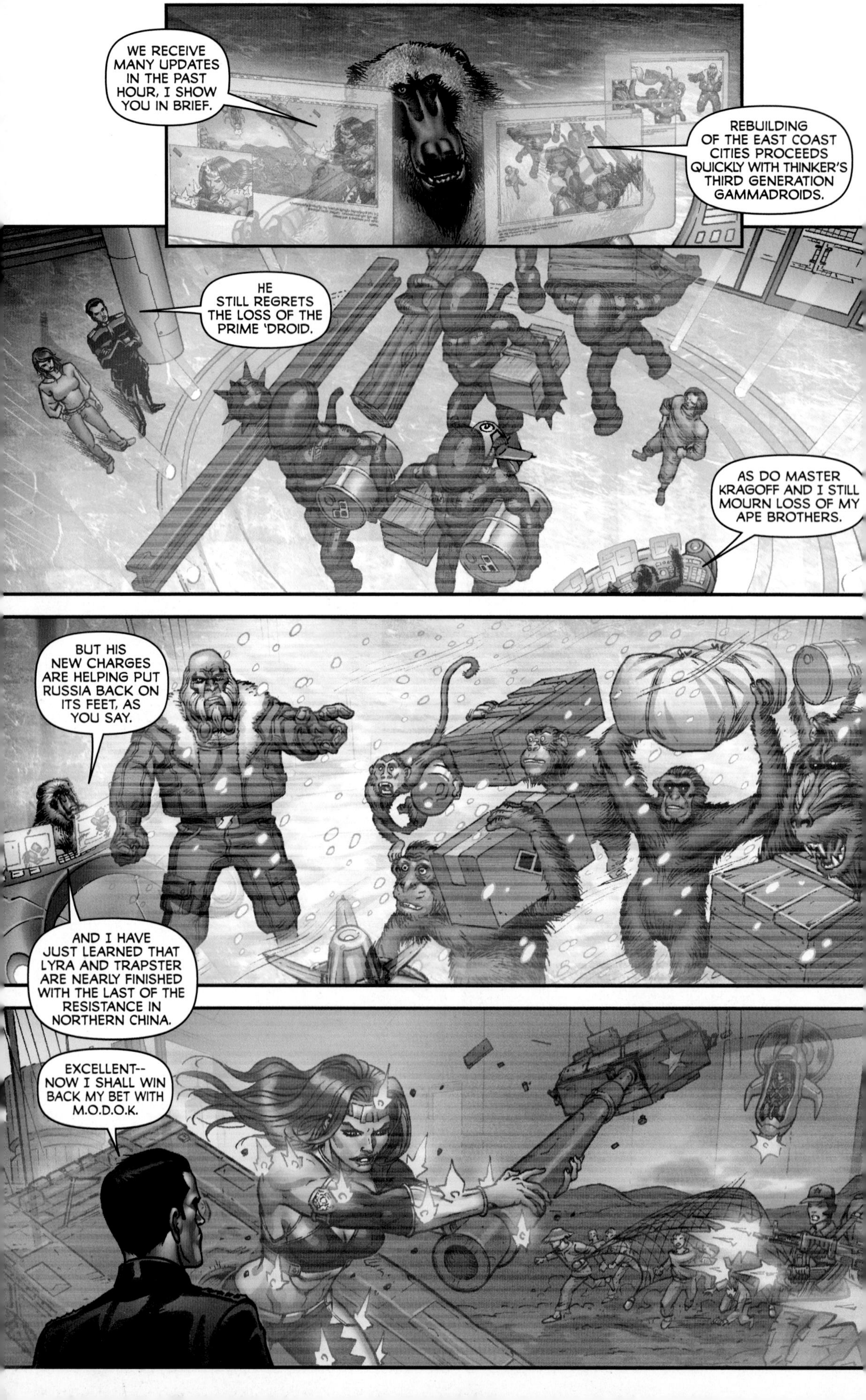

WE RECEIVE MANY UPDATES IN THE PAST HOUR, I SHOW YOU IN BRIEF.
REBUILDING OF THE EAST COAST CITIES PROCEEDS QUICKLY WITH THINKER'S THIRD GENERATION GAMMADROIDS.
HE STILL REGRETS THE LOSS OF THE PRIME 'DROID.
AS DO MASTER KRAGOFF AND I STILL MOURN LOSS OF MY APE BROTHERS.
BUT HIS NEW CHARGES ARE HELPING PUT RUSSIA BACK ON ITS FEET, AS YOU SAY.
AND I HAVE JUST LEARNED THAT LYRA AND TRAPSTER ARE NEARLY FINISHED WITH THE LAST OF THE RESISTANCE IN NORTHERN CHINA.
EXCELLENT-- NOW I SHALL WIN BACK MY BET WITH M.O.D.O.K.

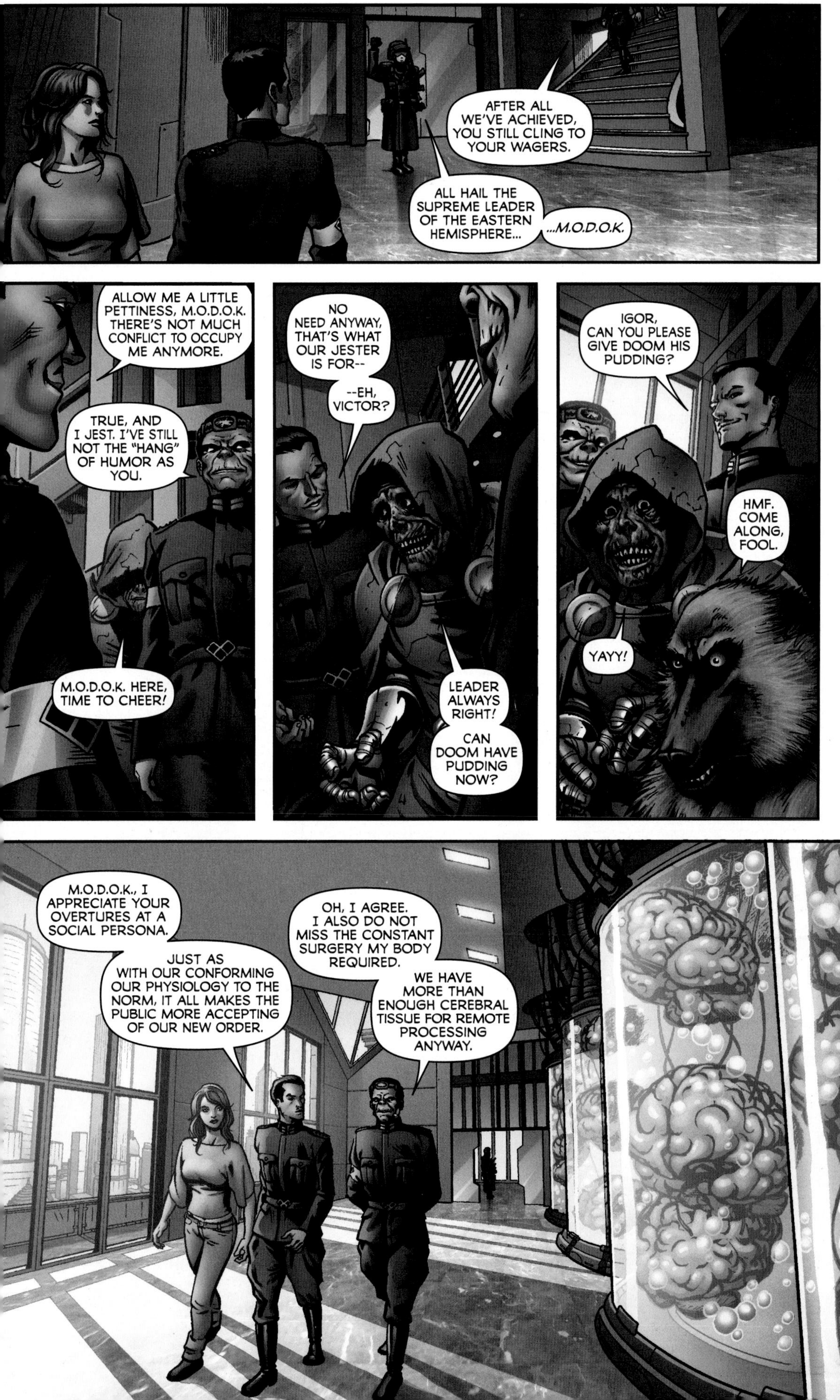
AFTER ALL WE'VE ACHIEVED, YOU STILL CLING TO YOUR WAGERS.
ALL HAIL THE SUPREME LEADER OF THE EASTERN HEMISPHERE...
...M.O.D.O.K.
ALLOW ME A LITTLE PETTINESS, M.O.D.O.K. THERE'S NOT MUCH CONFLICT TO OCCUPY ME ANYMORE.
TRUE, AND I JEST. I'VE STILL NOT THE "HANG" OF HUMOR AS YOU.
M.O.D.O.K. HERE, TIME TO CHEER!
NO NEED ANYWAY, THAT'S WHAT OUR JESTER IS FOR--
--EH, VICTOR?
LEADER ALWAYS RIGHT!
CAN DOOM HAVE PUDDING NOW?
IGOR, CAN YOU PLEASE GIVE DOOM HIS PUDDING?
HMF. COME ALONG, FOOL.
YAYY!
M.O.D.O.K., I APPRECIATE YOUR OVERTURES AT A SOCIAL PERSONA.
JUST AS WITH OUR CONFORMING OUR PHYSIOLOGY TO THE NORM, IT ALL MAKES THE PUBLIC MORE ACCEPTING OF OUR NEW ORDER.
OH, I AGREE. I ALSO DO NOT MISS THE CONSTANT SURGERY MY BODY REQUIRED.
WE HAVE MORE THAN ENOUGH CEREBRAL TISSUE FOR REMOTE PROCESSING ANYWAY.

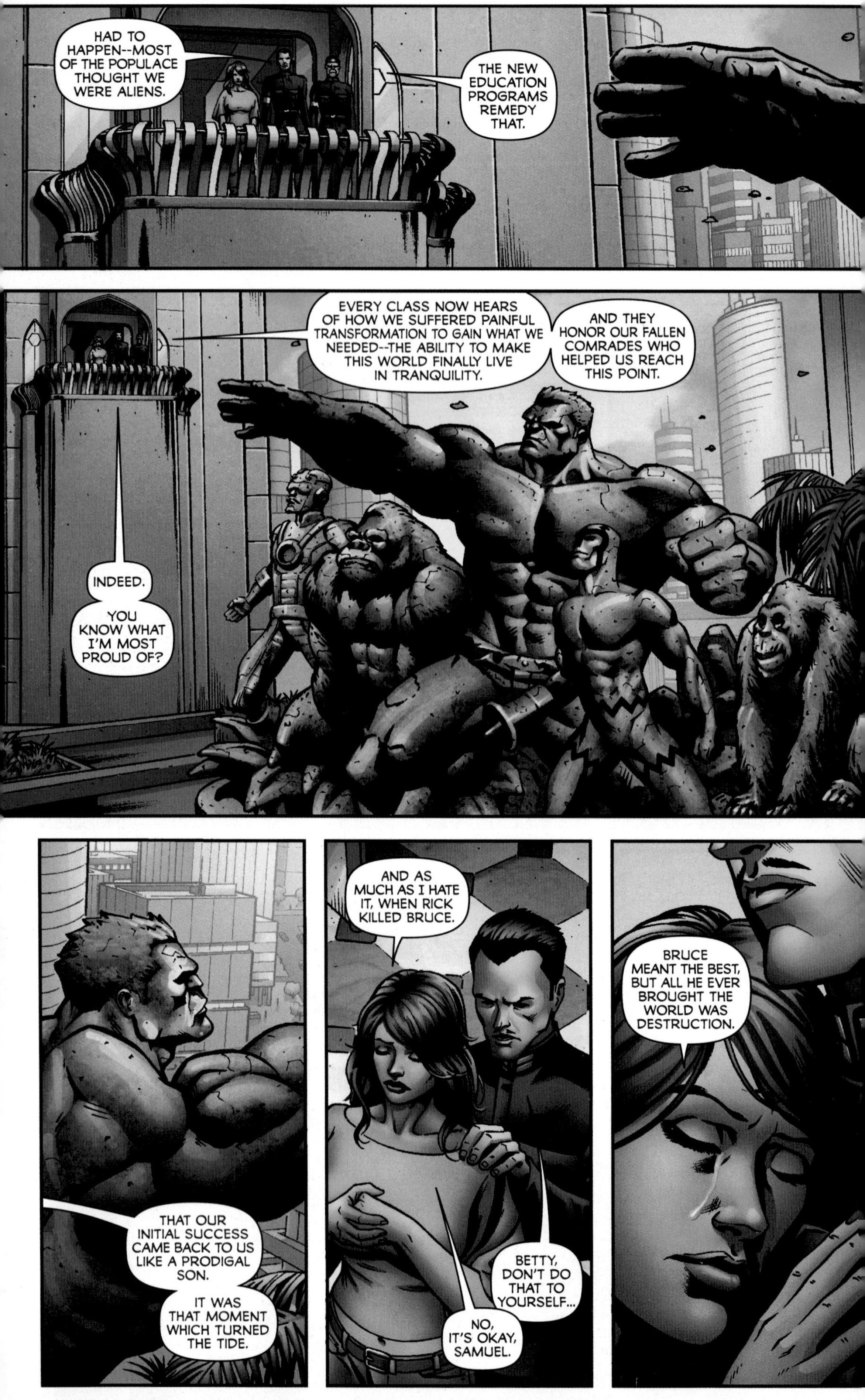

HAD TO HAPPEN--MOST OF THE POPULACE THOUGHT WE WERE ALIENS.
THE NEW EDUCATION PROGRAMS REMEDY THAT.
EVERY CLASS NOW HEARS OF HOW WE SUFFERED PAINFUL TRANSFORMATION TO GAIN WHAT WE NEEDED--THE ABILITY TO MAKE THIS WORLD FINALLY LIVE IN TRANQUILITY.
AND THEY HONOR OUR FALLEN COMRADES WHO HELPED US REACH THIS POINT.
INDEED.
YOU KNOW WHAT I'M MOST PROUD OF?
THAT OUR INITIAL SUCCESS CAME BACK TO US LIKE A PRODIGAL SON.
IT WAS THAT MOMENT WHICH TURNED THE TIDE.
AND AS MUCH AS I HATE IT, WHEN RICK KILLED BRUCE.
BETTY, DON'T DO THAT TO YOURSELF...
NO, IT'S OKAY, SAMUEL.
BRUCE MEANT THE BEST, BUT ALL HE EVER BROUGHT THE WORLD WAS DESTRUCTION.

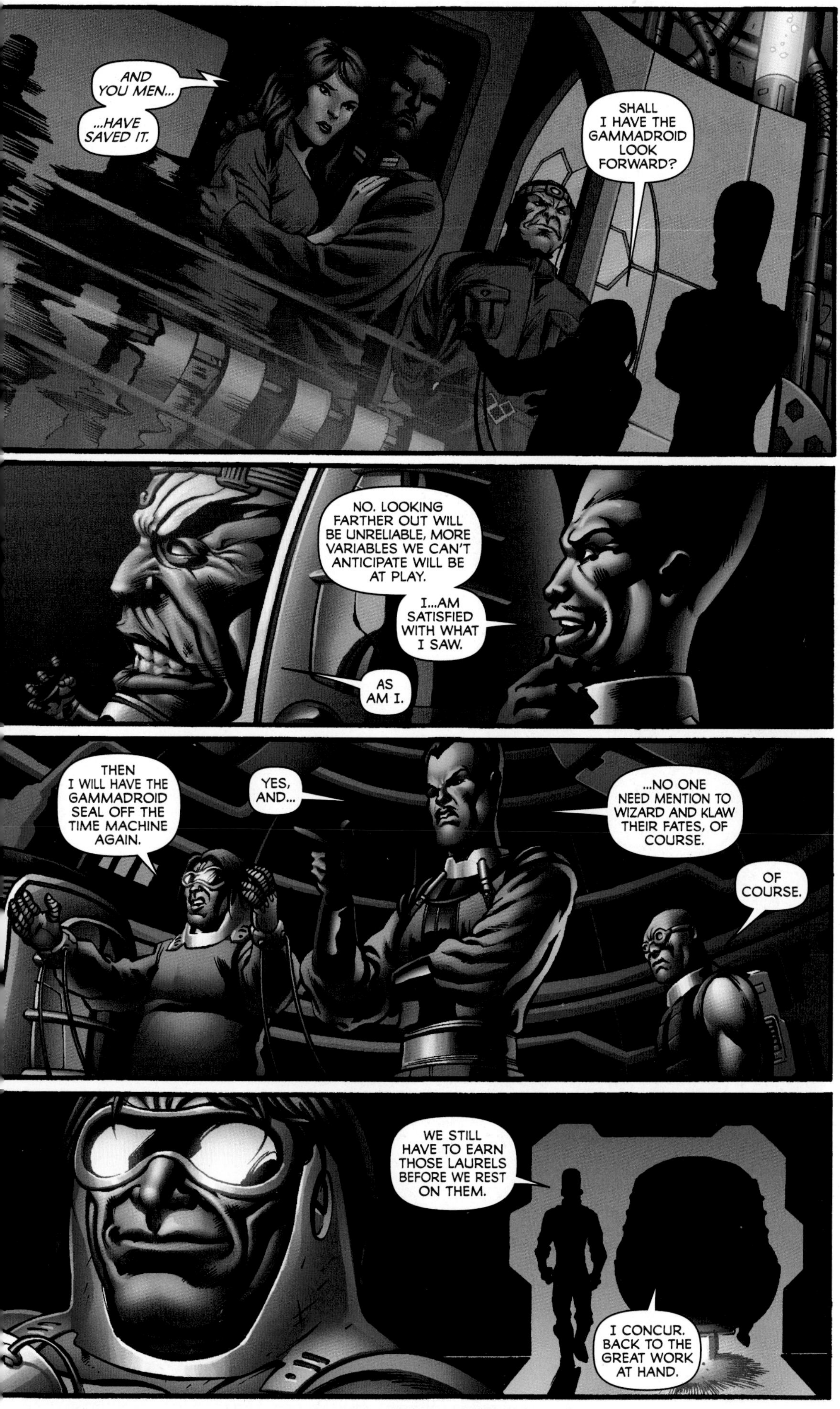
AND YOU MEN...
...HAVE SAVED IT.
SHALL I HAVE THE GAMMADROID LOOK FORWARD?
NO. LOOKING FARTHER OUT WILL BE UNRELIABLE, MORE VARIABLES WE CAN'T ANTICIPATE WILL BE AT PLAY.
I...AM SATISFIED WITH WHAT I SAW.
AS AM I.
THEN I WILL HAVE THE GAMMADROID SEAL OFF THE TIME MACHINE AGAIN.
YES, AND...
...NO ONE NEED MENTION TO WIZARD AND KLAW THEIR FATES, OF COURSE.
OF COURSE.
WE STILL HAVE TO EARN THOSE LAURELS BEFORE WE REST ON THEM.
I CONCUR. BACK TO THE GREAT WORK AT HAND.

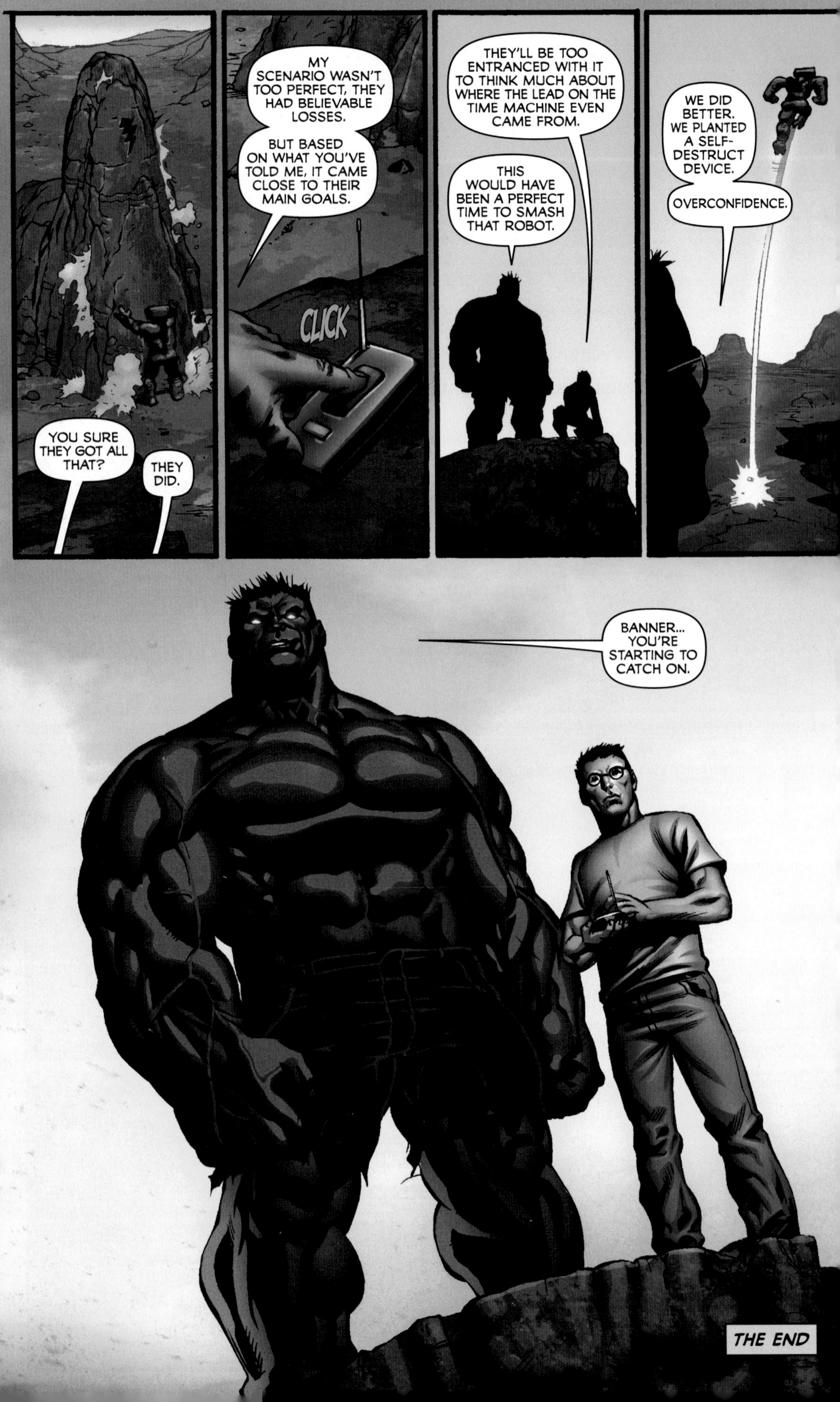
YOU SURE THEY GOT ALL THAT?
THEY DID.
MY SCENARIO WASN'T TOO PERFECT, THEY HAD BELIEVABLE LOSSES.
BUT BASED ON WHAT YOU'VE TOLD ME, IT CAME CLOSE TO THEIR MAIN GOALS.
CLICK
THEY'LL BE TOO ENTRANCED WITH IT TO THINK MUCH ABOUT WHERE THE LEAD ON THE TIME MACHINE EVEN CAME FROM.
THIS WOULD HAVE BEEN A PERFECT TIME TO SMASH THAT ROBOT.
WE DID BETTER. WE PLANTED A SELF-DESTRUCT DEVICE.
OVERCONFIDENCE.
BANNER... YOU'RE STARTING TO CATCH ON.
THE END

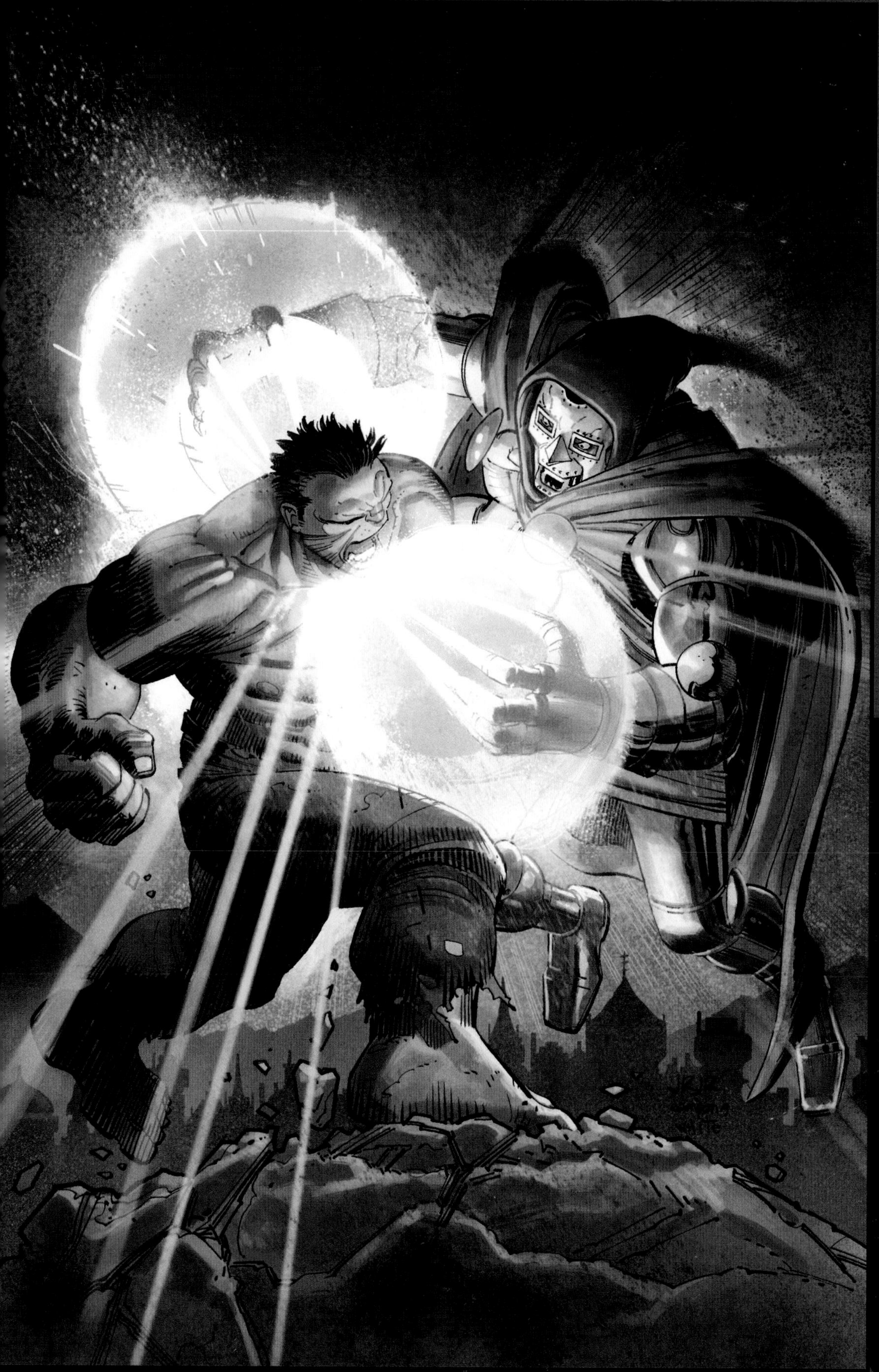

INCREDIBLE HULK #606

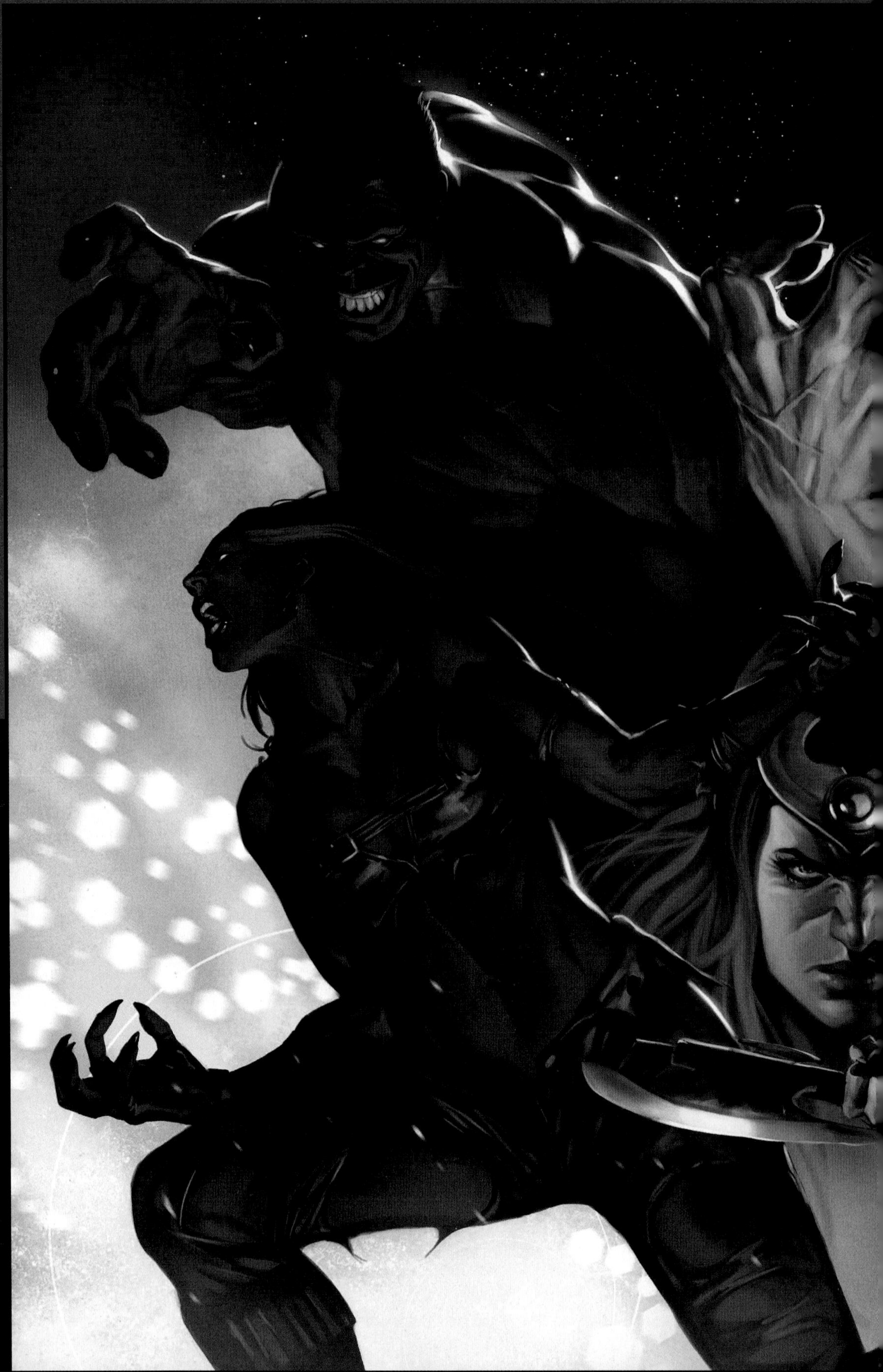

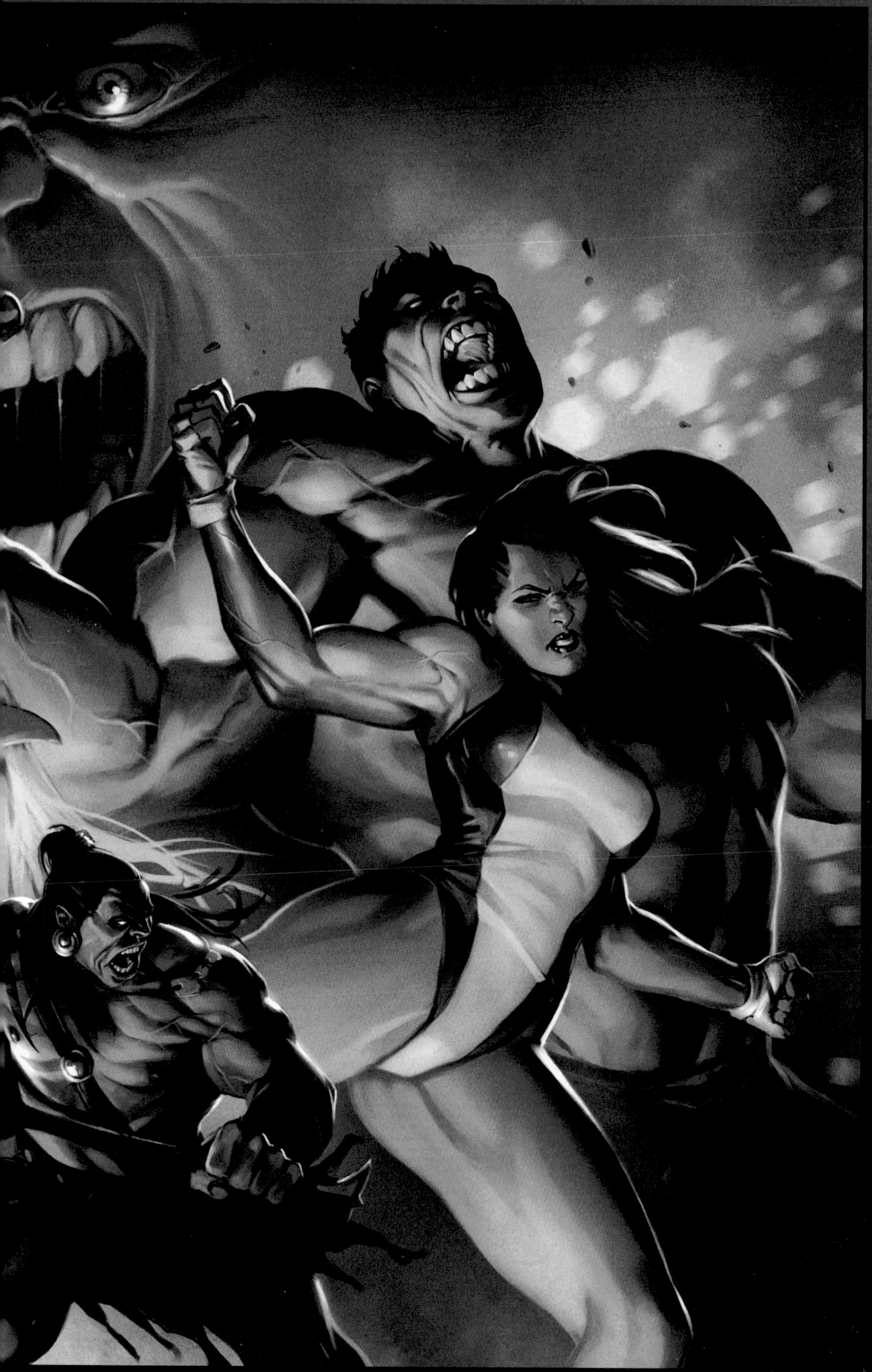

INCREDIBLE HULK #606 Variant by Marko Djurdjevic

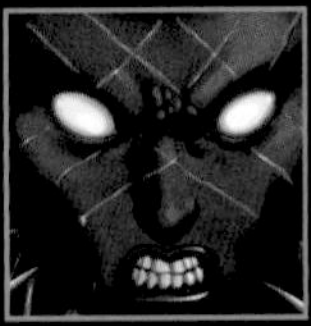

RED SHE-HULK

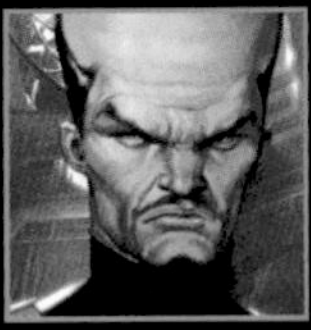

THE LEADER

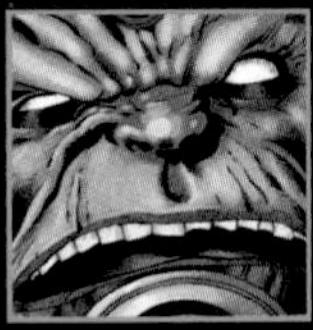

M.O.D.O.K.

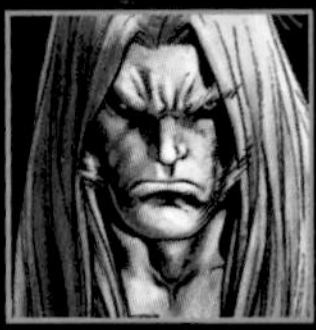

SAMSON

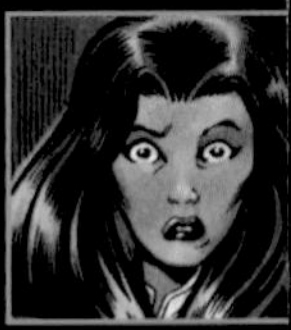

SHE-HULK

PREVIOUSLY ON FALL OF THE HULKS

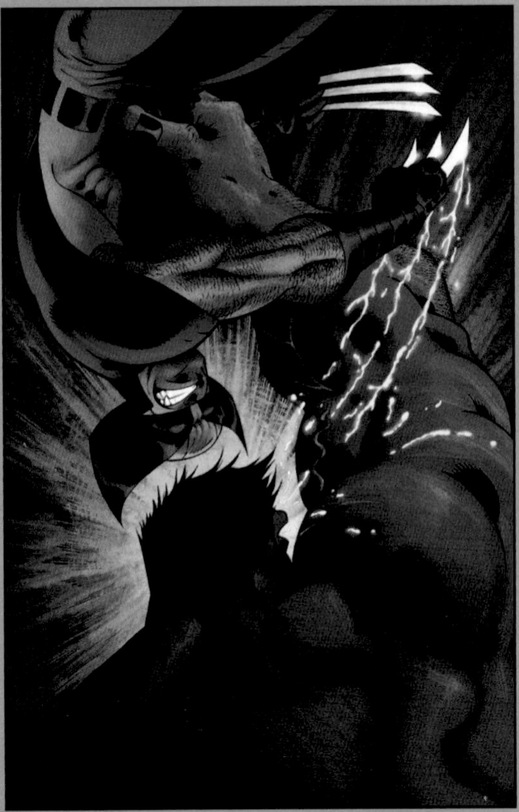

RED HULK WAS FIGHTING WOLVERINE...

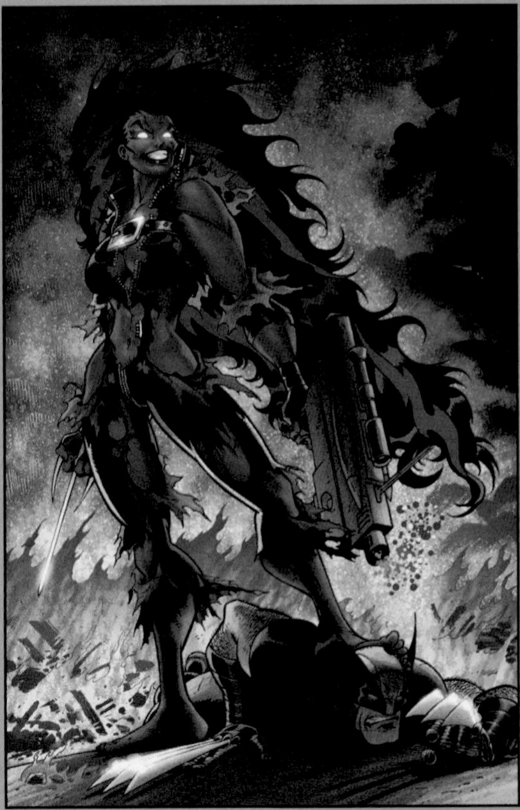

...WHEN A RED SHE-HULK SHOWED UP.

HERE'S HOW SHE GOT THERE...

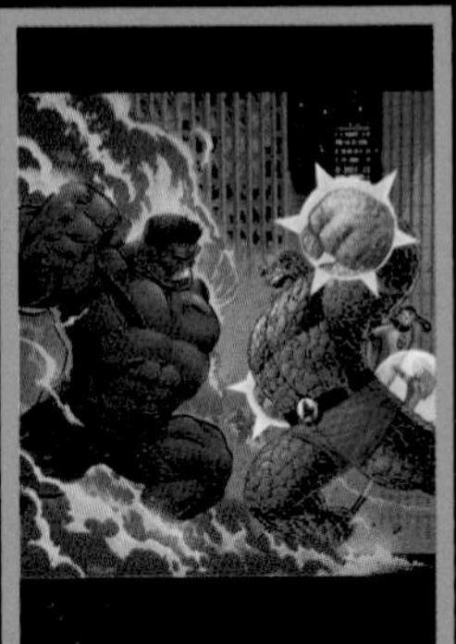

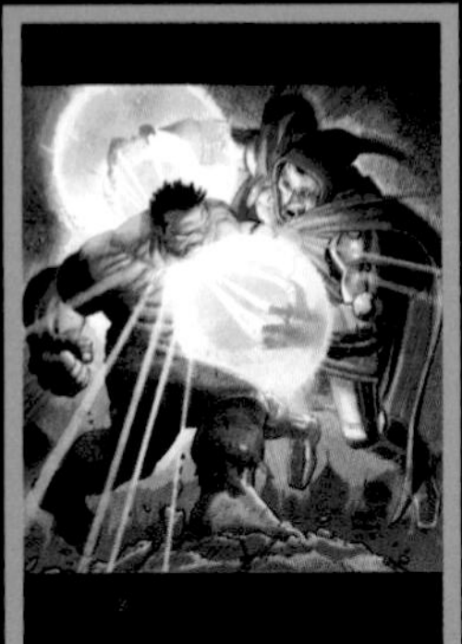

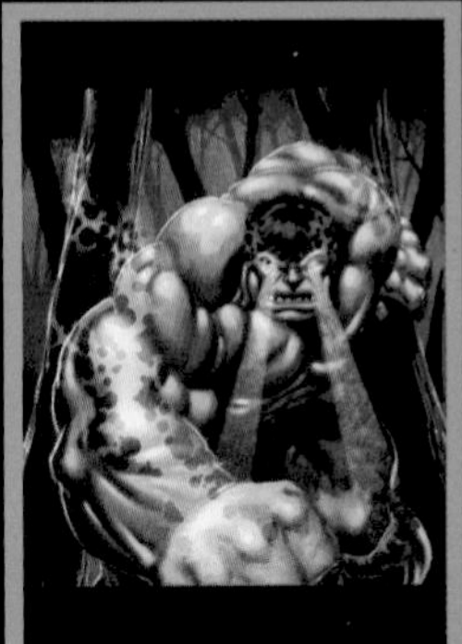

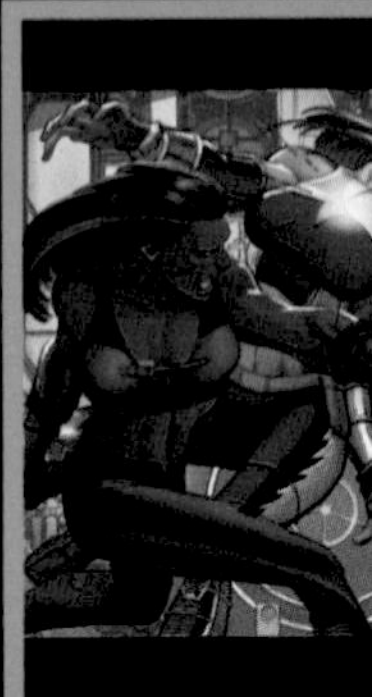

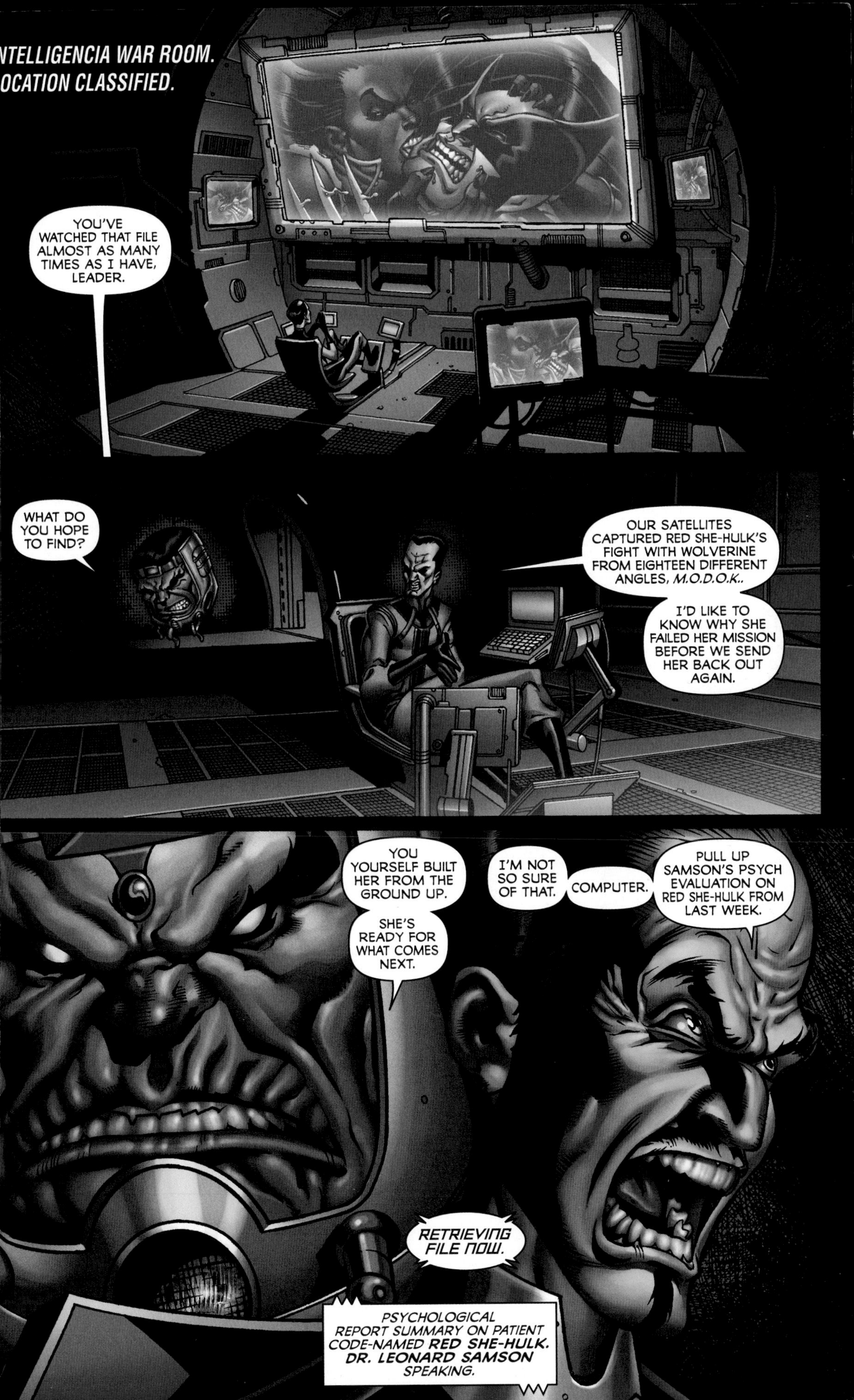

NTELLIGENCIA WAR ROOM.
OCATION CLASSIFIED.
YOU'VE WATCHED THAT FILE ALMOST AS MANY TIMES AS I HAVE, LEADER.
WHAT DO YOU HOPE TO FIND?
OUR SATELLITES CAPTURED RED SHE-HULK'S FIGHT WITH WOLVERINE FROM EIGHTEEN DIFFERENT ANGLES, M.O.D.O.K..
I'D LIKE TO KNOW WHY SHE FAILED HER MISSION BEFORE WE SEND HER BACK OUT AGAIN.
YOU YOURSELF BUILT HER FROM THE GROUND UP.
SHE'S READY FOR WHAT COMES NEXT.
I'M NOT SO SURE OF THAT.
COMPUTER.
PULL UP SAMSON'S PSYCH EVALUATION ON RED SHE-HULK FROM LAST WEEK.
RETRIEVING FILE NOW.
PSYCHOLOGICAL REPORT SUMMARY ON PATIENT CODE-NAMED RED SHE-HULK. DR. LEONARD SAMSON SPEAKING.

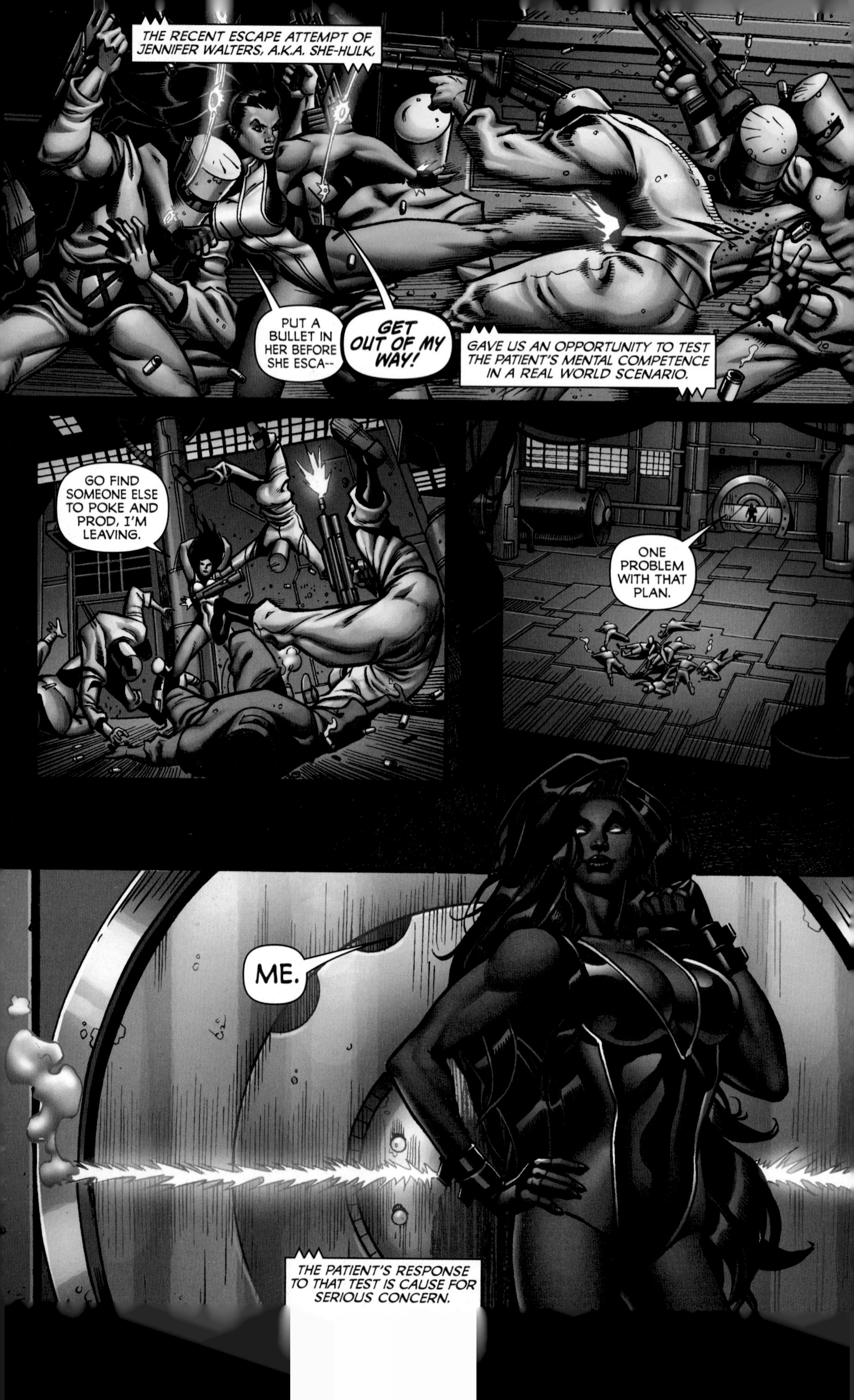
THE RECENT ESCAPE ATTEMPT OF JENNIFER WALTERS, A.K.A. SHE-HULK,
PUT A BULLET IN HER BEFORE SHE ESCA--
GET OUT OF MY WAY!
GAVE US AN OPPORTUNITY TO TEST THE PATIENT'S MENTAL COMPETENCE IN A REAL WORLD SCENARIO.
GO FIND SOMEONE ELSE TO POKE AND PROD, I'M LEAVING.
ONE PROBLEM WITH THAT PLAN.
ME.
THE PATIENT'S RESPONSE TO THAT TEST IS CAUSE FOR SERIOUS CONCERN.

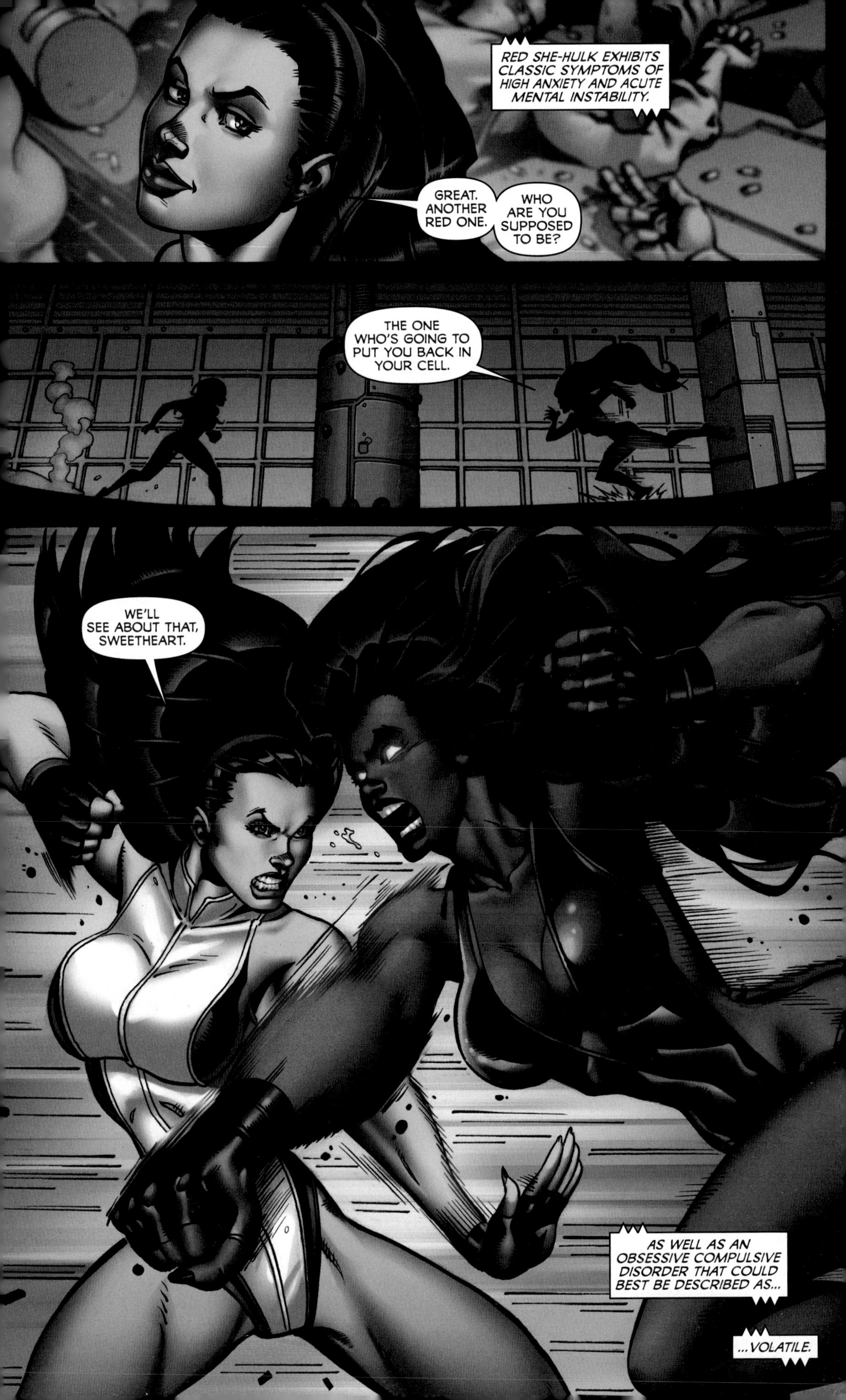
RED SHE-HULK EXHIBITS CLASSIC SYMPTOMS OF HIGH ANXIETY AND ACUTE MENTAL INSTABILITY.
GREAT. ANOTHER RED ONE.
WHO ARE YOU SUPPOSED TO BE?
THE ONE WHO'S GOING TO PUT YOU BACK IN YOUR CELL.
WE'LL SEE ABOUT THAT, SWEETHEART.
AS WELL AS AN OBSESSIVE COMPULSIVE DISORDER THAT COULD BEST BE DESCRIBED AS...
...VOLATILE.

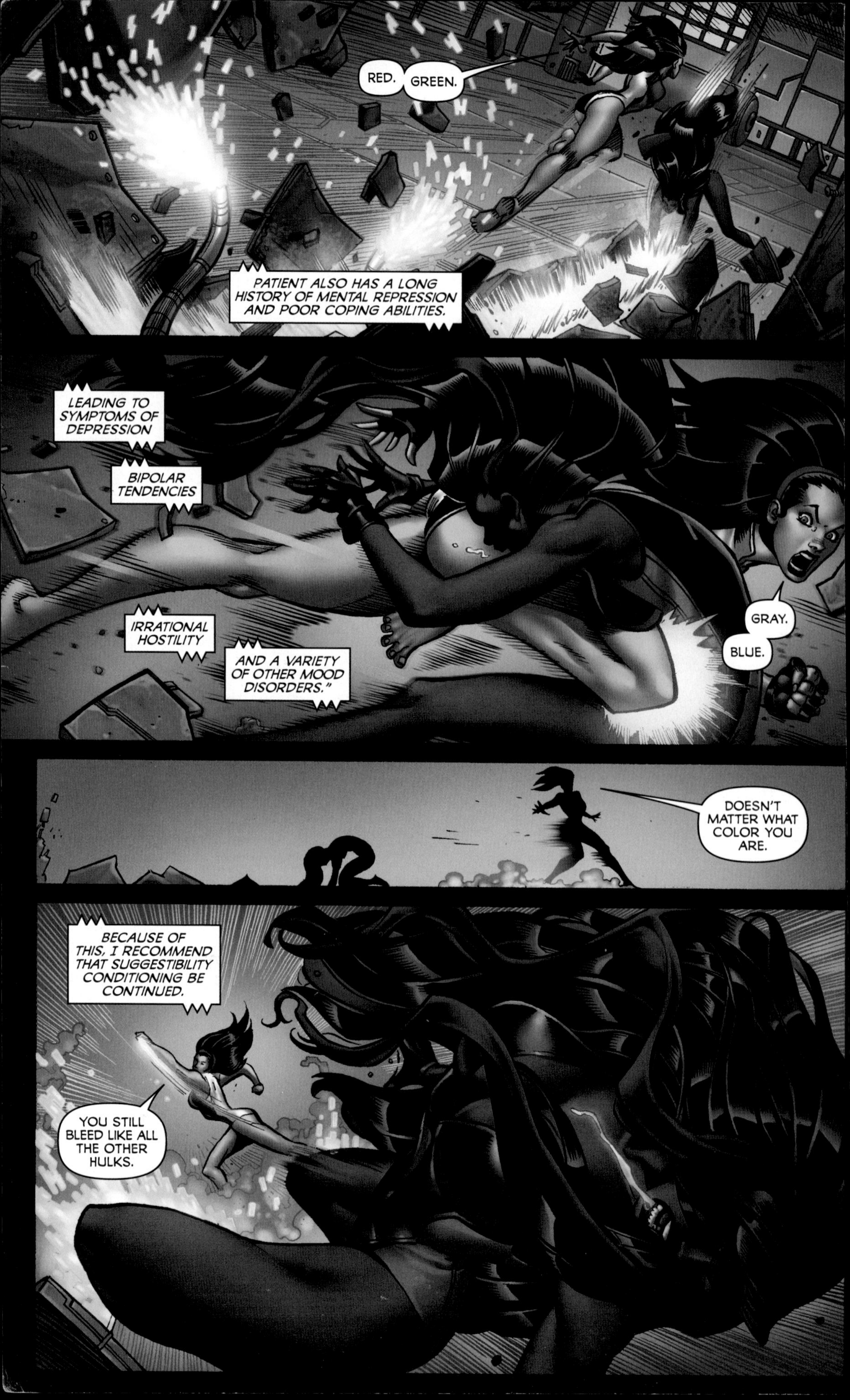
RED.
GREEN.
PATIENT ALSO HAS A LONG HISTORY OF MENTAL REPRESSION AND POOR COPING ABILITIES.
LEADING TO SYMPTOMS OF DEPRESSION
BIPOLAR TENDENCIES
IRRATIONAL HOSTILITY
AND A VARIETY OF OTHER MOOD DISORDERS."
GRAY.
BLUE.
DOESN'T MATTER WHAT COLOR YOU ARE.
BECAUSE OF THIS, I RECOMMEND THAT SUGGESTIBILITY CONDITIONING BE CONTINUED.
YOU STILL BLEED LIKE ALL THE OTHER HULKS.

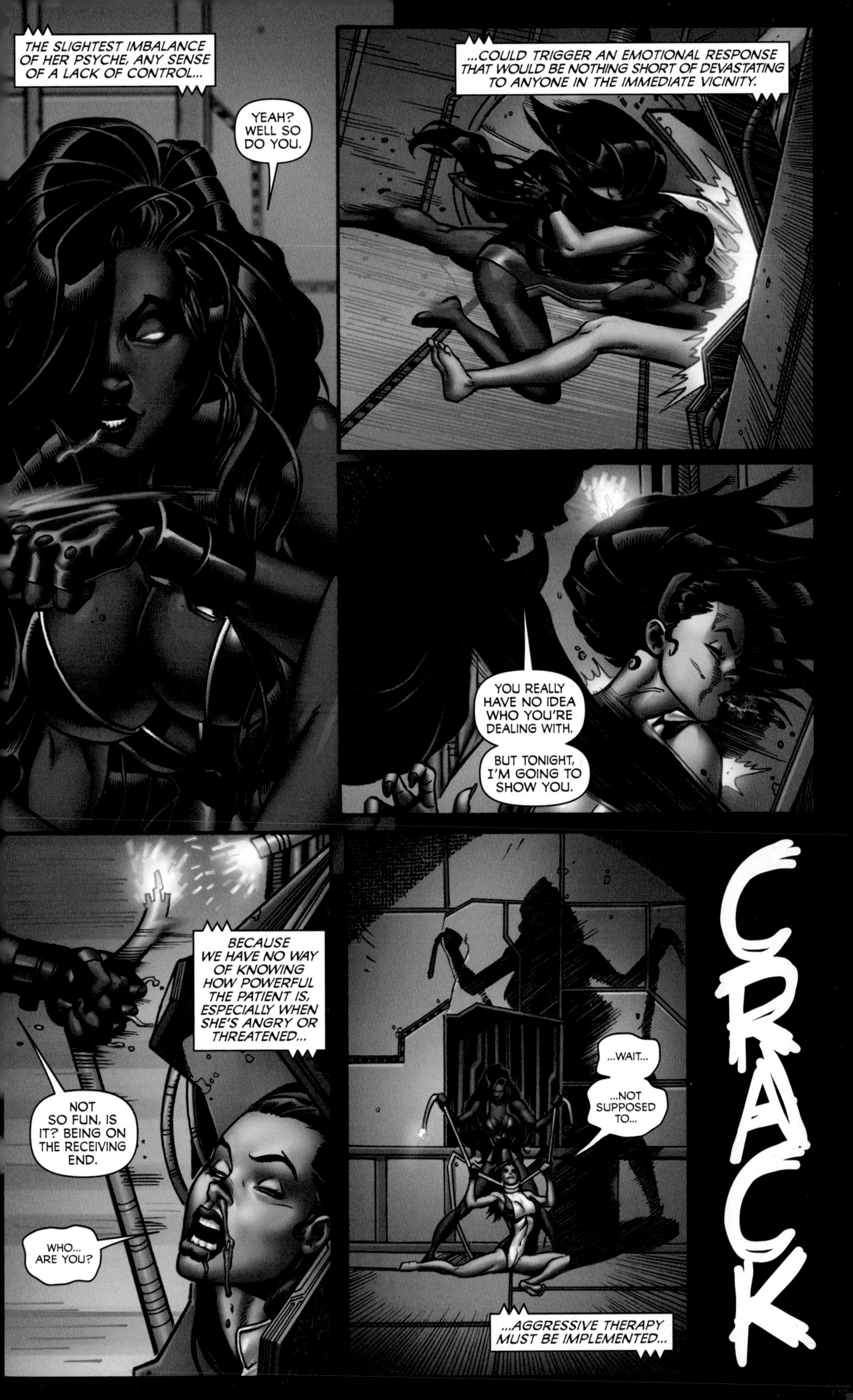
THE SLIGHTEST IMBALANCE OF HER PSYCHE, ANY SENSE OF A LACK OF CONTROL...
YEAH? WELL SO DO YOU.
...COULD TRIGGER AN EMOTIONAL RESPONSE THAT WOULD BE NOTHING SHORT OF DEVASTATING TO ANYONE IN THE IMMEDIATE VICINITY.
YOU REALLY HAVE NO IDEA WHO YOU'RE DEALING WITH.
BUT TONIGHT, I'M GOING TO SHOW YOU.
BECAUSE WE HAVE NO WAY OF KNOWING HOW POWERFUL THE PATIENT IS, ESPECIALLY WHEN SHE'S ANGRY OR THREATENED...
NOT SO FUN, IS IT? BEING ON THE RECEIVING END.
WHO... ARE YOU?
...WAIT...
...NOT SUPPOSED TO...
...AGGRESSIVE THERAPY MUST BE IMPLEMENTED...
CRACK

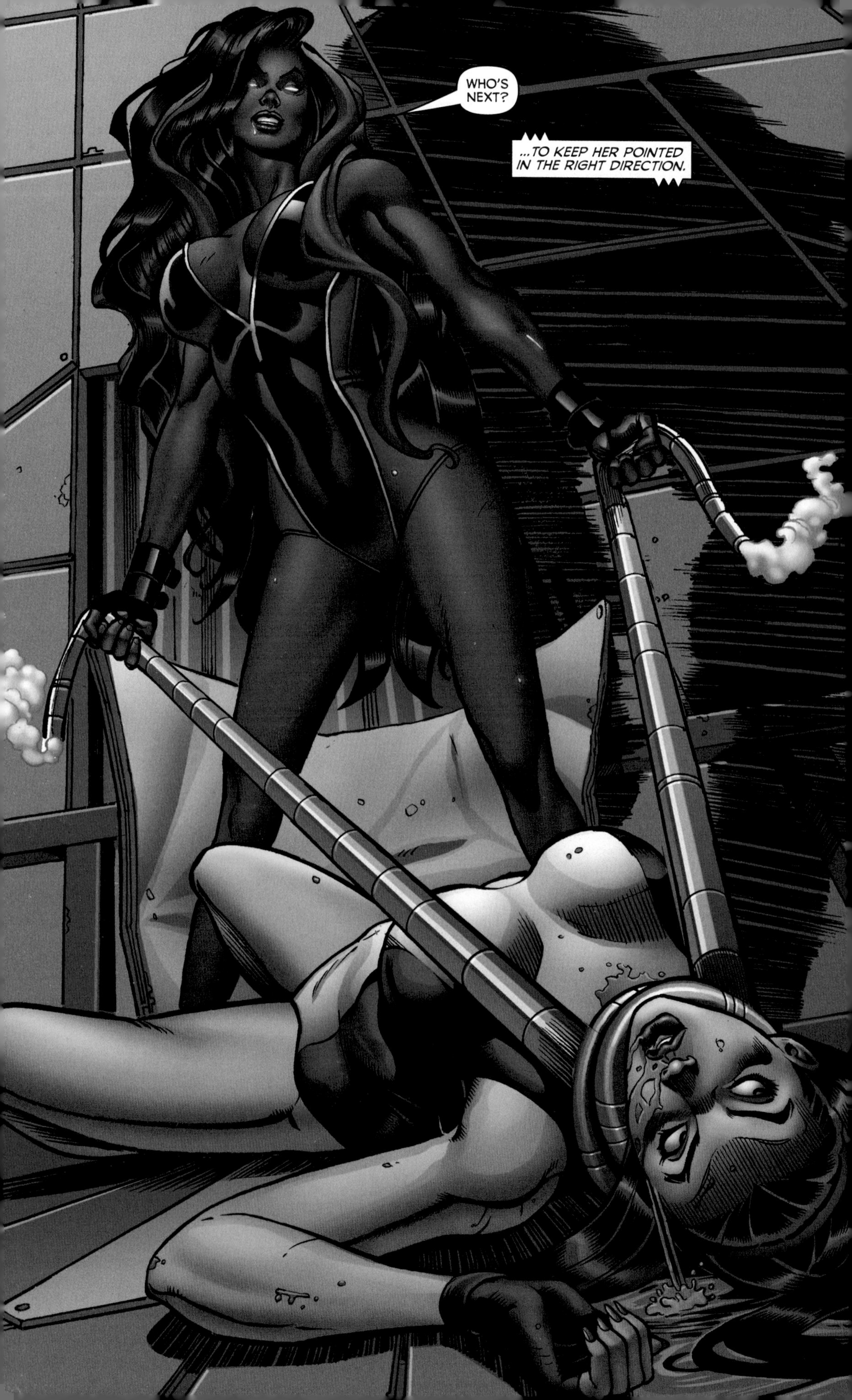
WHO'S NEXT?
...TO KEEP HER POINTED IN THE RIGHT DIRECTION.

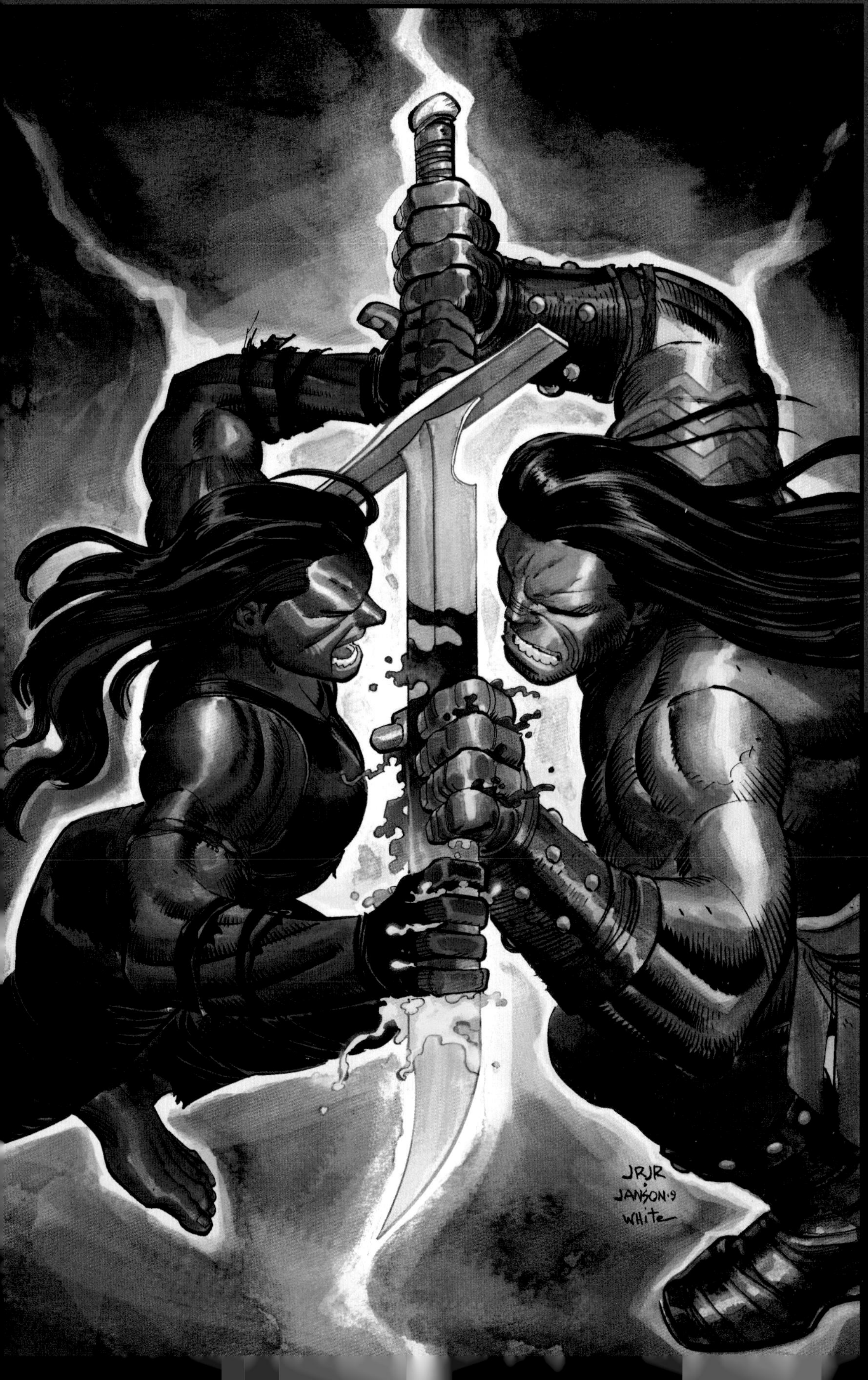
JRJR
JANSON·9
WHITE

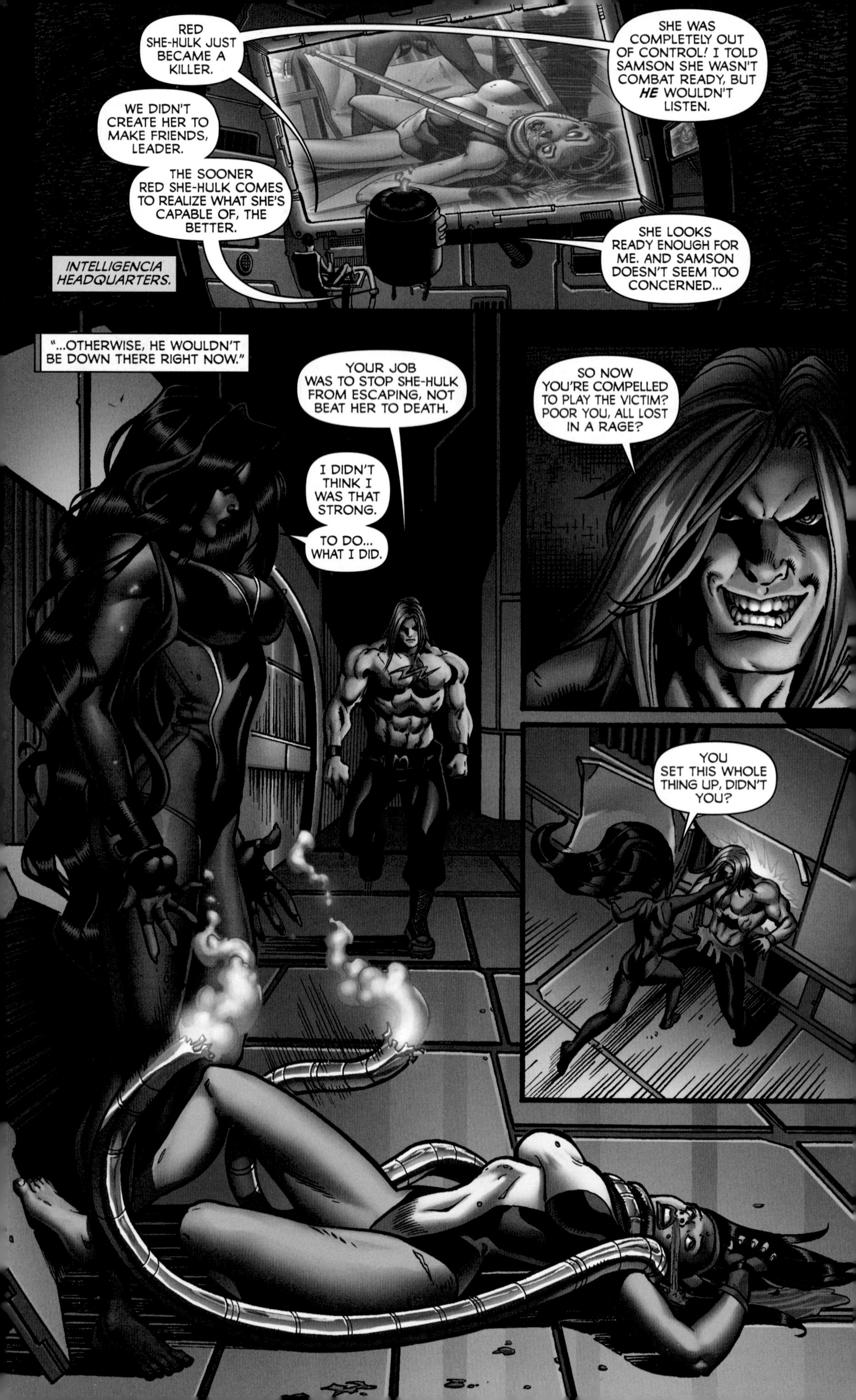
RED SHE-HULK JUST BECAME A KILLER.
SHE WAS COMPLETELY OUT OF CONTROL! I TOLD SAMSON SHE WASN'T COMBAT READY, BUT *HE* WOULDN'T LISTEN.
WE DIDN'T CREATE HER TO MAKE FRIENDS, LEADER.
THE SOONER RED SHE-HULK COMES TO REALIZE WHAT SHE'S CAPABLE OF, THE BETTER.
INTELLIGENCIA HEADQUARTERS.
SHE LOOKS READY ENOUGH FOR ME. AND SAMSON DOESN'T SEEM TOO CONCERNED...
"...OTHERWISE, HE WOULDN'T BE DOWN THERE RIGHT NOW."
YOUR JOB WAS TO STOP SHE-HULK FROM ESCAPING, NOT BEAT HER TO DEATH.
I DIDN'T THINK I WAS THAT STRONG.
TO DO... WHAT I DID.
SO NOW YOU'RE COMPELLED TO PLAY THE VICTIM? POOR YOU, ALL LOST IN A RAGE?
YOU SET THIS WHOLE THING UP, DIDN'T YOU?

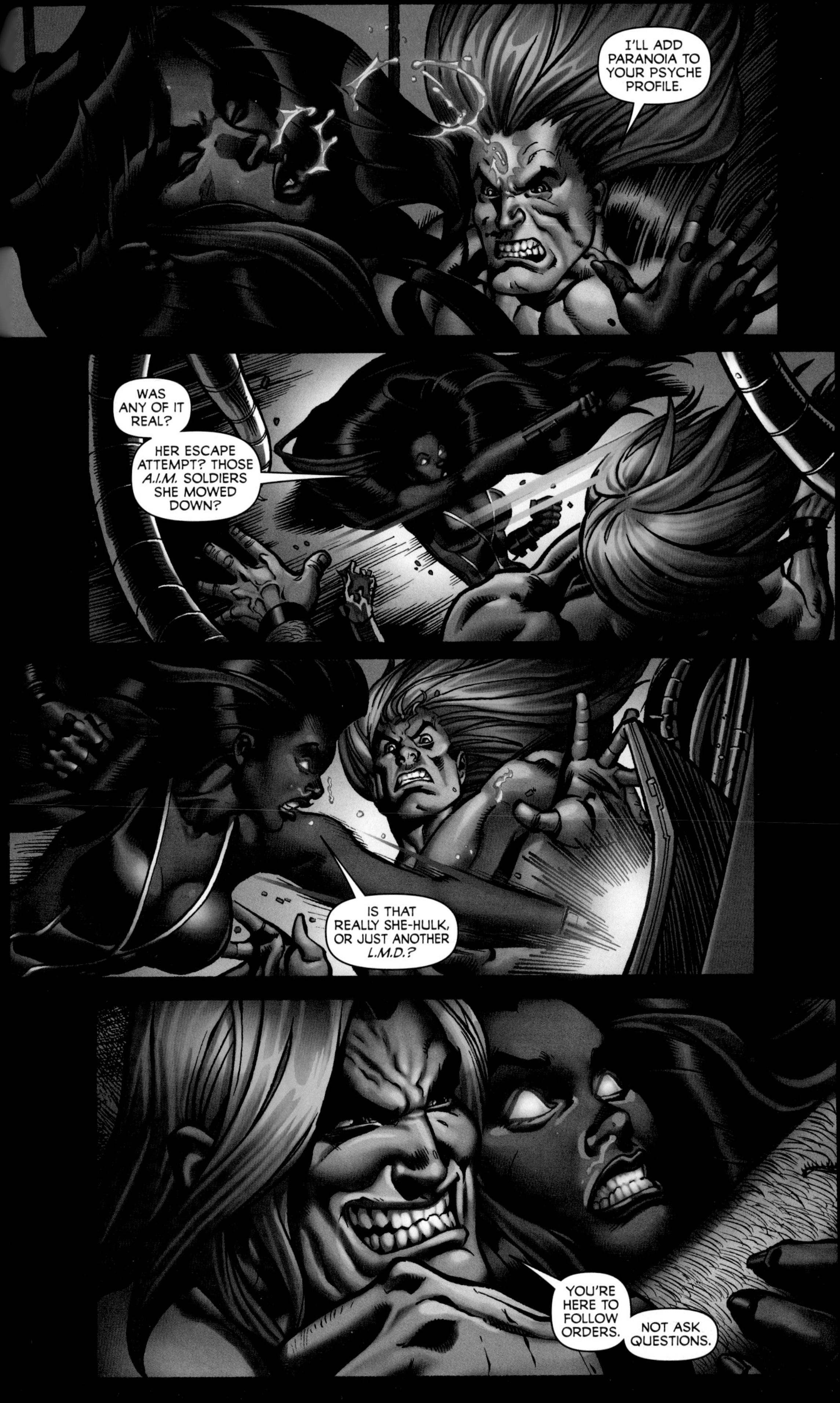
I'LL ADD PARANOIA TO YOUR PSYCHE PROFILE.
WAS ANY OF IT REAL?
HER ESCAPE ATTEMPT? THOSE *A.I.M.* SOLDIERS SHE MOWED DOWN?
IS THAT REALLY SHE-HULK, OR JUST ANOTHER *L.M.D.?*
YOU'RE HERE TO FOLLOW ORDERS.
NOT ASK QUESTIONS.

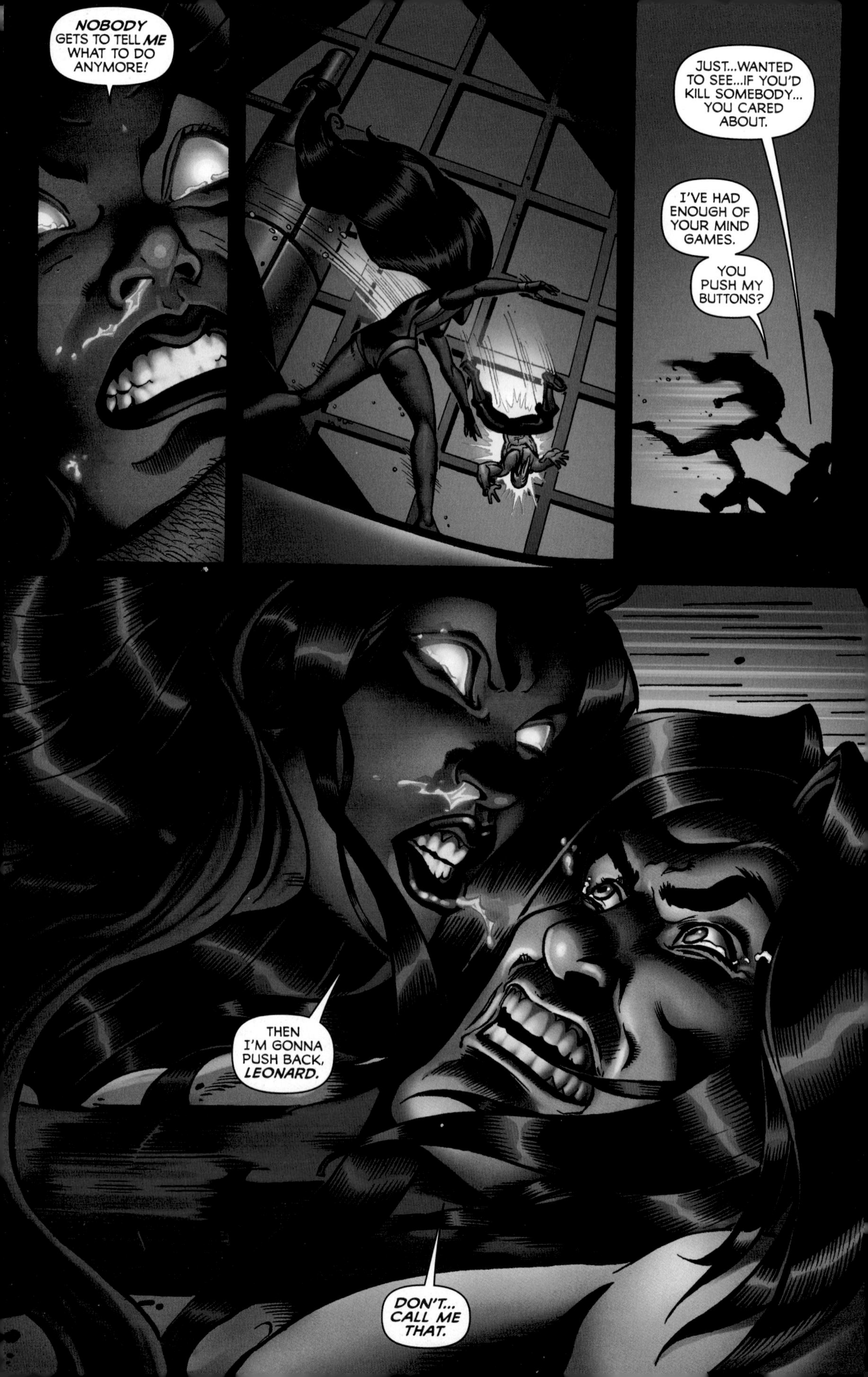
NOBODY GETS TO TELL ME WHAT TO DO ANYMORE!
JUST...WANTED TO SEE...IF YOU'D KILL SOMEBODY... YOU CARED ABOUT.
I'VE HAD ENOUGH OF YOUR MIND GAMES.
YOU PUSH MY BUTTONS?
THEN I'M GONNA PUSH BACK, LEONARD.
DON'T... CALL ME THAT.

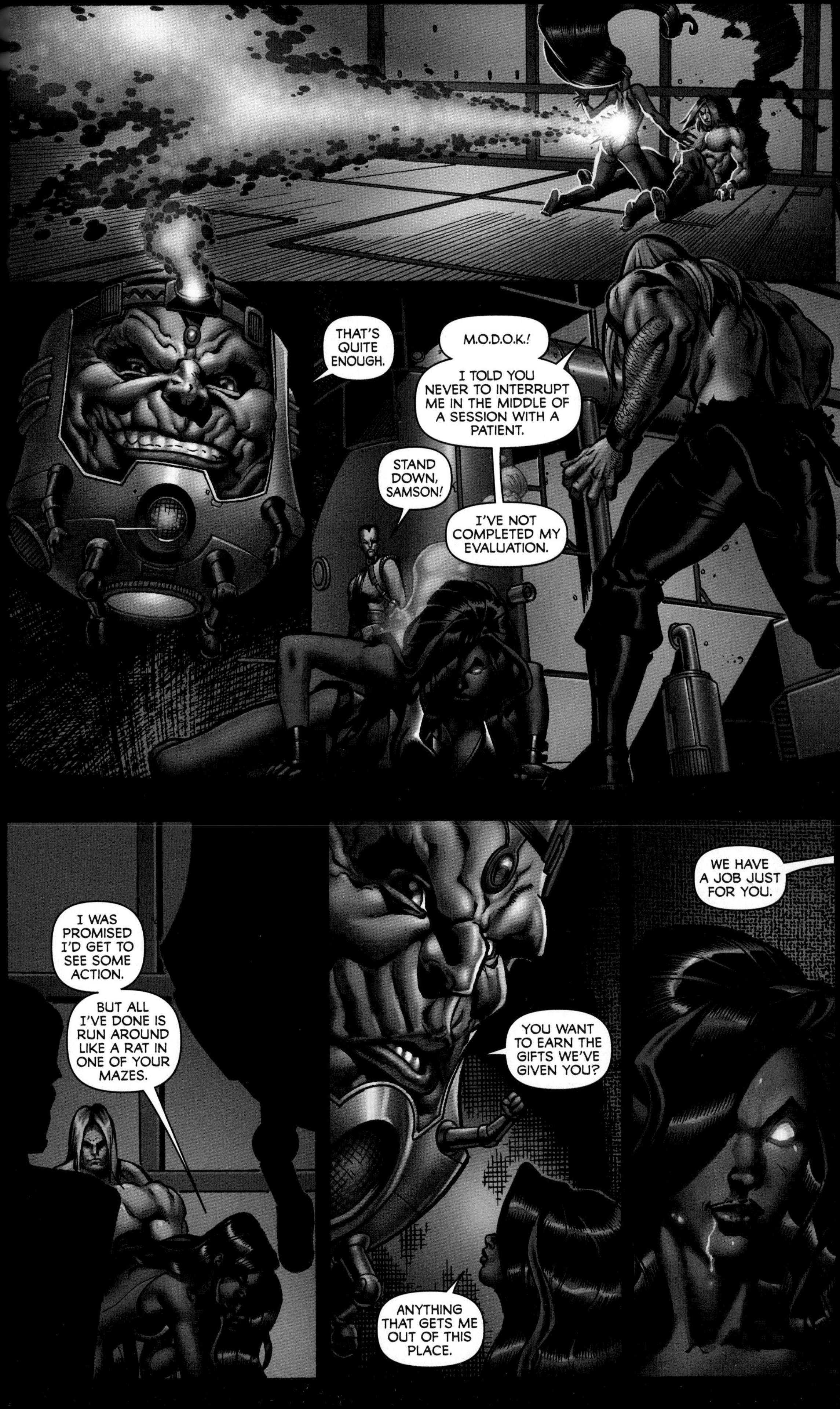
THAT'S QUITE ENOUGH.
M.O.D.O.K.!
I TOLD YOU NEVER TO INTERRUPT ME IN THE MIDDLE OF A SESSION WITH A PATIENT.
STAND DOWN, SAMSON!
I'VE NOT COMPLETED MY EVALUATION.
I WAS PROMISED I'D GET TO SEE SOME ACTION.
BUT ALL I'VE DONE IS RUN AROUND LIKE A RAT IN ONE OF YOUR MAZES.
YOU WANT TO EARN THE GIFTS WE'VE GIVEN YOU?
ANYTHING THAT GETS ME OUT OF THIS PLACE.
WE HAVE A JOB JUST FOR YOU.

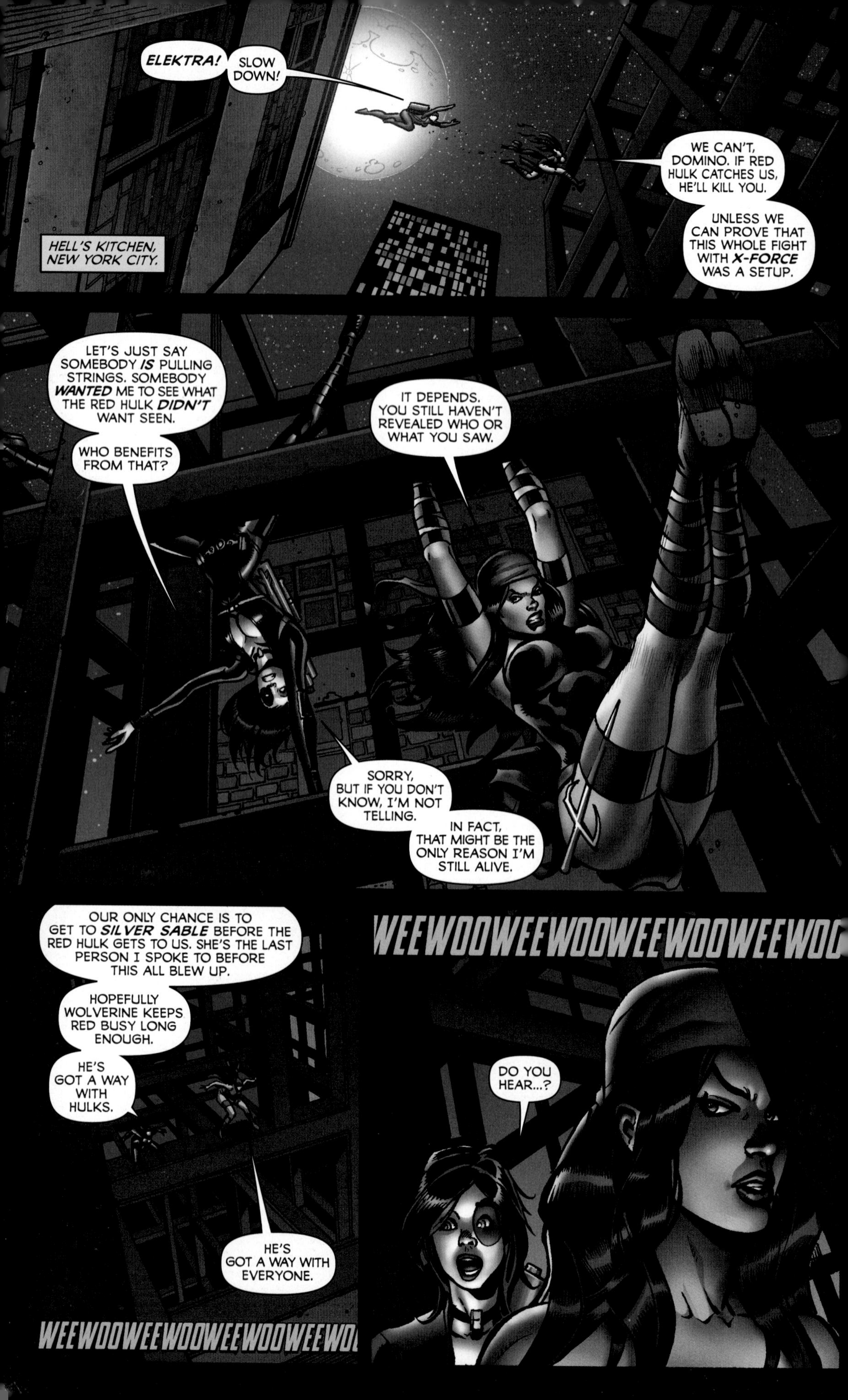
HELL'S KITCHEN, NEW YORK CITY.
ELEKTRA!
SLOW DOWN!
WE CAN'T, DOMINO. IF RED HULK CATCHES US, HE'LL KILL YOU.
UNLESS WE CAN PROVE THAT THIS WHOLE FIGHT WITH X-FORCE WAS A SETUP.
LET'S JUST SAY SOMEBODY IS PULLING STRINGS. SOMEBODY WANTED ME TO SEE WHAT THE RED HULK DIDN'T WANT SEEN.
WHO BENEFITS FROM THAT?
IT DEPENDS. YOU STILL HAVEN'T REVEALED WHO OR WHAT YOU SAW.
SORRY, BUT IF YOU DON'T KNOW, I'M NOT TELLING.
IN FACT, THAT MIGHT BE THE ONLY REASON I'M STILL ALIVE.
OUR ONLY CHANCE IS TO GET TO SILVER SABLE BEFORE THE RED HULK GETS TO US. SHE'S THE LAST PERSON I SPOKE TO BEFORE THIS ALL BLEW UP.
HOPEFULLY WOLVERINE KEEPS RED BUSY LONG ENOUGH.
HE'S GOT A WAY WITH HULKS.
HE'S GOT A WAY WITH EVERYONE.
WEEWOOWEEWOOWEEWOOWEEWO
WEEWOOWEEWOOWEEWOOWEEWO
DO YOU HEAR...?

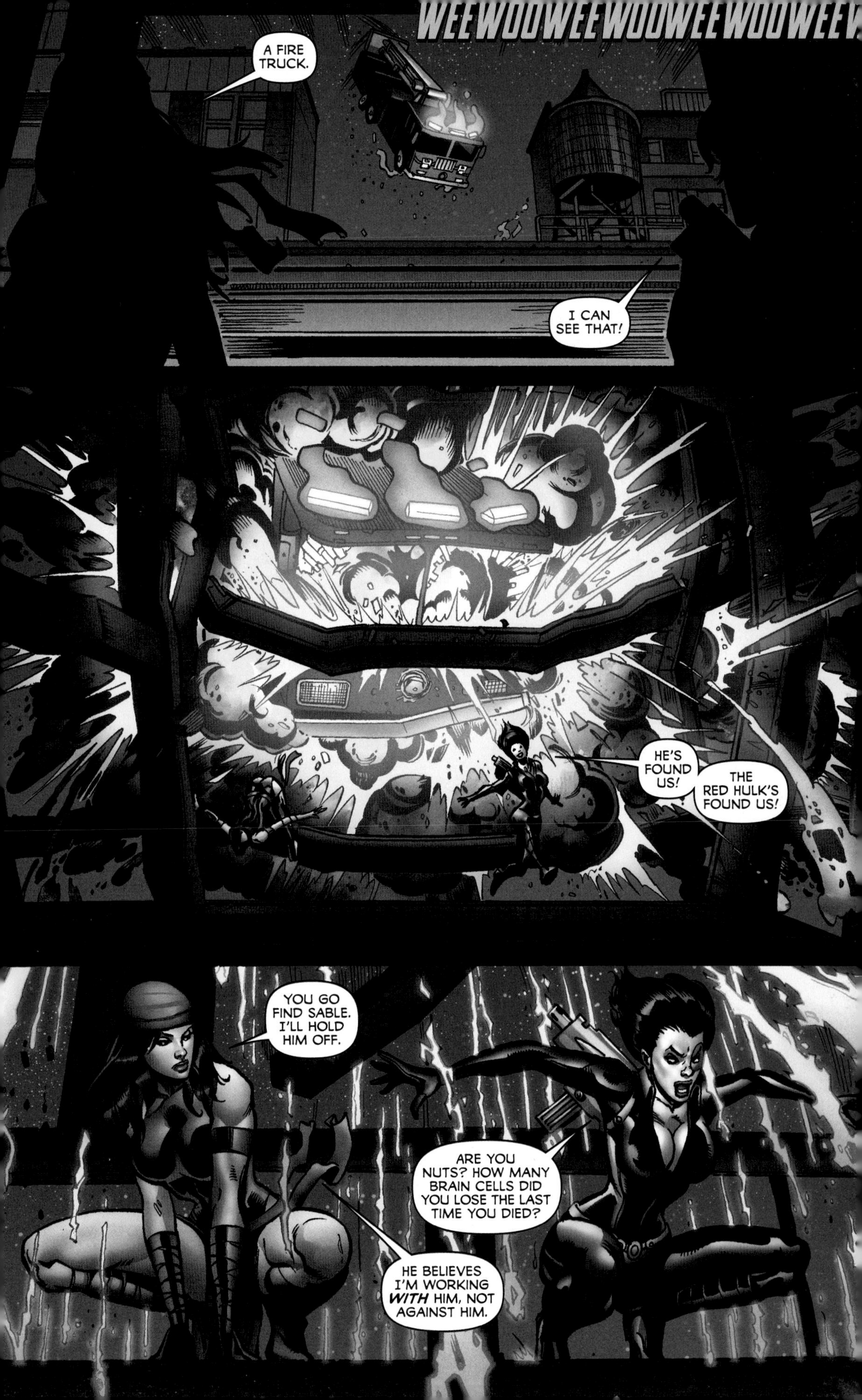
WEEWOOWEEWOOWEEWOOWEEW
A FIRE TRUCK.
I CAN SEE THAT!
HE'S FOUND US!
THE RED HULK'S FOUND US!
YOU GO FIND SABLE. I'LL HOLD HIM OFF.
ARE YOU NUTS? HOW MANY BRAIN CELLS DID YOU LOSE THE LAST TIME YOU DIED?
HE BELIEVES I'M WORKING ***WITH*** HIM, NOT AGAINST HIM.

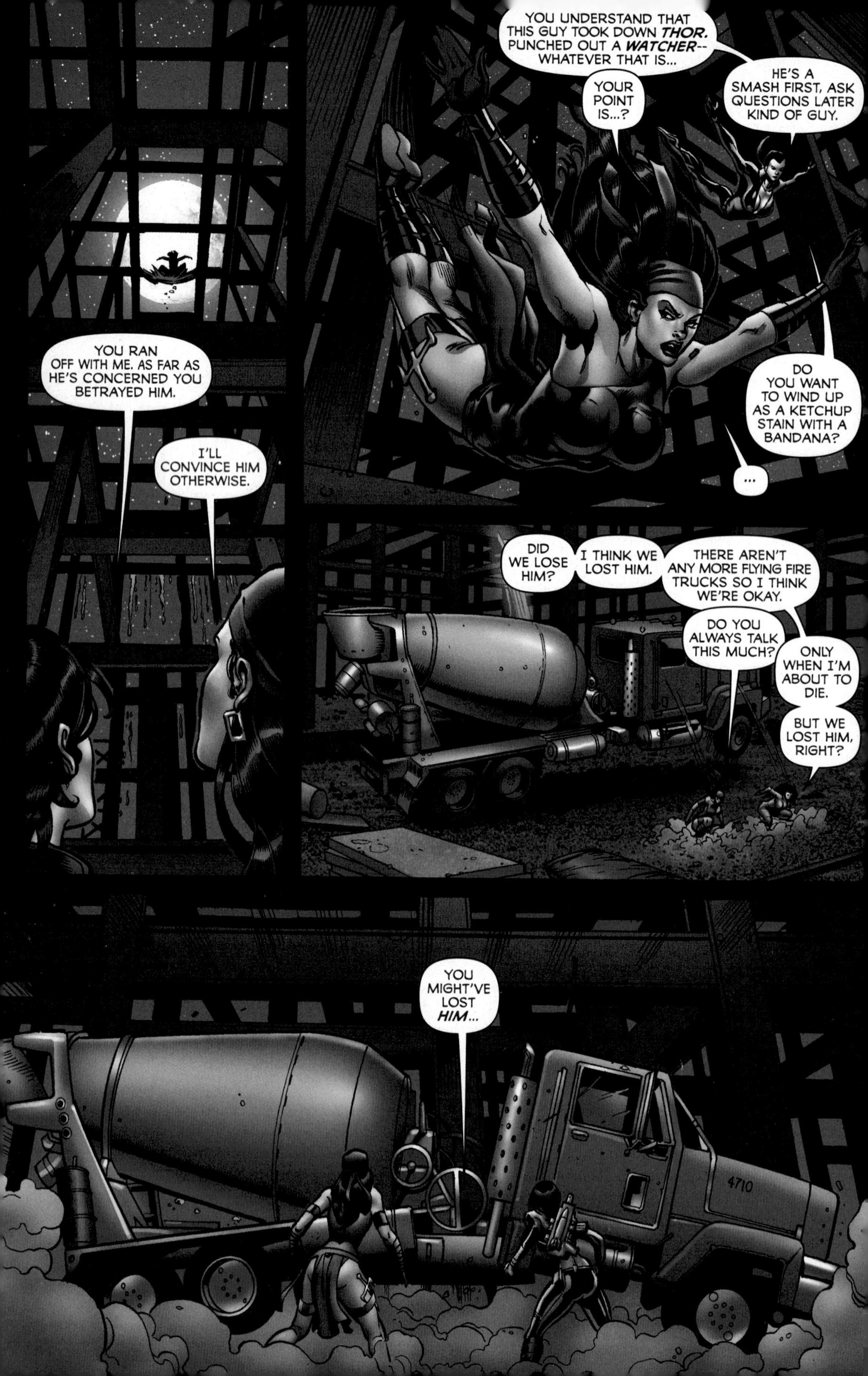
YOU UNDERSTAND THAT THIS GUY TOOK DOWN THOR. PUNCHED OUT A WATCHER-- WHATEVER THAT IS...
YOUR POINT IS...?
HE'S A SMASH FIRST, ASK QUESTIONS LATER KIND OF GUY.
DO YOU WANT TO WIND UP AS A KETCHUP STAIN WITH A BANDANA?
...
YOU RAN OFF WITH ME. AS FAR AS HE'S CONCERNED YOU BETRAYED HIM.
I'LL CONVINCE HIM OTHERWISE.
DID WE LOSE HIM?
I THINK WE LOST HIM.
THERE AREN'T ANY MORE FLYING FIRE TRUCKS SO I THINK WE'RE OKAY.
DO YOU ALWAYS TALK THIS MUCH?
ONLY WHEN I'M ABOUT TO DIE.
BUT WE LOST HIM, RIGHT?
YOU MIGHT'VE LOST HIM...
4710

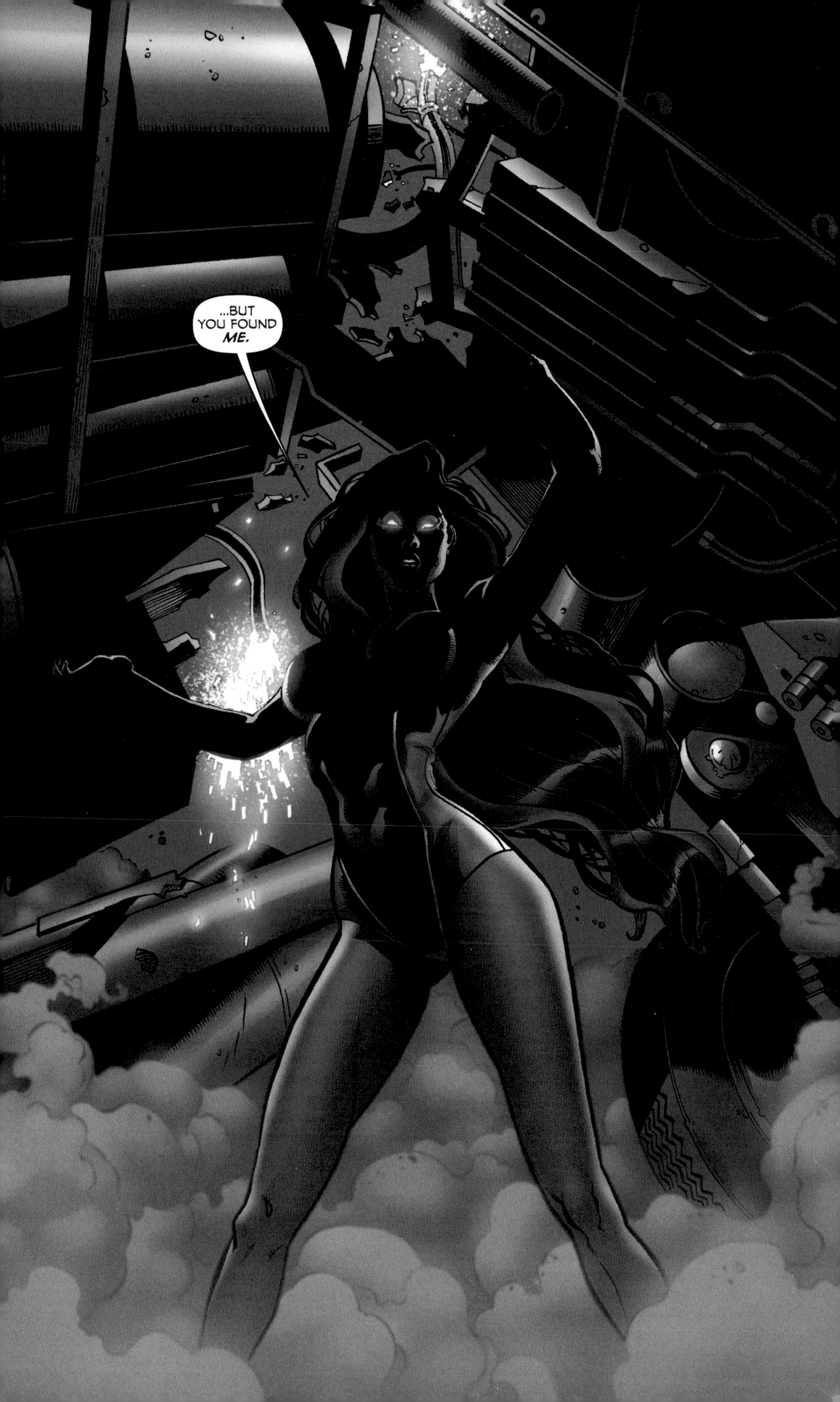
...BUT YOU FOUND *ME.*

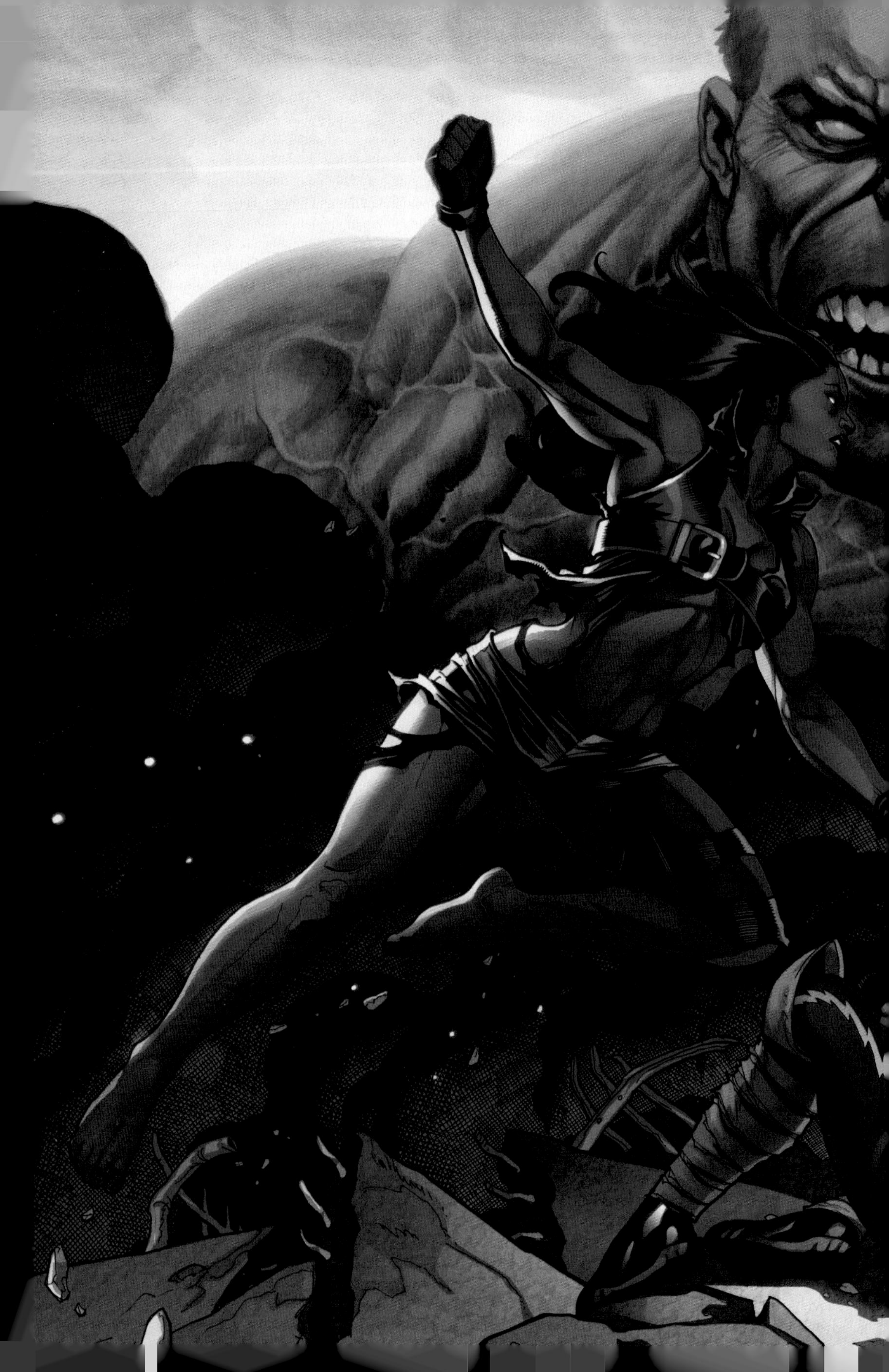

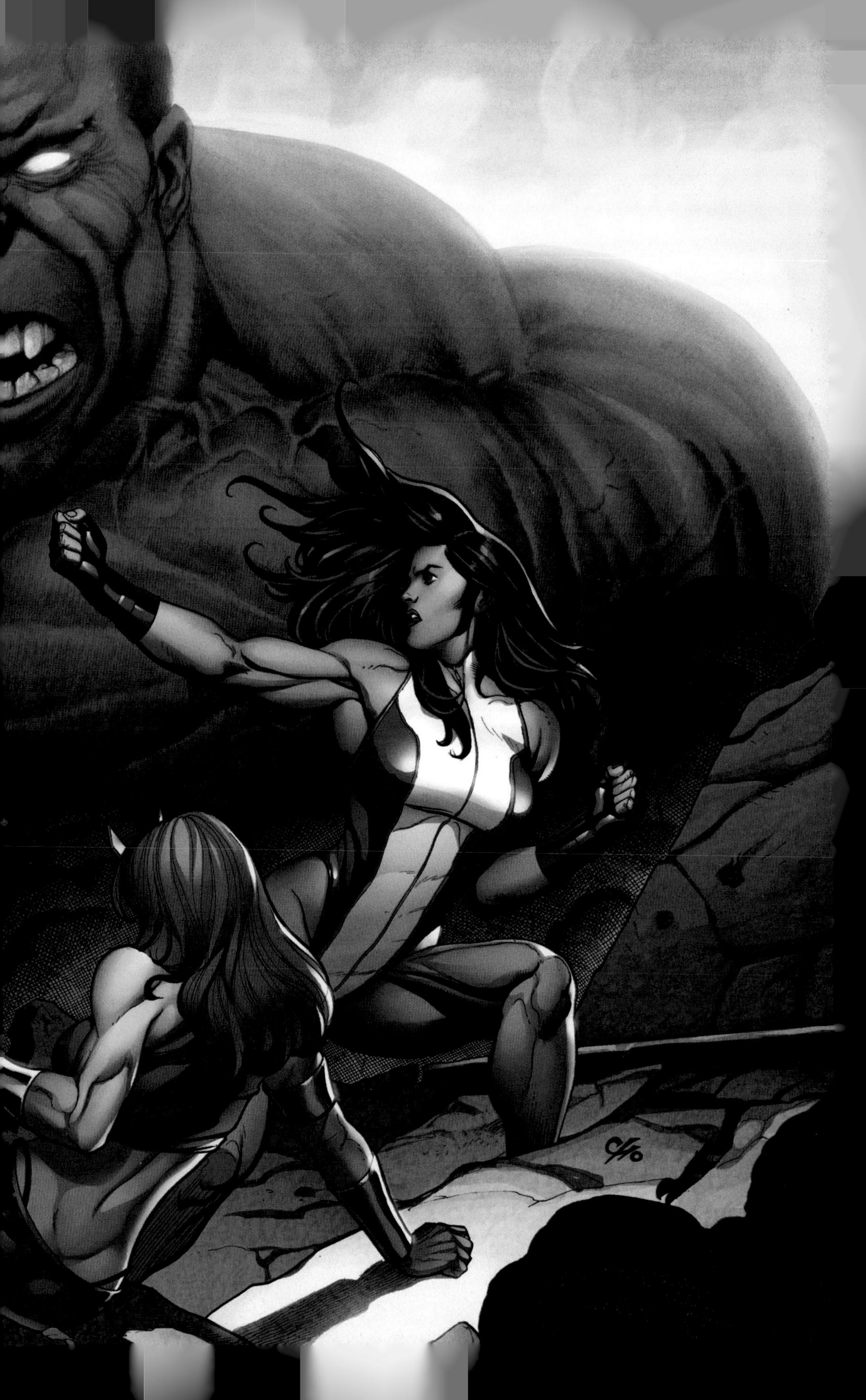

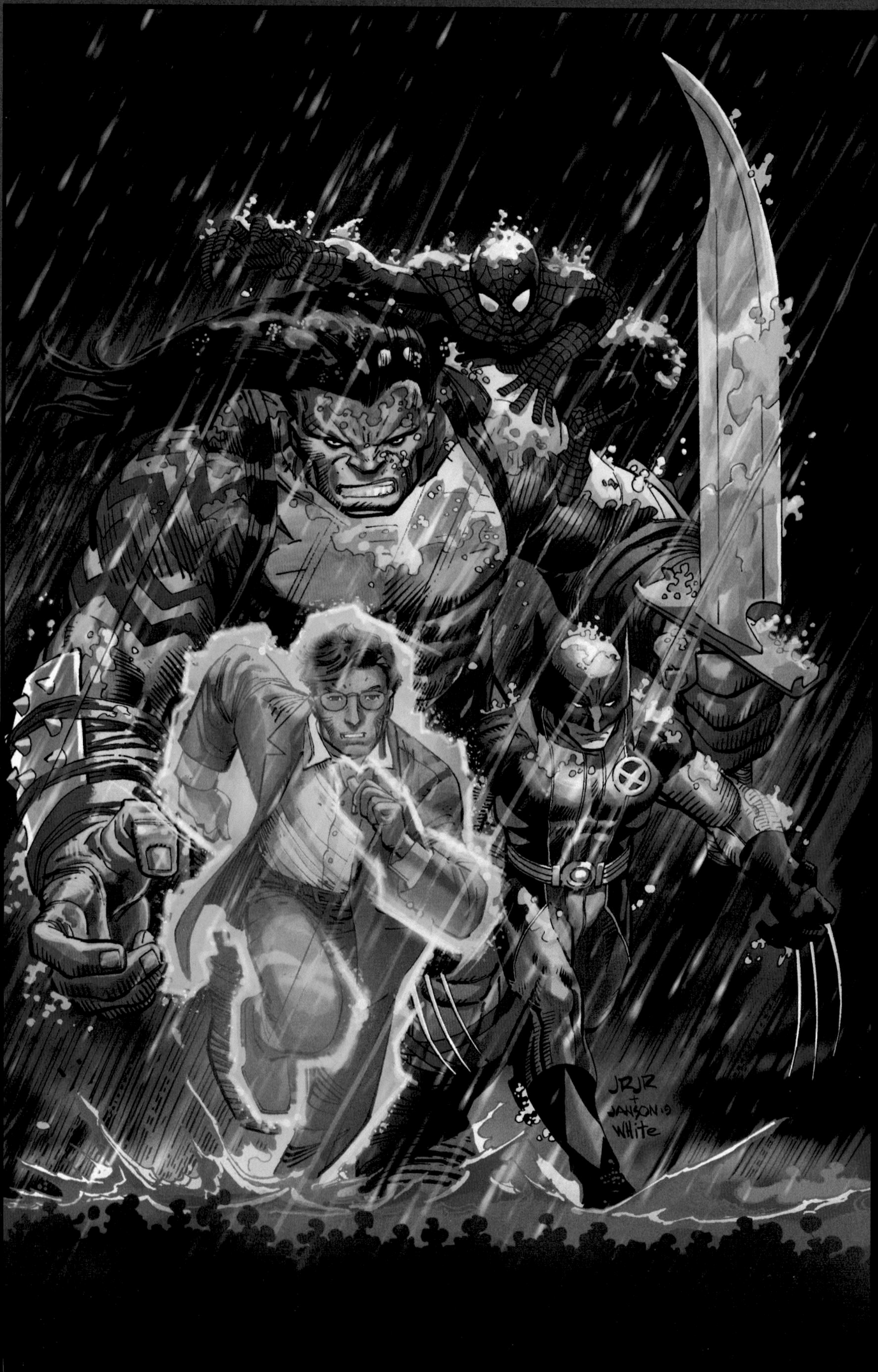
JRJR
+
JANSON '19
White

INCREDIBLE HULK #608

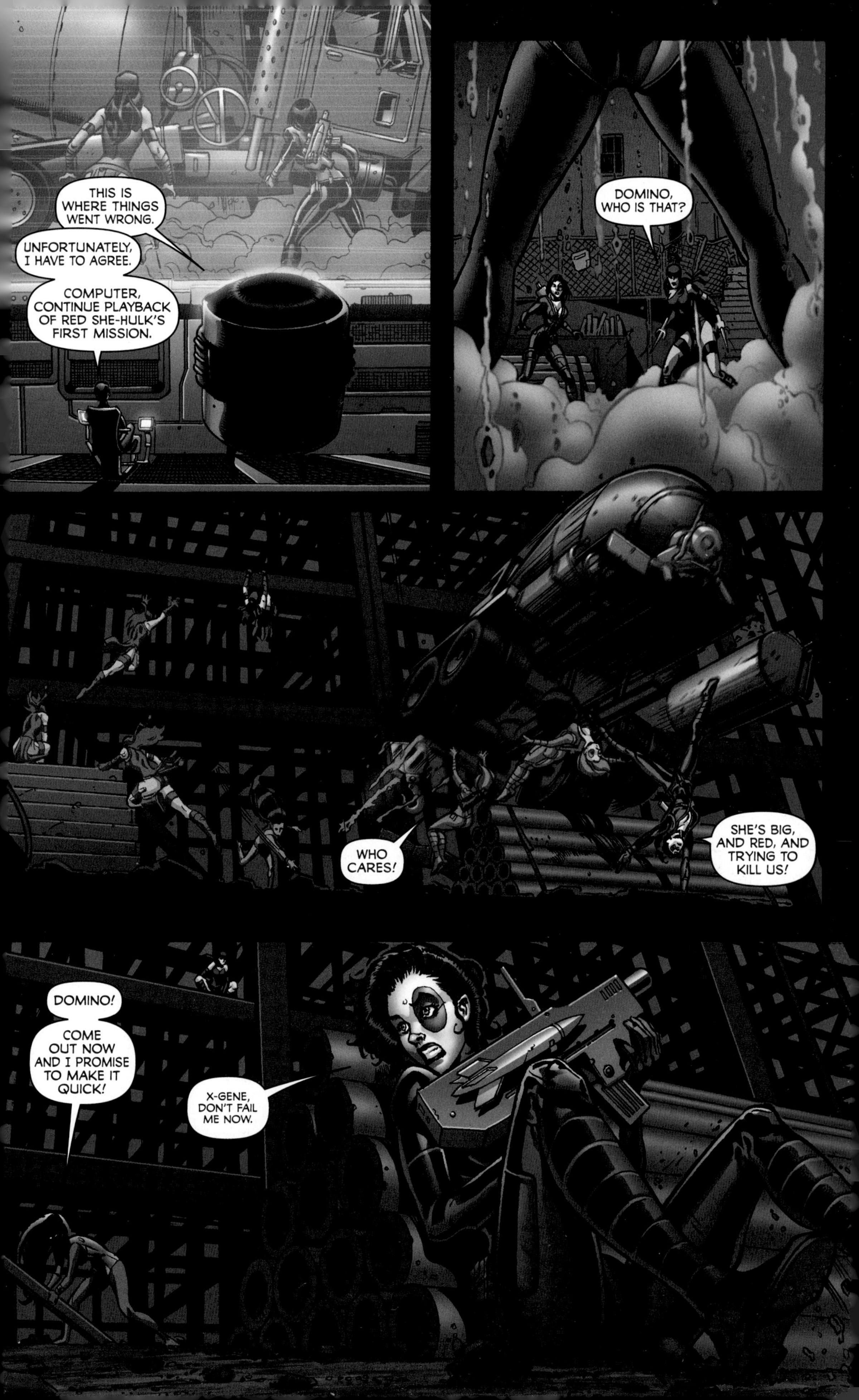
THIS IS WHERE THINGS WENT WRONG.
UNFORTUNATELY, I HAVE TO AGREE.
COMPUTER, CONTINUE PLAYBACK OF RED SHE-HULK'S FIRST MISSION.
DOMINO, WHO IS THAT?
WHO CARES!
SHE'S BIG, AND RED, AND TRYING TO KILL US!
DOMINO!
COME OUT NOW AND I PROMISE TO MAKE IT QUICK!
X-GENE, DON'T FAIL ME NOW.

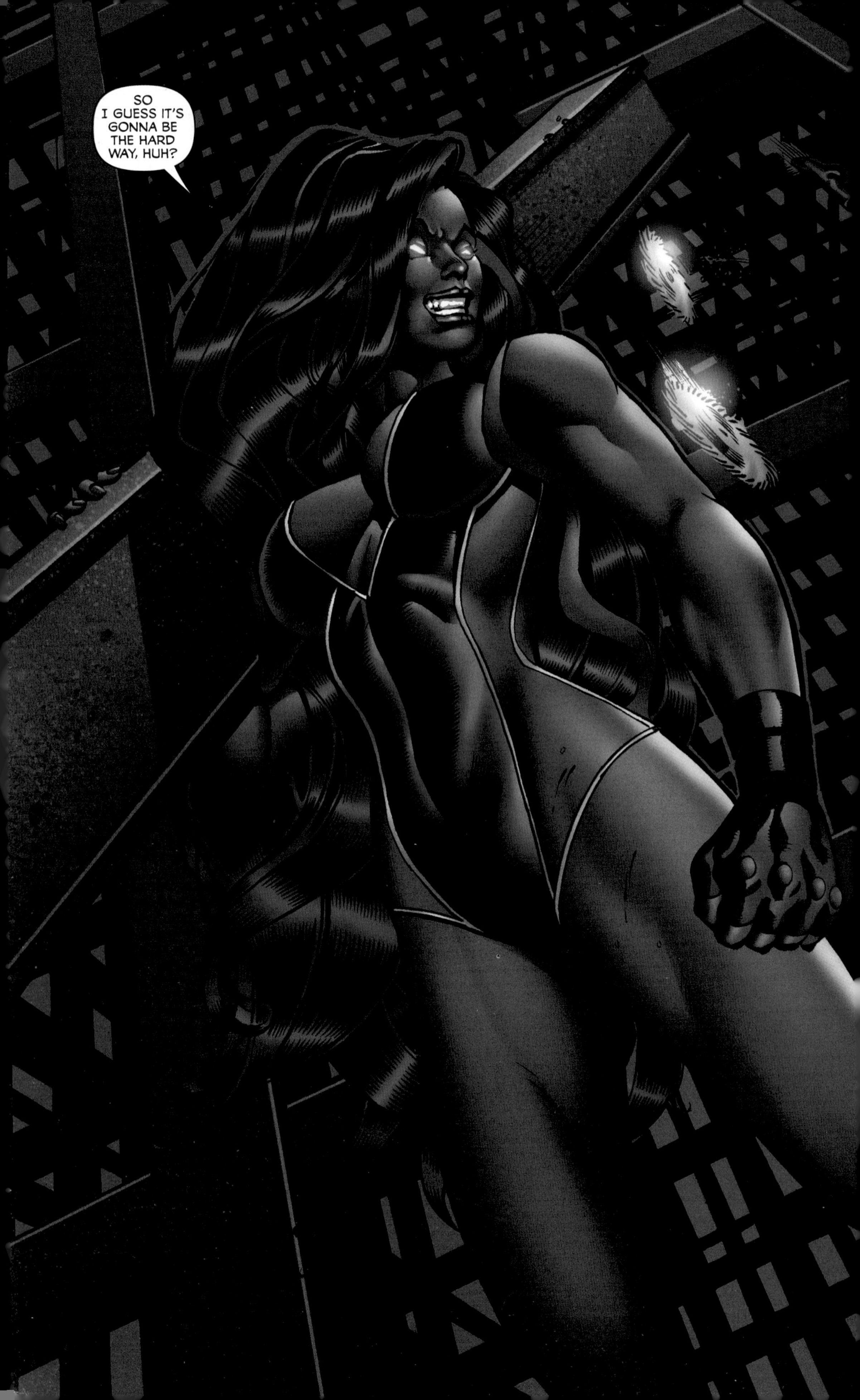
SO I GUESS IT'S GONNA BE THE HARD WAY, HUH?

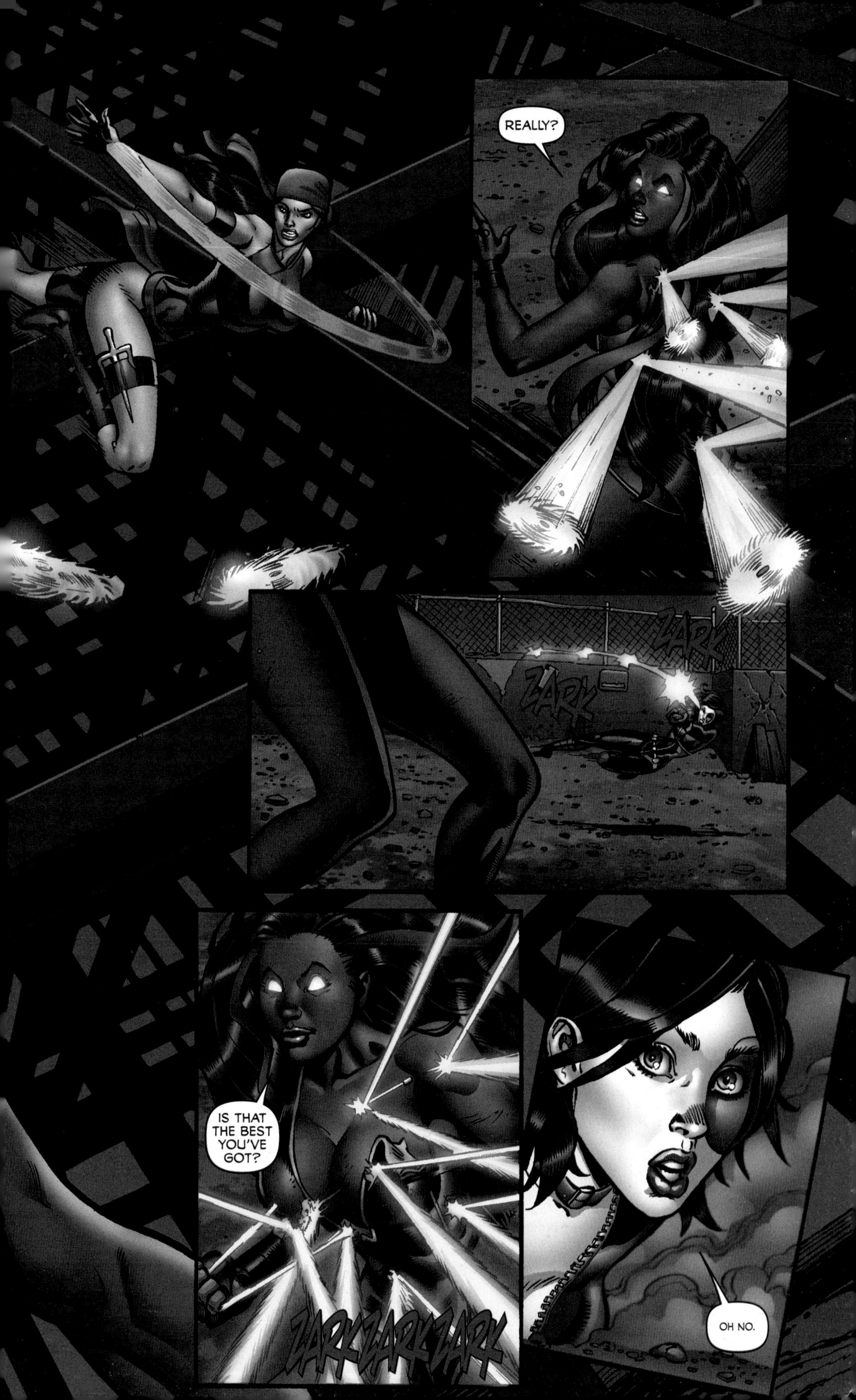
REALLY?
ZARK
ZARK
IS THAT THE BEST YOU'VE GOT?
ZARK ZARK ZARK
OH NO.

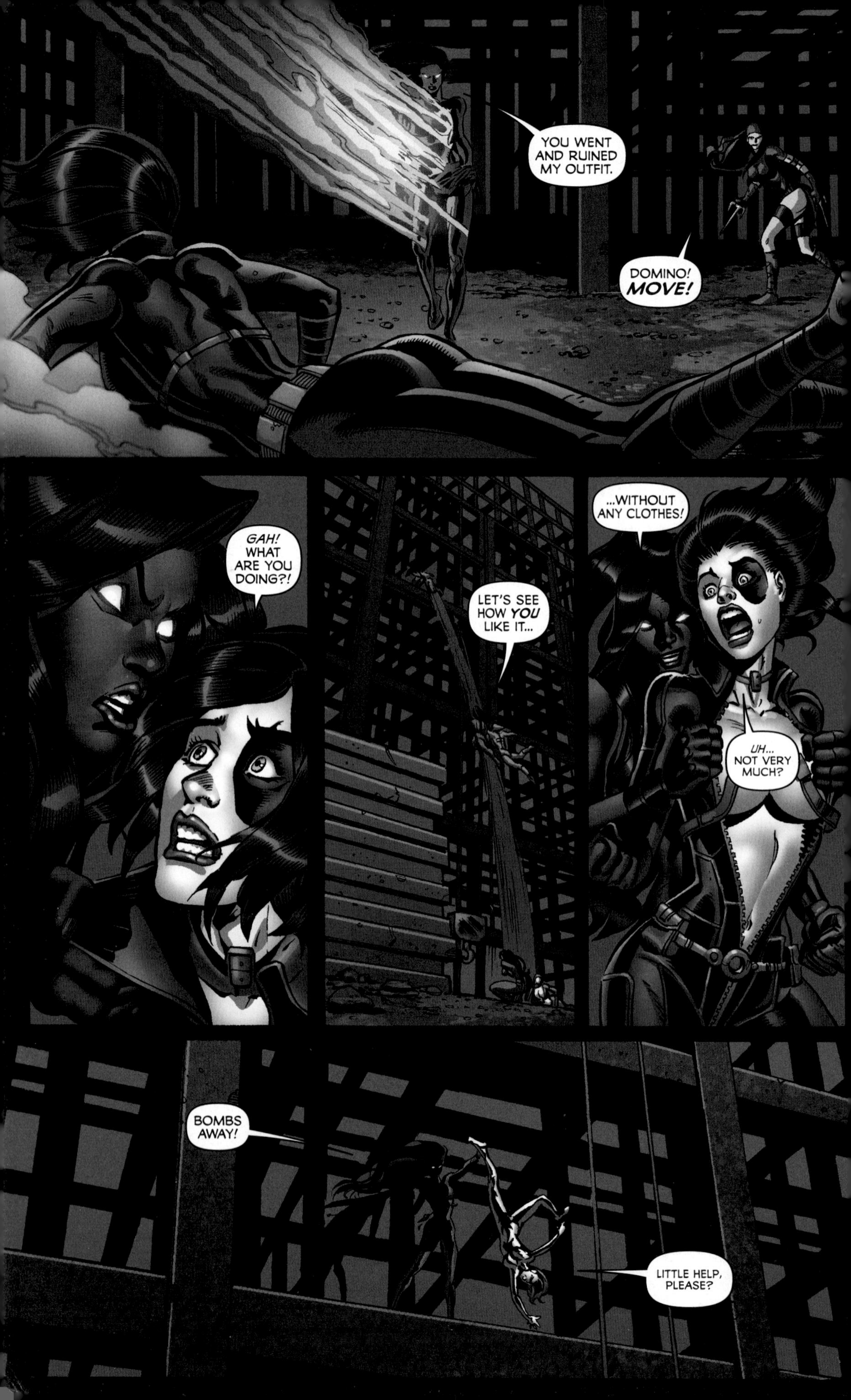
YOU WENT AND RUINED MY OUTFIT.
DOMINO! *MOVE!*
GAH! WHAT ARE YOU DOING?!
LET'S SEE HOW *YOU* LIKE IT...
...WITHOUT ANY CLOTHES!
UH... NOT VERY MUCH?
BOMBS AWAY!
LITTLE HELP, PLEASE?

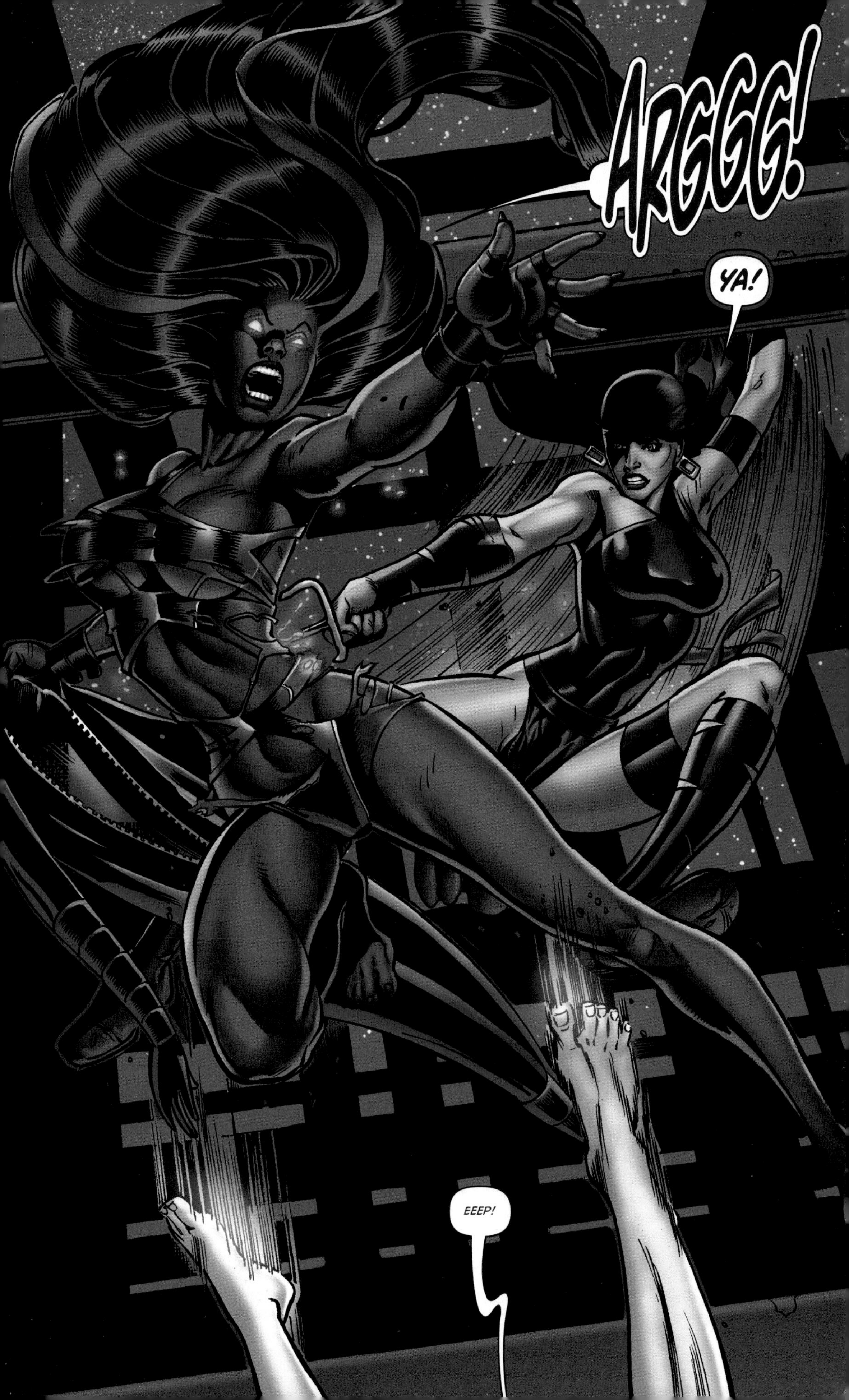
ARGGG!
YA!
EEEP!

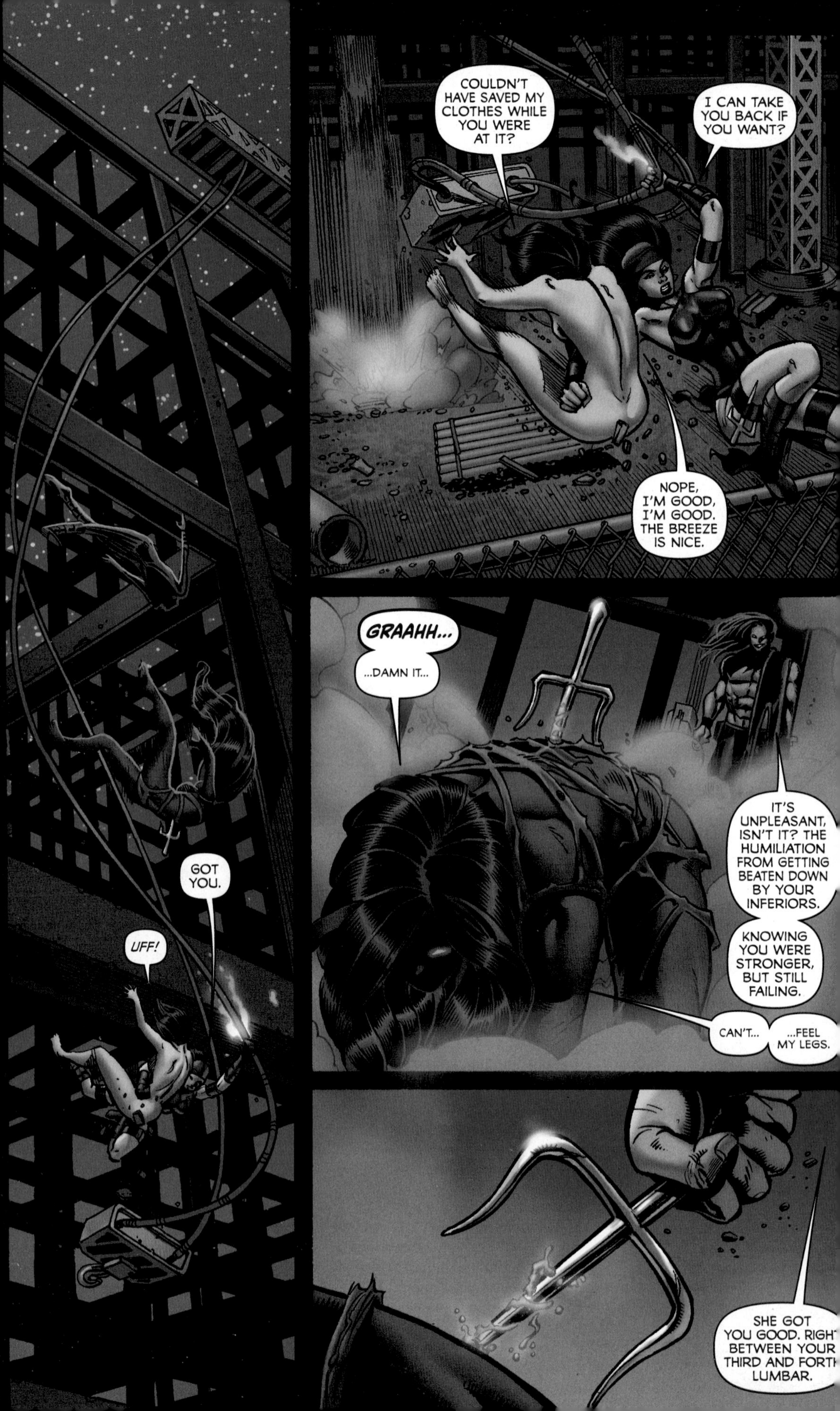
GOT YOU.
UFF!
COULDN'T HAVE SAVED MY CLOTHES WHILE YOU WERE AT IT?
I CAN TAKE YOU BACK IF YOU WANT?
NOPE, I'M GOOD, I'M GOOD. THE BREEZE IS NICE.
GRAAHH...
...DAMN IT...
IT'S UNPLEASANT, ISN'T IT? THE HUMILIATION FROM GETTING BEATEN DOWN BY YOUR INFERIORS.
KNOWING YOU WERE STRONGER, BUT STILL FAILING.
CAN'T...
...FEEL MY LEGS.
SHE GOT YOU GOOD. RIGHT BETWEEN YOUR THIRD AND FORTH LUMBAR.

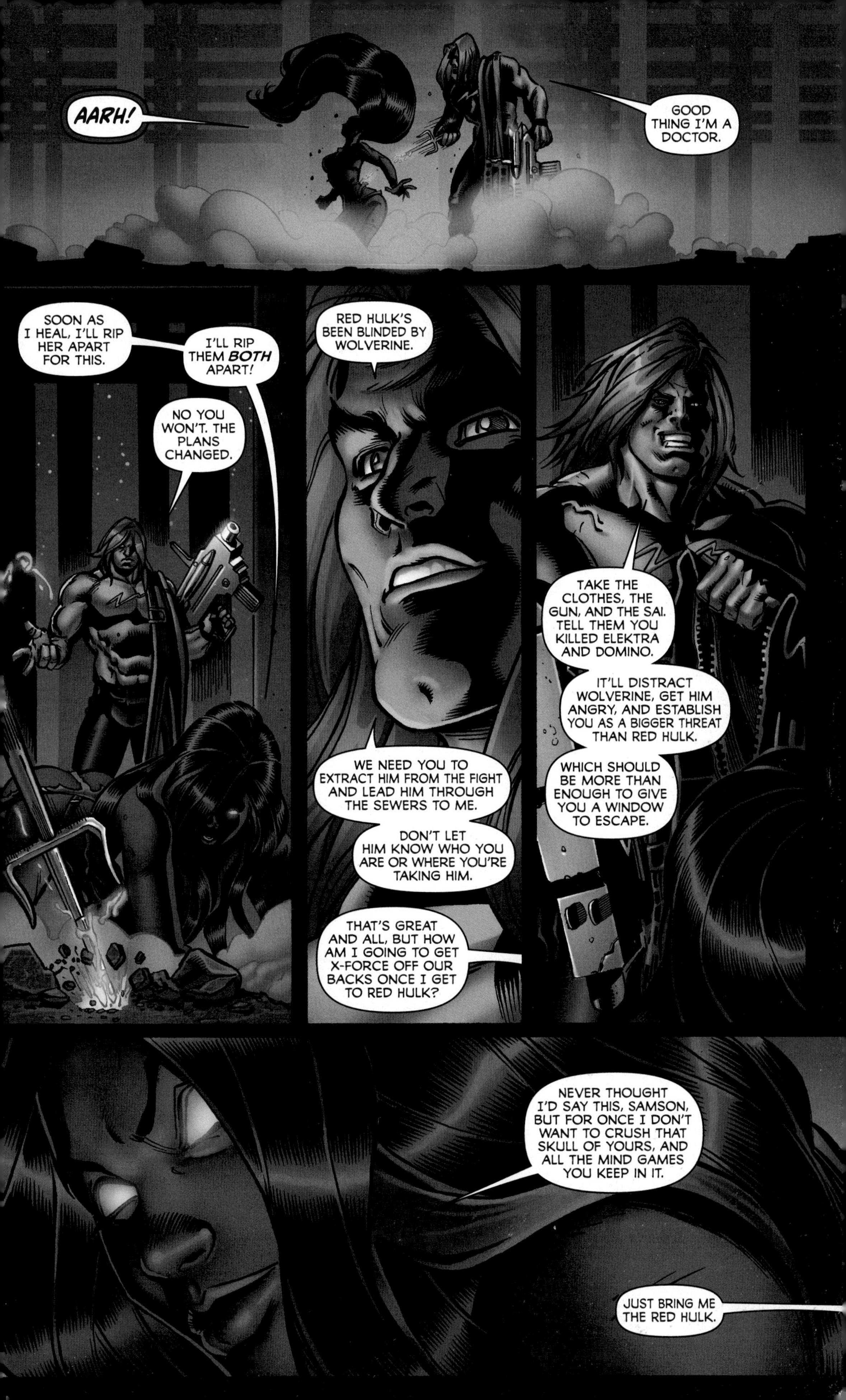
AARH!
GOOD THING I'M A DOCTOR.
SOON AS I HEAL, I'LL RIP HER APART FOR THIS.
I'LL RIP THEM BOTH APART!
NO YOU WON'T. THE PLANS CHANGED.
RED HULK'S BEEN BLINDED BY WOLVERINE.
WE NEED YOU TO EXTRACT HIM FROM THE FIGHT AND LEAD HIM THROUGH THE SEWERS TO ME.
DON'T LET HIM KNOW WHO YOU ARE OR WHERE YOU'RE TAKING HIM.
THAT'S GREAT AND ALL, BUT HOW AM I GOING TO GET X-FORCE OFF OUR BACKS ONCE I GET TO RED HULK?
TAKE THE CLOTHES, THE GUN, AND THE SAI. TELL THEM YOU KILLED ELEKTRA AND DOMINO.
IT'LL DISTRACT WOLVERINE, GET HIM ANGRY, AND ESTABLISH YOU AS A BIGGER THREAT THAN RED HULK.
WHICH SHOULD BE MORE THAN ENOUGH TO GIVE YOU A WINDOW TO ESCAPE.
NEVER THOUGHT I'D SAY THIS, SAMSON, BUT FOR ONCE I DON'T WANT TO CRUSH THAT SKULL OF YOURS, AND ALL THE MIND GAMES YOU KEEP IN IT.
JUST BRING ME THE RED HULK.

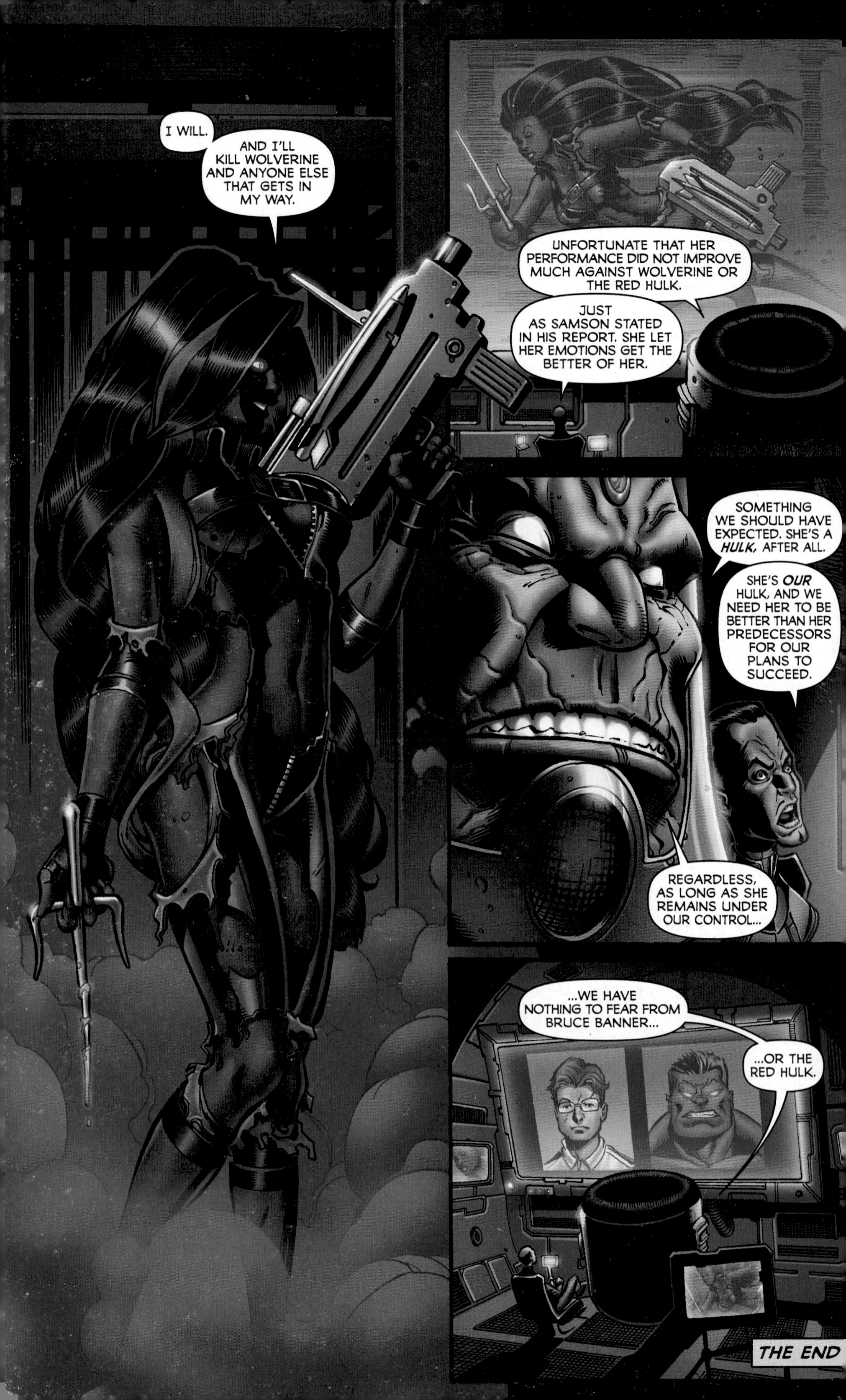
I WILL.
AND I'LL KILL WOLVERINE AND ANYONE ELSE THAT GETS IN MY WAY.
UNFORTUNATE THAT HER PERFORMANCE DID NOT IMPROVE MUCH AGAINST WOLVERINE OR THE RED HULK.
JUST AS SAMSON STATED IN HIS REPORT. SHE LET HER EMOTIONS GET THE BETTER OF HER.
SOMETHING WE SHOULD HAVE EXPECTED. SHE'S A *HULK,* AFTER ALL.
SHE'S *OUR* HULK, AND WE NEED HER TO BE BETTER THAN HER PREDECESSORS FOR OUR PLANS TO SUCCEED.
REGARDLESS, AS LONG AS SHE REMAINS UNDER OUR CONTROL...
...WE HAVE NOTHING TO FEAR FROM BRUCE BANNER...
...OR THE RED HULK.
THE END